VOLUME 17

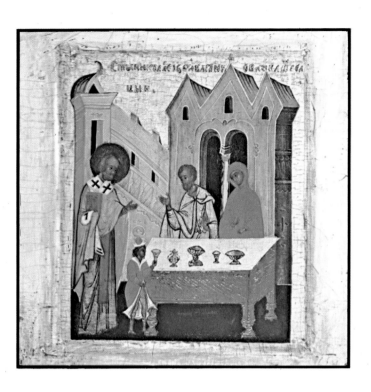

DISCOVERING ANTIQUES

THE STORY OF WORLD ANTIQUES

GREYSTONE PRESS/NEW YORK · TORONTO · LONDON

This superb full-color work is brought to you in its entirety from the original publisher, The British Publishing Corporation. Only the arrangement has been slightly altered. In fact, rather than disturb the text in any way, you will find the English monetary system used throughout the set. Here is a handy conversion table showing the value of a Pound (£) in terms of U.S. dollars.

DATES	U.S. Dollars equal to one Pound (£)
1939	$3.92 to 4.68
1940 to Sept. 1949	4.03
Sept. 1949 to Nov. 1967	2.80
Nov. 1967 to Aug. 1971	2.40
Aug. 1971 to June 1972	2.60
June 1972 to present	2.45 (floating rate)

20 shillings = one Pound (£)
21 shillings = one guinea

In February, 1971, the guinea was taken out of circulation.

TITLE PAGE PHOTO CREDIT: *Scene from the Life of St. Nicholas,* possibly Rostov school, sixteenth century. Tempera on wood, 15 x 13 inches. (Temple Gallery, London.)

© 1973 by the GREYSTONE PRESS.
© BPC Publishing Limited MCMLXXII
All rights reserved.
Published by the Greystone Press
225 Park Avenue South
New York, N.Y. 10003

Library of Congress Catalog Card Number: 72-90688

Cover Design: Harold Franklin

MANUFACTURED IN THE UNITED STATES OF AMERICA.

Contents

The Magnificent Reign of Shah 'Abbas

Olga Ford

Fig. 1 **Shah 'Abbas receiving Nazir Muhammad, Khan of Turan.** Shah 'Abbas the Great (1588–1628) was a far-sighted ruler who encouraged contacts with other lands, and welcomed their ambassadors at his own Court. (British Museum, London.)

*Persia in the 16th
and 17th Centuries*

Shah Isma'il 1502–24
Shah Tahmasp
1524–76
Shah 'Abbas
the Great 1588–1628

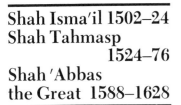

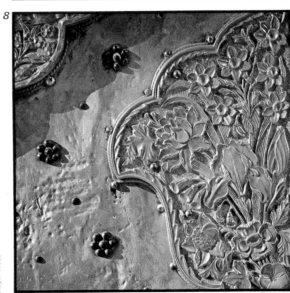

Fig. 2 **Courtyard of the Madrasa Madar-i-Shah, or Theological School,** *built between 1706 and 1714 by Shah Sultan Husayn.*

Fig. 3 **Detail of the 'stalactites' in** *the West Iwan, or Portal, open to the courtyard of the old Friday Mosque in Isfahan, redecorated by the last Safawid sovereign, Shah Sultan Husayn.*

Fig. 4 **Dome of the Mosque of the Shah,** *Isfahan, the most important building of the reign of Shah 'Abbas the Great, begun by him in 1612 and finished, after his death, in 1630.*

Fig. 5 **Pigeon tower,** *near Isfahan. In the time of Shah 'Abbas the Great, there were some three thousand towers of this sort. They were built to provide roosting niches for thousands of pigeons, and the resulting fertilizer was collected for use in the fields.*

Fig. 6 **Vault of a Porcelain Room,** *Ali Qapu Palace, Isfahan. The walls and vaults are covered with cut-out woodwork in the shape of bottles. Real porcelain was inserted into the walls, but the vault bottles were only painted.*

Fig. 7 **Courtyard of the Madrasa Madar-i-Shah,** *also seen in Fig. 2. This fine monument marks the end of the great building period of the Safawids.*

Fig. 8 **Detail of a door in the Madrasa Madar-i-Shah.** *Gold and silver.*
These doors to the entrance of the Theological School are covered with finely worked precious metals, and bear a close resemblance to book-covers of the period.

Fig. 9 **Old Friday Mosque,** *Isfahan. The dome and main fabric are of the early eleventh century, but the tile mosaic on the face of the South-west Iwan dates from the reign of Shah Tahmasp, c.1531, according to an inscription on one of the panels.*

Shah 'Abbas the Great inherited a weak and vulnerable monarchy. Before he died he built a strong and invincible empire

At the beginning of the sixteenth century, one of the dark periods of Persian history, a new dynasty came to power. They were the Safawids, who claimed descent from the prophet Muhammad. They were destined to give Iran national unity and to vanquish its enemies, the Ottoman Turks and the Uzbeks in the east. They raised the country to the highest level of prosperity it has ever attained, and inspired a new interest and enthusiasm that found expression in the arts.

9

Olga Ford

Shah Isma'il (1502–24) officially introduced the Shi'ite doctrine, which recognised only the descendants of Muhammad, as the State Religion, whereas the Sunnite enemies of Iran believed in the election of their civil and religious ruler. Shah Isma'il was perpetually involved in war during his short reign and, because of the destruction of his capital, Tabriz, by the Ottoman Turks, few of his buildings have survived. Those which have, although fine, are distinguished by their decorative tile mosaics rather than by great architectural qualities.

His son and successor, Shah Tahmasp (1524–76) was an amateur painter and carpet designer whose interests lay in textiles, carpets, book-covers and miniature paintings, which all attained a high degree of perfection under both Shah Isma'il and Shah Tahmasp. Since the latter frequently used mud brick for his buildings, very little has survived in this earthquake region and the great building period started with Shah 'Abbas the Great (1588–1628), who had enough energy and enthusiasm to bring about a renaissance in architecture in the grand manner.

When Shah 'Abbas I came to the throne at the age of sixteen, the outlook for his reign was not very auspicious. After the weak Shah Tahmasp, the authority of the Safawids over the tribal chiefs had been lost. The hereditary enemies, the Ottoman Turks and the Uzbeks, threatened the country. Nevertheless, Shah 'Abbas, by creating a new standing army directly paid by the treasury, and by forming an artillery with the technical advice of an Englishman, Robert Sherley, was successful in his military operations and left the country to his successors with frontiers similar to those it has today. Despite continuous warfare, this far-sighted ruler found the time to further trade and public security by his ruthless suppression of highwaymen, and by building roads, bridges, caravansarais and bazaars.

Before the discovery of a direct route to the East around the Cape of Good Hope, the Eastern trade to Europe was compelled to go overland by caravan through Turkey. This meant that Iran had to pay high customs rates to an enemy. Later, the Portuguese settled on an island in the Persian Gulf and monopolised the whole of the Eastern trade. Shah 'Abbas expelled them with the reluctant help of the English and encouraged contact with Europe in order to promote direct trade and to form an alliance against the Ottoman Turks. The very existence of a powerful Iran in their rear prevented the Turks from making even further inroads into Europe.

Shah 'Abbas was renowned for his hospitality to visiting ambassadors

Ambassadors from all parts of the world were hospitably and generously received. Reports from many travellers made Shah 'Abbas well known throughout Europe and much admired. Christian missionaries were allowed to establish themselves and to build churches, although Shah 'Abbas was a fervent believer in Islam and had even made the long pilgrimage from Isfahan to the shrine of Imam Riza in Meshed on foot.

The character and personality of the Shah is well known to us from the many descriptions of European travellers. He was an energetic, audacious and resolute man, cruel (he blinded and killed his sons and brothers), passionate and dangerous when enraged, shrewd, well-informed and intelligent. He had a macabre sense of humour. His more endearing qualities were his generosity and hospitality. He was an informal man, easily accessible, and could hold his own with the remarkable European sovereigns who were reigning at that time.

An interesting light on Shah 'Abbas' Court and on the pomp and ceremony of the time is shed by the description of the reception of the Sherley brothers' Mission to Qazwin in 1599, which was sent and paid for by the Earl of Essex and which was the first to come from Europe. It consisted of Sir Anthony Sherley, his brother Robert, and twenty-five of his retinue. Preceded by his marshal with a white baton, Sir Anthony is reported to have looked very splendid, dressed in a stuffed and quilted doublet woven with silver threads, his head covered with a huge turban, his shoes stitched with pearls and garnets, and carrying a sword covered with precious stones. His brother Robert followed him as his page and the other members were similarly dressed in velvet, damask, and silver *lamé*. The colours were brilliant yellows, blues and scarlet reds.

All this magnificence appears to have pleased the Shah greatly. He rushed with enthusiasm to his camp to fetch his wives and dancers and dancing-women on horseback, who welcomed the strangers with exuberant cries. Sir Anthony presented the Shah with twelve emeralds mounted as ear-rings,

Fig. 10 *'Abbas, King of Persia.*
Engraving from Herbert's
Travels, *published in 1638.
This ferocious portrait of Shah
'Abbas the Great (1588–1628)
comes from one of the many
travel books which were
published as records by early
European voyagers to the exotic
lands of the East.*

Mansell Collection

two other jewels with topazes, a cup made of gold and enamel, a crystal salt-cellar and a water jug with a lid in the form of a dragon. After the Shah had welcomed Sir Anthony and his retinue, all proceeded to the royal palace, the whole population of Qazwin lining the streets on their knees and kissing the soil along the Shah's route.

Magnificent entertainments were arranged

Shah 'Abbas gave immediate audience to Sir Anthony, who came with unofficial proposals of an alliance against the Ottomans and of direct trade. The same evening, the Shah invited his guests to attend the public celebrations of his victory over the Uzbeks. The Shah on his throne, surrounded by his Amirs, watched the march-past of his troops and again called for his dancers, dancing-women and music. Against a background of precious hangings, carpeted floors, thousands of lights arranged in festoons and the flicker of smoking torches, this spectacle must have been fairy-like and almost ethereal. Afterwards the Shah, who liked to mix with his people, showed his guests around the streets and bazaars. Preceded by musicians and dancers, he stopped on all corners to look at athletic and camel combats, acrobatics and other side-shows.

The festivities went on for many days; on the

twelfth day the Shah presented Sir Anthony with twelve camels, three complete tents, sixteen mules laden with, in all, sixty-four carpets of which twelve were silk; fourteen horses saddled and harnessed and sixteen thousand ducats. Since all the expenses of Sir Anthony and his suite were paid by the treasury, he had a generous return for his own presents.

Last but not least, Shah 'Abbas was a great builder and town planner and had an enthusiastic and genuine interest in the arts. He himself was, as were so many Oriental monarchs, an able and versatile craftsman. His new capital, a mile to the south of the prosperous town of Isfahan, was one of the most magnificent towns the world had yet seen. Little remains of its former glory to remind us of the time when, according to Chardin, a reliable seventeenth-century traveller, Isfahan had one hundred and sixty-two mosques, forty-eight colleges, one thousand, eight hundred and two caravansarais and two hundred and seventy-three baths. The most important monuments which are still standing today testify, however, to the high artistic quality of the architecture during his reign and the zeal with which the Shah searched his own country and as far as India for the best architects and ceramists.

Architecture under Shah 'Abbas reached its last phase of richness and flamboyance

Around the enormous square, the *maydan*, surrounded by a wall of arcading in two storeys, were grouped the covered bazaar, the Ali Qapu Palace, the entrance to the numerous palaces and gardens of the Shah opposite the mosque of the Shaykh Lutf Allah, and, at the south end, the Shah's mosque.

To the west, parallel to the *maydan*, ran the Chahar Bagh Avenue, seventeen hundred yards long, leading through two parks to the river and beyond, to a hunting-lodge of the Shah. It was three alleys broad and planted with eight rows of poplars and plane trees. Between rose hedges and jasmine bushes, water rushed in onyx channels to feed fountains and pools in the middle of the promenade. The gay palaces of ministers, with their balconies and galleries, lined the Chahar Bagh and could be perceived through open arcades. On festive days brocades were spread out and a sand and flower-strewn path was made for the Shah to ride upon. The rest of the town was laid out on a grid system, each street having its trees and water channel.

During Shah 'Abbas' reign architecture reached its last flamboyant phase of magnificence and richness in decoration before decay set in. The mosques' high entrance portals, the sanctuaries, the prayer chambers, the domes, the four portals opening on to the courtyards and the courtyards themselves were covered inside and out with painted tiles or tile mosaics.

The colourful domes of the mosques around the *maydan* seem to float over the white-washed, niched facades surrounding the square, landmarks which would be seen from afar by the weary traveller who, in Shah 'Abbas' time, had probably spent weeks, or even months in the monotonous fawn-coloured desert and, having arrived in Isfahan, would make his way to the mosque where he would be transported into another world of cool colours, quiet beauty and splendour.

Persian Potters and their Wares

Oliver Hoare

Standing at the gateway to the Orient, Persian potters were strongly influenced by the porcelain of China. Nevertheless, the indigenous Islamic tradition imbued their work with a highly individual character

The most frequently encountered types of Persian pottery of the sixteenth and seventeenth centuries are those decorated in blue on a white ground, in the Chinese style. It has been argued that the Chinese potters originally took the idea, along with the cobalt ore they imported, from Persia, where, from the early thirteenth century onwards, blue decoration, outlined in black to prevent running, was common. As black would not have withstood the high temperature in the porcelain kilns, the Chinese had to omit it, making the outlines in darker blue instead. It is not known when the Chinese blue and white porcelain first started arriving in the Middle East, but there is evidence in miniature paintings to show that it was known in the fourteenth century, and certainly it had become the prevalent fashion by the fifteenth century. It was the fourteenth- and fifteenth-century Ming porcelain which gave the main inspiration for design.

The Persians never mastered the art of making porcelain themselves, but they admired and valued it to such an extent that, as Thomas Herbert, an Englishman in Isfahan in the early seventeenth century, remarked, 'they commonly eat in earth [enware] and porcelain, not valuing silver', and the word *Chini* (Chinese) came to be used to describe anything of fine quality, regardless of the material

Fig. 1 **Base of a qalian, or hookah,** Meshed, first half of the seventeenth century. Height 8½ ins. Water which was kept in the qalian base provided a cool smoke. (Christie, Manson and Woods, London.)

of which it was made. Shah 'Abbas thought it sufficiently important to dedicate a collection of 1,162 pieces of Chinese porcelain to the shrine of his revered ancestor, Shaykh Safi, in 1611, of which eight hundred and five pieces remain, forming one of the world's finest collections. A curious incident is related by the official chronicler of the occasion, namely that when Shah 'Abbas entered the kitchens at Ardabil, 'the lid of a nearby saucepan lifted itself about nine inches and crashed down on the saucepan with such a noise . . . much to the astonishment of those present'. If this amazing saucepan could be found, it would no doubt be a valuable collector's item.

In 1682, the British East India Company recorded

intense black and filled in with shades of a slightly violet transparent blue. Usually on the bottom there is an attempt to imitate a Chinese mark in black, taking the form of concentric squares, which illustrates the lengths to which the Persians went in their emulation of the Chinese.

The earliest examples are extremely rare, dating from the second half of the sixteenth century and showing long-legged cranes flying among trailing clouds and delicately observed birds perched beside rather limp flowers. About 1600, the style became less individual and lasted in a similar vein until the end of the century, tending to become more and more sloppy towards 1700. Human figures sometimes appear, intended as Chinese, but some-

2

3

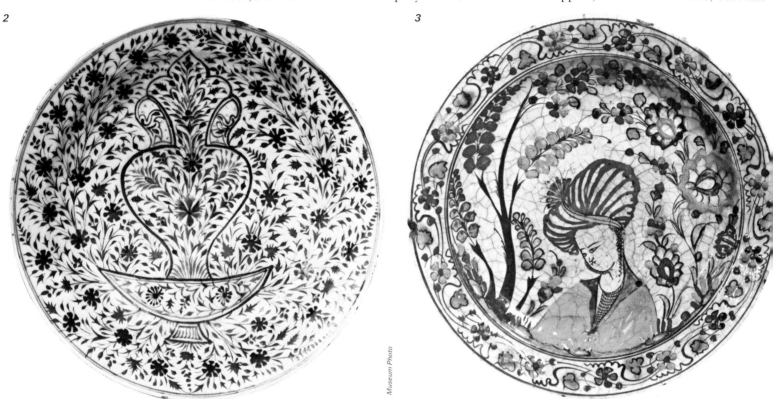

Museum Photo

Fig. 2 **Plate**, *Kirman, seventeenth century.*
Kirman was noted for its celadon wares which were reputed to change colour on contact with poison and were thus considered suitable for kings, who were frequently subject to this kind of assassination attempt.
(Victoria and Albert Museum, London.)

Fig. 3 **Plate**, *Kubachi, c.1600. Sometimes plates were decorated with portraits, but it is not known if the figure here represents a specific person.*
(Victoria and Albert Museum.)

that Kirman and Meshed were the two places where really good imitations of Chinese porcelain could be obtained. The shapes, as well as the designs, followed the Chinese example – big dishes and bowls, jars, vases and bottles. Even the shape of a Chinese pouring vessel was adapted to the needs of the *qalian* (hookah), the side hole receiving the wooden mouthpiece, and the tall stem holding the tobacco cup fixed on top (Fig. 1).

The Chinese influence on Meshed and Kirman wares

Although deceptive at first, a close examination will always distinguish Persian wares. The pottery, however fine, does not have the hard, compact, vitreous quality of porcelain, and often is softer and manifestly coarser in grain. In order to achieve a similarity to porcelain, the painted decoration of the pottery was covered in a hard and brilliant transparent glaze.

The best technique was evolved in Meshed (this is a generally accepted attribution for the group rather than an established fact), where the potters employed a hard white body and a clear thin glaze. The glaze has a greenish tinge more evident where it is thicker; the designs are sharply outlined in

how looking more European, and the figure of a drunken Chinaman hugging a winebottle and showing his legs seems to have been a hugely appreciated joke at this time. A bowl in the Staatliche Museen, Berlin, is particularly interesting, showing an adaptation of a European painting of a Virgin and Child. The *qalian* base in Figure 1 has a more usual decoration of panels enclosing animals, and a relatively restricted vocabulary of floral types. Also serving as *qalian* bases are the particularly charming animal figures such as the duck in the Victoria and Albert Museum, London, complete with the legs painted underneath.

The wares attributed to Kirman have fine and relatively soft white bodies, often thickly potted, with a bright and warm blue painted under a thickish, rather uneven glaze full of tiny bubbles which tend to run into green drops. The outlines are usually executed in darker blue, rather than black as at Meshed, and frequently look blurred 'like ink lines on blotting paper', as Lane describes it in his *Later Islamic Pottery*. Again one finds imitation Chinese marks on the base, called 'tassel marks' because of their odd trailing shapes. The drawing became more Persian as the seventeenth century progressed and there was a great simplification and stylisation of Chinese designs.

Pieces from the sixteenth century are hardly

Fig. 4 **Ewer**, *late seventeenth century. Honey-coloured with a clear glaze.*
(Victoria and Albert Museum.)

Fig. 5 **Painted tile wall decoration** *from the Chihil Sutun Palace, Isfahan, seventeenth century.*
This type of large-scale wall decoration was inspired by the frescos and wall paintings of Europe and indeed, several European painters were recorded in Persia at this period. The figures themselves, however, were inspired by the work of miniaturists such as Riza-i-'Abbasi' whose unctuous rhythms would appear obscene even without the occasional help from the subject matter'. (Arthur Lane, Later Islamic Pottery.)

Fig. 6 **Bottle**, *seventeenth century. Lustreware, height 8½ ins.*
The 'leaf-specimen' treatment is very unusual in the decoration of this period.
(Christie's.)

Fig. 7 **Beaker**, *late seventeenth century. Turquoise glaze.*
This beaker was almost certainly designed to hold toilet accessories. The colour is opaque and very well preserved.
(Victoria and Albert Museum.)

known. The repertoire of shapes included the usual bowls and dishes, but also many-faceted forms such as octagonal trays and plates. Sometimes the design was a simple outline, and occasionally figurative subjects were outlined in black. A bottle of *c.*1550 in the Schloss Charlottenburg, Berlin, painted in blue and white with celadon green details and with a fantastic figure of a dragon, is worth mentioning as a splendid piece of decorative painting. The extraordinary decorative genius of the Persians which transformed all they touched is manifest here, because although the dragon closely resembles his Chinese original, he is unmistakably Persian in his placing and the power of the drawing.

More numerous than the Kirman blue and white are the polychrome pieces, although polychrome tends to be an addition to the basic blue and white scheme. The influence of Isnik pottery after 1550 is perhaps apparent in the choice of a thick tomato red slip, akin in appearance to the 'Armenian bole'. A celadon green, which turned to a *café au lait* colour when badly fired, was also used, as well as a chocolate brown, yellow and black. The blue and white decoration remains basically Chinese, but the colours are applied in a manner

more characteristically Persian, with sprays of thin flowers, often contained in elegant panels, and spirals incised through bands of colour (Fig. 2). Later in the seventeenth century, moulded designs were experimented with at both Kirman and Meshed.

The development of more specifically Persian pottery

Although by no means exhaustive, the examination of the two groups above give, perhaps, an idea of Chinese-inspired pottery in Persia. These groups were the most commonly found. The Kubachi group may be taken first of the more specifically Persian types. It is a homogeneous group, so named because a large number of intact pieces were found in the remote Caucasian hill-town of Kubachi, whose inhabitants probably exchanged them for weapons, and then kept them for wall decoration, piercing the bases for suspension. They may have been made in Tabriz, and have been found in widely dispersed areas. The white bodies are very soft and loose-grained, and where the glaze has not covered the entire surface they turn very dark as they are easily impregnated with dirt. The glaze is thin, and develops a wide crackle into which dirt also tends to seep, as can be seen in the marvellous portrait plate illustrated here (Fig. 3). It is in the extraordinary decorative flair that the interest of these wares lies; from the point of view of materials they are very rough. Some early pieces are decorated in the blue and white Chinese style under a clear glaze or, more rarely, under a yellow or green glaze; others have black incised panels under a turquoise glaze, such as the famous example dated 1468 with the inscription 'May this dish ever be full and surrounded by friends, may they never lack anything and eat their fill'.

A more typical polychrome decoration seems to have originated during the reign of Shah Tahmasp

Persian Pottery

Fig. 8 **Bowl**, Meshed, first half of
the seventeenth century.
Diameter 13 ins.
This bowl is in the Chinese
manner.
(Christie's.)

Fig. 9 **Bottle**, attributed to
Isfahan, seventeenth century.
Green glaze.
The vessel is moulded with an
elaborate animal scene.
(Victoria and Albert Museum.)

A. C. Cooper

Museum Photo

K. Hoddle

Museum Photo

(1524–76) with figures of musicians and dancers in the style of the miniatures of the period enclosed in cell patterns and leaf borders. After 1550 the palette of black outlines containing a deep, runny blue came into use with dull green, thick yellow ochre and thick brownish red. Occasionally, the yellow or a pale salmon red is used for the whole background, another Isnik-inspired trick. Tiles were decorated with portraits as on the plate illustrated in Figure 3 which has a typical narrow ring foot and flattened rim. The slightly inclined head is recognizably from the Shah 'Abbas period and the foliage has much the same Persian feel about it as already noted in the Kirman decoration. The production seems to have died out after Shah 'Abbas and was perhaps adversely affected by the move of the capital to Isfahan in 1598.

Lustring was a technique invented by the Islamic potters in Mesopotamia in the ninth century and was a jealously guarded secret brought to great fruition in Persia in the twelfth and

sprinkling themselves with rare perfumes from beak-spouted vessels. The bowl with small birds in the bottom which can just be glimpsed in Figure 8 was almost certainly a luxury ware for use in the bath and the ewers and slender-necked vases hint at a similar destination. The potting tends to be heavy, sometimes with a glassy, honey-coloured glaze (Fig. 4) or an array of subtle greens, blues, turquoise, purple or pink. Other vessels were carved with hunting scenes (Fig. 9) or animals, and one category has moulded panels outlined in relief containing different intense colours (Fig. 11). Figure 10 shows a type of monochrome ware painted with sprays of flowers which can be compared to Figure 2, painted in white or cut through the thick monochrome ground.

A last mention should be made of a group of delicate, very fine-grained, pure white pottery covered in a shiny glaze, often incised and carved beneath the glaze or decorated with cut away monochrome slips (Fig. 12).

Museum Photo

Fig. 10 **Qalian base**, *seventeenth century.*

The complicated ritual in the preparation of the qalian *for smoking was taken very seriously. The water contained in the base made the smoke cool enough to be fully inhaled; this made the head spin pleasantly.*
(Victoria and Albert Museum.)

Fig. 11 **Bottle**, *seventeenth century. Earthenware with turquoise glaze.*
This bottle recalls the so-called cloisonné wares of the Chinese Ming dynasty.
(Victoria and Albert Museum.)

Fig. 12 **Bowl**, *seventeenth century.*
Very fine pottery which closely approaches porcelain. The pierced decoration covered by a transparent glaze adds to the impression of flimsiness.
(Victoria and Albert Museum.)

thirteenth centuries. From the names of the potters we know of this period, it is almost as if the secret of lustreware was kept in one or two families, but it is very unlikely that the process was handed down continuously until its sudden re-emergence in the seventeenth century. The bodies of the vessels at this later period were very white, compact and rather heavy. The lustre, often of a deep brown colour, gives a range of rainbow reflections from gold to purple and ruby red, sometimes set against a deep blue ground, or, even more rarely, turquoise. Arthur Lane ingeniously suggested that the high proportion of winebottles may point to Shiraz as the centre of production because this city was so famous for its wines. The decoration is painted in silhouette showing nimble animals skipping amongst foliage and trees and is treated in a style not unrelated to Kirman. The bottle illustrated (Fig. 6) is unusual, the drawing much stronger showing two magnificent dragons, a fox and a bird and leaf shapes, and the Persian word for 'a believer' written in yellow lustre round the rim. This type is so far undocumented. Another similar piece is in the Teheran Museum, with lustre much paler in colour, and the fox and bird in much more obvious relation to each other, perhaps illustrating a fable.

Monochrome wares of the Safawid period again turn to China for inspiration. Celadon greens are common and many of the articles seem to have been destined for use in the Turkish bath *(hammam)*. Tile representations of bathing beauties show them

HOW TO RECOGNISE PERSIAN POTTERY

The question of fakes does not really arise, as attention has not been paid to the pottery of this period to the same extent as to the earlier productions by this very lucrative Persian industry. However, one danger arises for the beginner. The golden Safawid era has lived on in the imagination of the Persians, and all through the nineteenth century and even up to the present day the style has been endlessly copied. These copies are easily identified once they have been pointed out, and their outstanding characteristic is the lack of any artistic merit; the drawing and colours are bad, and the shapes heavy and monotonous. Perhaps the best advice is not to touch anything obviously coarse. Even if it is eighteenth-century, its value is much lower than that of a seventeenth-century piece.

British interests in the Middle East are of long standing, and a surprising number of Safawid works of art are to be found throughout the British Isles and Commonwealth. This means that there is a sufficient number available to make looking worthwhile, and the finest examples are still liable to be very cheap.

MUSEUMS AND COLLECTIONS
Persian pottery can be seen at the following:

GERMANY
Berlin: Staatliche Museen

GREAT BRITAIN
London: British Museum
            Victoria and Albert Museum

IRAN
Teheran: Iran Archaeological Museum

PORTUGAL
Lisbon: Calouste Gulbenkian Foundation

U.S.A.
New York: Metropolitan Museum of Art

FURTHER READING
Later Islamic Pottery by Arthur Lane, London, 1959.

ARTHUR NEGUS
COLLECTORS' ITEM

KELIM RUGS

The technique of *kelim,* that is slit tapestry weaving, is probably older than the better-known hand knotting of oriental pile carpets. But, apart from a few fifteenth- and sixteenth-century silk *kelims* from Kashan and the more commercially produced Persian *sehnas,* most were made by nomads and villagers throughout the Middle East for daily use, with the result that few have survived in good condition from before 1800. Those that can be found today have thus retained the simplicity and freedom of design only found in the very earliest pile carpets. Most impressive is the Caucasian *pallas* which often comes in large sizes up to eighteen feet by twelve feet, with powerful tarantula and scorpion symbols against the evil eye. Prices, depending on age, condition and size, vary between £80 and £200. Turkish *kelims* are more subtle, with gentle colours and more detailed designs often of stylised flowers. Especially interesting are the *karamanis* (£60–£150), which were woven in two halves on narrow looms in sizes up to twelve feet by six feet, and, rarer still, small, niche-design, prayer *kelims* which often use beautiful magentas, greens and traces of metal thread. Prices: £40 and upwards.

Kelims from Persia include thick Kurdish pieces from the north west and Kashgai tribal types from the Shiraz area at between £50 and £150. The latter often echo their pile relations using medallion designs, angular flowers and geometric forms. Old north west Persian *sehnas,* on the other hand, often use a single delicate medallion on a field of a curved and flowing pattern which is not found elsewhere in the Middle East. Prices range between £80 and £250, while those woven on silk warps start at £200.

Finally, some smaller groups. These include the Bessarabians from Rumania and the Balkans. Rarest types have large, realistic floral motifs (and sometimes human figures or animals) on plain grounds and are extremely tightly woven. Prices: £250–£1,000. The red and blue *Shaquiords* (£200–£400) from western Turkey are finely woven, come in large sizes with leaf and branch designs and, sometimes, a number of prayer-niche shapes across the field. Turkoman *kelims* are extremely rare, most flat-weaves from this area being embroidered or worked with a *sumakh* running stitch.

Collectors' Hints

Watch for a tight, canvas-like weave, using hand-spun wool. New types use cotton or machine-spun warps. The toughest *kelims* can be used on the floor but always put any old, fine or worn pieces on the wall as these are generally becoming harder to find. Colours should be of vegetable origin and rich with subtle variations in tone. Antique pieces acquire a definite silky patina. Avoid bright, hard colours, especially orange or muddy purple, which are usually chemical. Guard, too, against colours that have run on dry, brittle wool.

Bottom left: ***Antique Caucasian pallas*** with *scorpion design. Mid-nineteenth century.*

Bottom right: ***Unusual Kelim from Shiraz,*** *south west Persia. Late nineteenth century.*

Opposite: ***Antique prayer kelim.*** *Anatolian, c. 1800.*

David Black Oriental Carpets, London W.11

David Black Oriental Carpets, London W.11

David Black Oriental Carpets, London W.11

Masterpieces in Miniature

B. W. Robinson

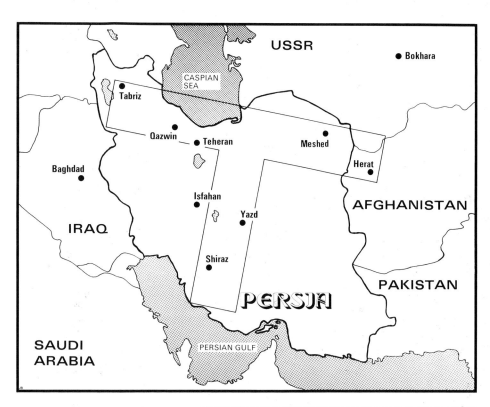

Above: **Map of Persia** *showing the main centres of miniature painting during the sixteenth and seventeenth centuries.*

Fig. 1 **Khusraw killing the lion** *by Shaykhzada, Tabriz school, c.1525. 12¾ x 8¾ ins. This miniature is an illustration to a poem by Nizami which celebrates the life of Khusraw, the last great king of the Sassanian (pre-Islamic) dynasty. The story of his love for the Armenian princess Shirin is one of the great romances of Persian literature. In this miniature he is seen killing a lion with his fist outside Shirin's tent. (Chester Beatty Library, Dublin.)*

Jewel-like miniatures of exceptionally high quality characterise Persian painting in the sixteenth and seventeenth centuries

During the sixteenth and seventeenth centuries, the king of Persia was known to Europe as the Grand Sophy, a slightly distorted echo of the family name of Safawi, borne by the ruling house throughout that period. The dynasty was founded by Isma'il who was swept to power by a wave of nationalist revival at the beginning of the sixteenth century. He had the great advantage of being able to trace his ancestry not only to the Prophet Muhammad's family, but also to the pre-Islamic Persian dynasty of the Sassanians; for after the overthrow of the latter by the Arabs in the middle of the seventh century, Shahr-banu, daughter of the last Sassanian monarch, is said to

have married Husayn, Muhammad's grandson, and from this union the Safawid family boasted its descent.

From the Arab conquest to the enthronement of Shah Isma'il – a period of 850 years – Persia had been in a fragmented state and under the domination of a succession of foreign invaders, Arabs, Turks, Mongols and Tartars. However, it was under the Mongol rulers in the fourteenth century that a truly Persian style of painting was first developed, and in the following century, under the Tartar Timurids (the family of Timur, or Tamburlaine), it achieved heights it was never to surpass, despite the increased elaboration and magnificence of Safawid Court painting in the period we are to consider.

It must be remembered that classical Persian painting was an art of book-illustration; some murals were produced, it is true, but only a few have survived, in a very damaged state, and they are, in effect, simply enlarged miniatures. The painter's status was relatively humble. He was just one among the body of craftsmen upon whose varied skills the production of a fine book depended, a body that included the calligrapher or scribe, the paper-makers, colour-men and grinders of gold, the illuminator, the ruler of margins and column-lines, and the binder.

The scribe, whose craft gave him the privilege of inscribing the Word of God, enjoyed considerably higher standing than the others; the painter, on the contrary, was always under something of a cloud, as his profession was abhorred by strict Muslims who shared the Semitic horror of idolatry embodied in the Second Commandment, and were taught to believe that in portraying human beings and animals the painter was usurping the functions of the Creator. This explains why, in many Persian paintings, the faces and figures have been wilfully defaced. Nevertheless, the tradition of pictorial art in Persia had remained so firmly embedded in the national character for two thousand years that painting was not only tolerated, but actively encouraged and patronised by the great majority of Persian rulers.

If we superimpose a large capital T on the map of Persia, it will give us a rough idea of the relative positions of the three main centres of painting on the eve of Shah Isma'il's accession. The right-hand end of the horizontal will rest on Herat, now within the borders of Afghanistan, but then capital of the great province of Khurasan. Fine manuscripts and miniatures had been produced there throughout the fifteenth century under the Timurid rulers, the last of whom, Sultan Husayn Mirza (1468–1506), was the patron of Bihzad, the most celebrated of all Persian painters. The Herat style was exquisite, precise, and slightly academic.

The left-hand end of the horizontal of the giant T rests on Tabriz. During the latter half of the fifteenth century this city had been the capital of the Turkman princes who, taking advantage of the increasingly confused state of the Timurid empire, had gradually moved in from the West and established their power over the whole of Persia, excepting only Khurasan. Painting under the later Turkman rulers was brilliant in colour, sometimes uneven in execution, and often markedly original in concept and treatment.

The base of our capital T rests on Shiraz. This most Persian of all Persian cities had been under

A. C. Cooper

Fig. 2 *Suicide of Shirin on the corpse of the murdered Khusraw,* possibly by Sultan Muhammad, Tabriz, c.1505. $11\frac{3}{4} \times 8\frac{3}{4}$ ins.
Sultan Muhammad's style evolved in the Turkman court where he began his career. This final episode in the love story of Khusraw shows Shirin killing herself on the corpse of her murdered husband.
(*Keir Collection, London.*)

Fig. 3 **Bahram Gur Hunting** by *Sultan Muhammad, Tabriz, c.1540.*
Bahram Gur ruled Persia from 420 to 438 A.D. He is commemorated by Omar Khayyam as 'The Great Hunter'. Sultan Muhammad's style at this stage in his career was less exuberant and more academic than his earlier work illustrated in Fig. 2.
(*British Museum, London.*)

Turkman rule since the middle of the fifteenth century, by which time it seems already to have assumed the role of purveyor of illustrated manuscripts on a commercial scale to those who could not afford to maintain a library staff of their own. For this purpose a fairly simple but generally satisfactory style had been evolved from a blend of Turkman court painting with elements of the Shiraz style as practised earlier under the Timurids. This 'utility' style was broad and effective, though without much refinement or elaboration, and is found in countless illustrated volumes of the works of Firdausi, Nizami and other favourite authors during the last quarter of the fifteenth century.

It was from Herat and Tabriz that Shah Isma'il, once he had settled in the latter city as his capital, recruited his library staff, which eventually included the aging Bihzad. The traditions of the two cities are separately recognisable in many of the paintings executed in his reign and in the early years of his son Tahmasp, who succeeded him in 1524, and are personified, as it were, in the work of Shaykhzada and of Sultan Muhammad. Shaykhzada was a pupil of Bihzad and a native of Khurasan; his work is exquisitely fine and often expressive. He had all his master's perfection of technique, but lacked the vital spark of genius (Fig. 1). Sultan Muhammad, a Tabrizi, may well have begun his career under the Turkman princes before taking

service with the conquering Isma'il, and his work at this stage exemplifies the Turkman strain in the evolving Safawid court style (Fig. 2). He brought to it a feeling for fantasy, a fertile imagination, and a bubbling sense of humour. His brilliant and exuberant paintings are in strong contrast to the meticulous academic style of Shaykhzada.

Tahmasp (1524–1576), the second Safawid king, was a keen patron of painting in the earlier part of his reign, and actually took lessons from Sultan Muhammad. From his accession until about 1550 he maintained a library staff of unequalled brilliance, and during this period the court style of painting was 'ironed out', so that by the late 1530s even Sultan Muhammad had been persuaded, or driven, to drop his exuberant idiosyncrasies and conform to the smooth and resplendent academic norm, as can be seen from his work in the famous British Museum Nizami manuscript of 1539–43.

In the latter part of Tahmasp's reign, the capital was moved from Tabriz (uncomfortably near the Turkish frontier) to Qazwin, further to the east. But the king had by now become a religious bigot, and had ceased to take any interest in painting, and though a certain amount of work was done in the new capital under the patronage of the nobility, the best painters seem to have transferred their services to the able and cultured young prince Ibrahim Mirza, who held his court at Meshed

Fig. 4 **Rustam in battle** *from the*
Shahnama *(Book of Kings) by*
Firdausi, Shiraz school, 1566.
14 x 8 ins. (Private Collection.)

Fig. 5 **Bahram Gur hunting**
from the Shahnama *of Firdausi*
by Mu'in, 1693.
(Metropolitan Museum of Art,
New York.)

Fig. 6 **The Vizier pleads for the**
life of a boy bandit, *Bokhara*
school, 1548. 8 x 5 ins.
This miniature is an illustration
to the Gulistan *(Rose Garden) by*
Sa'di.
(Private Collection.)

Fig. 7 **Two Lovers** *by Riza-i-*
Abbasi, Isfahan school, 1629.
7 x 4½ ins.
(Metropolitan Museum of Art,
Francis M. Weld Fund, 1950.)

Fig. 8 **Lovers in a garden**
pavilion, *Meshed school,*
c.1560. 18½ x 12¾ ins.
(Keir Collection.)

Fig. 9 **'She would and she would**
not' *by Muhammadi, Qazwin*
school, c.1575. 7¼ x 3½ ins.
Muhammadi is said to have been
the son of the Sultan Muhammad.
(Museum of Fine Arts, Boston,
Massachusetts.)

(Fig. 8). The style was becoming harder in outline, and the human figures slimmer and more supple, with a tendency towards longer necks and rounder faces. We find an increasing number of drawings, often lightly tinted and usually of single figure subjects. This style is generally associated with the painter Muhammadi of Herat, who is said to have been a son of Sultan Muhammad (Fig. 9).

Meanwhile at Shiraz and at Bokhara, distinct styles of painting flourished. As we have seen, Shiraz was the centre, at the end of the fifteenth century, of the simplified 'commercial' Turkman style, and during the first years of Safawid rule this style continued virtually unchanged except for the incorporation of the characteristic Safawid turban with its slender baton, usually coloured red, rising from the centre. By the middle of the sixteenth century Shiraz painting had approached the metropolitan style more closely, but its colouring remained paler and the general effect is often rather flat and provincial (Fig. 4). The number of Shiraz manuscripts surviving from the sixteenth century indicates that the city continued its busy commercial activities in book-production.

Bokhara, in the land of the Uzbeks, was the capital of the Shaybanid dynasty during the sixteenth century. The founder of the dynasty, Shaybani Khan, sacked Herat in 1507, abducting a number of painters and other craftsmen who were

Fig. 10 **Picnic scene** *by Riza-i-'Abbasi, Isfahan school, 1629. 8½ x 5½ ins.*
This miniature is one of a group which has played an important part in the reconstruction of the career of Riza-i-'Abbasi, the most distinguished painter of the seventeenth century Persian school.
(Keir Collection.)

Fig. 11 **Combat of the Lion and the Ox** *by Sadiqi Beg, Qazwin school, 1591. 11¾ x 8¼ ins. This miniature is taken from a manuscript of the* Anwar i Suhayli *(Lights of Canopus), a book of popular fables. (Library of the Marquess of Bute.)*

set to work for their new masters. Although Shaybani Khan was defeated and killed by Shah Isma'il in 1510, the Uzbeks continued to give trouble on the north-eastern frontier, and in 1535 they again raided Herat, transporting a further body of artists and craftsmen across the Oxus. Bokhara painting thus began as almost indistinguishable from the Herat style of Bihzad and his school, and this style continued to be its model till well after the middle of the sixteenth century. Sultan 'Abd al-'Aziz (1540–50) was the greatest patron of the arts of the book among the Shaybanid rulers (Fig. 6). But soon after this, Bokhara painting became lifeless and sterile; the imported Herat artists were dead, and their Uzbek pupils do not seem to have had the ability to keep the style alive, far less to develop it.

Returning to the metropolitan style of Qazwin and Meshed, we find the slim and exquisite youths and girls of Muhammadi and his followers throughout the 1570s and 1580s, disporting themselves elegantly at picnics and hunting parties, as well as in the inevitable court scenes. One or two distinguished new artists, such as Sadiqi Beg (Fig. 11) and Siyawush the Georgian, made their appearance at this time. A simplified form of Muhammadi's style is also found in the illustrations of a number of manuscripts from Khurasan, and it seems likely that they were produced in much the same commercial manner as were the Shiraz manuscripts already mentioned.

In 1598 Shah 'Abbas the Great established his capital at Isfahan, in the very centre of Persia, and at that time a very distinguished painter was coming into prominence under whose influence Persian painting underwent a gradual but profound change. This was Riza, whose work under the patronage of Shah 'Abbas earned him the epithet of 'Abbasi. Ever since Persian painting was first seriously studied in the West, some sixty years ago, he has been the centre of controversy. The nub of the problem is this: are the exquisite drawings and miniatures bearing the signature or attribution 'Riza' or 'Aqa Riza' and dating from the 1590s and early 1600s by the same hand as the rather different, coarser, but still masterly works signed 'Riza-i-'Abbasi' between about 1620 and 1635, or are these two groups the work of two different men of the same name? This is no place to rake over the embers of this old dispute; suffice it to say that many who, like the present writer, were formerly 'dualists' have been converted to the view that Aqa Riza and Riza-i-'Abbasi are one and the same painter at different stages of his career. This has been brought about partly by the discovery and publication of several important 'bridge' works (Fig. 10), and partly by the forceful and scholarly writings of Dr. Ivan Stchoukine of Beirut, perhaps the foremost living authority on Persian painting.

In Riza's work, then, we can trace the transition from the slim figures, fluent draughtsmanship, and pure colours of Muhammadi to the distinctly plumper young men and women (often, indeed, with a discreet indication of a double-chin), rapidly sketched with nervous calligraphic strokes, or strongly coloured with purples, yellows and browns. These youths have more than a hint of decadence in their languid postures, curling whiskers and affected gestures. Indeed, after the death of Shah 'Abbas the Great (1628), the

Safawid dynasty rapidly sank into a state of weakness and corruption under a succession of ineffectual or dissipated monarchs.

The style of Riza-i-'Abbasi had many followers in the middle and later years of the seventeenth century, amongst whom Muhammed Qasim was one of the most noteworthy, but the best of the master's successors was probably his pupil Mu'in whose exceptionally long working life stretched from about 1635–1707 (Fig. 5). At first he followed Riza very closely – indeed, he was not above forging his master's signature – but as the century progressed he evolved a fluent and effective style of his own and remained the last great master of the traditional Persian style.

In about 1675, when Mu'in was still in his prime, a younger painter, Muhammed Zaman, was sent to study painting in Italy. The late seventeenth century was not, of course, by any standards the golden age of Italian painting, but Muhammed Zaman conscientiously absorbed the canons of perspective, modelling, and chiaroscuro, and on his return to Persia produced a number of highly finished miniatures in an Italianate style. These immediately 'caught on', and by the end of the century had determined the course of Persian painting for the next two hundred years. But by 1700 the glorious Safawid dynasty was all but played out. In 1722 a comparatively small band of Afghan marauders was able to invade the country, rout the vastly superior Persian army, besiege and sack Isfahan, the capital, and bring the dynasty to an ignominious end.

FURTHER READING
Painting in Islam by Sir T. W. Arnold, reprinted New York, 1965.
Les Peintures des Manuscrits de Shah Abbas Ier **à la fin des Safavis** by Ivan Stchoukine, Paris, 1964.
Persian Painting by Basil Gray, Geneva, 1961.
Les Peintures des Manuscrits Safavis de 1502–1587 by Ivan Stchoukine, Paris, 1959.
Persian Miniature Painting by Laurence Binyon, J. V. S. Wilkinson and Basil Gray, London, 1933.

The Carpets of Persia

Edmund de Unger

Persian carpets cover the floors of homes throughout the world. Their owner may know nothing else about Persian art, yet the delicate design and warm colours of Persian carpets will immediately delight him

It is in carpets that the Persians achieved artistic supremacy. Persian pottery, despite the magnificence of its lustre and colours, may have to contend with China. Western architecture may be preferred to that of Persia. Persian miniatures are within their self-imposed limitations unsurpassed but again the delicate brush-work of the Chinese or Japanese masters or early fourteenth century French miniatures may have just as much appeal.

Persian carpets, on the other hand, have no real rivals and world opinion has rightly awarded supremacy to them.

The origin of carpet-making goes back far into early history. The oldest existing carpet was found in 1949 by the Russian archaeologist, Rudenko, in one of the burial mounds of the Pazyryk valley of the Altai mountains. This carpet, which is in the Hermitage in Leningrad, is knotted and is believed to have been made in the fourth or fifth century B.C. Its intricate and elaborate design presupposes a long tradition of carpet-making. The design is strongly influenced by the style of the Achaemenid dynasty which ruled over Persia from the sixth to the fourth century B.C.

This particular carpet has been preserved because of exceptional climatic circumstances – the relentless frost of the Altai mountains – for carpets are by their very nature perishable. Consequently, we have no substantial knowledge of any Persian carpets made before the beginning of the sixteenth century, although from miniature illustrations it would seem that the patterns in the fourteenth and fifteenth centuries were geometrical.

In one of the most celebrated Persian manuscripts, the *Khwaju Kimani* (dated 1396) which is now preserved in the British Museum, there are several miniatures showing carpets. These are decorated with a geometrical pattern consisting of star shapes and octagonal compartments. The borders of most of these carpets have stylised *Kufic*

writings. In another famous manuscript, the *Shahnama Book of the Kings of Firdausi* (copied about 1375) known as the *Demotte Shah Name* after its original owner, an animal which looks like a dragon is depicted. This design may have originated in China, whence Persian artists of the great period of carpets – the sixteenth and seventeenth centuries – often borrowed motifs.

Apart from miniature paintings, we also have the evidence of travellers who mention carpets. Ruy Gonzales de Clavijo, ambassador of the King of Castille to Timur, or Tamburlaine, describes in his account of 1404, the beautiful carpets he saw in Timur's capital of Samarkand. Another ambassador, Barbaro, who was sent by the Republic of Venice to the 'White Sheep' Prince Uzun Hasan (1466–78) in 1471 to Tabriz, is more explicit: 'The ground was covered with most beautiful carpets between which carpets and those of Cairo and Borsa (in my judgment) there is as much difference as between the cloth made of English wool and those of Saint Matthew's'. By 'Borsa', Barbaro refers to the ancient Turkish capital of Bursa, which was celebrated for its carpets.

This testimonial is one of the earliest confirming the supremacy of Persian carpets over the Turkish and Cairene carpets.

As we do not know of any surviving Persian carpets from this period, we can only observe from the representation of Persian miniature paintings that a change of carpet design took place towards the end of the fifteenth century. In the miniatures of the famous Persian painter, Bihzad and his pupils, we see new types of carpets decorated with arabesques and floral scrolls, medallions and compartments. These changes may be attributed to the Timurid Sultan Husayn Mirza (1468–1506) who, like his Florentine contemporary Lorenzo de' Medici, gathered the best artists and poets to his Court. The carpets shown in the miniatures of this period became the prototype of the great period of the subsequent two centuries.

In 1502, Shah Isma'il established the Safawid dynasty. He reunited the country, and under him and his son, Shah Tahmasp (1524–76), Persia enjoyed a period of great prosperity in which the arts and crafts flourished.

In the sixteenth century Persian carpets made of wool and silk were produced by first-class craftsmen, often from cotton prototypes designed by famous artists. There was close co-operation between the painters and weavers, and the magnificent result is not surprising. The Court itself

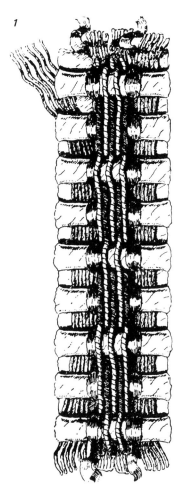

Oxford University Press

Fig. 1 *Diagram showing metal
threads cloth-woven over two
and under two warps in the
manner characteristic of many
'Polonaise' carpets.*

played an important part by establishing royal looms which were supported by large orders.

The Persian carpet designers' great achievement was, above all, harmony. The different motifs, such as scrolls and palmettes, were ingeniously moulded into a unity; the colours are subtle, often subdued, but always delicate. Persian carpets of the sixteenth century are well balanced and never overcrowded.

The seventeenth century in Persia started with the great Shah 'Abbas (1588–1628), a grandson of Shah Tahmasp. He transferred the capital in 1598 from Qazwin to near Isfahan where some of the mosques and palaces built by him still evoke our admiration and give us an idea of the splendour of his reign.

Unfortunately, from the point of view of carpets, this period was already one of decline. The majority are still splendid, but compared with the products of the sixteenth century they lack the strength and simplicity of earlier designs. The motifs become more and more elaborate and repetitive and sometimes even ostentatious. Even so, this period produced the magnificent 'Polonaise' carpets.

Under the successors of Shah 'Abbas, the manufacture of carpets continued, and we have the testimony of many European travellers such as Chardin and Piero de Valla who were struck by the beauty of Persian carpets.

In 1722 Isfahan was overrun by the Afghans and the Safawid dynasty came to an end. Carpet-making continued on a village and tribal basis, but without the Court's patronage. The great age of Persian carpets was over.

When examining the carpets of the sixteenth and seventeenth centuries, we have to bear in mind that comparatively few examples have survived. Another point to remember is that, even among those which have survived, they have suffered the wear and tear and neglect of centuries. Only a few are really first class and these can without any doubt be attributed to royal patronage.

The classification of Persian carpets of this period is not without difficulty. We assume that there were royal looms in great cities like Tabriz, Qazwin and Kashan, but with the exception of Isfahan, we have no documentary evidence of this. Nor do we know which type of carpets were made in which towns. Therefore it seems safest to classify carpets by their design and decoration rather than by their assumed place of origin.

The dating of carpets is equally difficult. We have only a few examples which are authoritatively dated, such as the 'Ardabil' carpet, which is dated 1539, and the hunting carpet in the Poldi Pezzoli Museum in Milan, dated 1521. Other carpets were documented by the date of arrival of a Persian ambassador bringing them as presents. Again, the representation of carpets of the sixteenth and seventeenth centuries on Persian or Indian miniatures or on contemporary European paintings can be a useful guide.

Broadly speaking, the carpets of the sixteenth and seventeenth centuries can be classified in the following way: hunting carpets, animal carpets, medallion carpets with flower or scroll decoration, vase carpets, garden carpets, prayer carpets and the so-called 'Polonaise' carpets.

Hunting carpets are truly the most magnificent carpets in the world. Among them, one of the finest and most famous is in the Museum of Applied Arts in Vienna. It belonged to the former Imperial House and is reputed to have been a present from Peter the

Great of Russia (1672–1725) to the Emperor Leopold I (1640–1705). In fact, it was probably a present made to the Russian Court by an earlier Shah in the sixteenth century. In its centre field, Persian riders chase antelopes, boars, gazelles, foxes and other animals. The superb border consists of *peris* (angels) surrounded by parrots and Chinese cloudbands. The entire colour scheme is salmon pink, the material silk. The cartoon of this carpet may have been designed by the famous miniature painter, Sultan Muhammad. The size of the carpet is one hundred and twenty-six inches by two hundred and sixty-seven inches and it must have taken fifteen to twenty years to make.

There is a similar though not quite so sumptuous carpet which is now in the Boston Museum of Fine Arts. This belonged formerly to the Torrigiani family in Florence, who, not realising its value or beauty, covered the floor of their hot-house with it. A smaller but very beautiful carpet is preserved in the Royal Palace at Stockholm. The hunting carpet in the Poldi Pezzoli Museum in Milan is dated but its design is not as spontaneous as that of the one in Vienna. Probably it is a provincial copy of a court carpet.

Successful collaboration between painters and weavers

Animal carpets follow hunting carpets most closely. Among these, perhaps the finest is a fragment (Fig. 11) which depicts in its medallion a court scene in a pavilion. The colour of the medallion is light blue and in the background there are bay trees. The whole scene bears a close resemblance to Persian miniatures of the mid-sixteenth century and this fragment is a striking proof of the successful collaboration between painters and weavers; the result is a stupendous scene in wool. The size of this unique fragment is seventy-seven inches by eighty-two inches. It belonged to Baron F. Hatvani in Budapest and was seized during the siege of Budapest in 1945. Its present location is unknown.

Another superb carpet designed with a central medallion and animals is in the Musée des Arts Décoratifs in Paris (Fig. 3). The colouring of the border and medallion is red and the field is a delicate yellow, decorated with beautifully shaped trees, some of them in blossom, birds and animals. The border contains Chinese cloudbands, and pheasants, which in a different way figure on the Vienna hunting carpet.

One of the most famous carpets designed with a medallion and plants is the so-called 'Ardabil' carpet, which is preserved in the Victoria and Albert Museum, London (Fig. 7). Originally it was in Ardabil (North West Persia) where it decorated the shrine of Shaykh Safi, the ancestor of the Safawid dynasty. It is dated 1539, and was sold in 1893 in order to raise money to restore the dilapidated shrine. The size of the carpet is two hundred and eight inches by four hundred and thirty-seven inches, which renders it the largest surviving carpet from the sixteenth century. It has three hundred and forty knots in every square inch. Two mosque lamps appear to hang from the centre medallion and the colours of the field are mainly different shades of blue. The centre medallion is mainly in shades of yellow, and is so delicately designed that it recalls the luminous stained glass rosette windows of

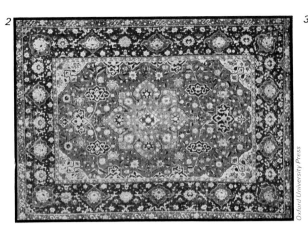

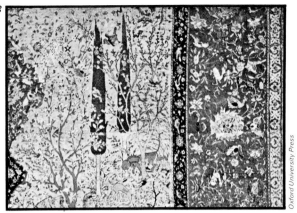

Oxford University Press

Oxford University Press

Fig. 2 **Medallion carpet**, c.1600. *Silk.*
(Collection of J. Widener.)

Fig. 3 **Medallion carpet** *(detail), sixteenth century.*
Decorated with trees in blossom, birds and animals on a yellow ground which contrasts with the red border and medallion, this is one of the most beautiful wool carpets of the period.
(Musée des Arts Décoratifs, Paris.)

Museum Photo

A. C. Cooper

Fig. 4 **Silk carpet,** *possibly from Kashan, c.1600.*
(Metropolitan Museum of Art, New York. Bequest of Benjamin Altman.)

Fig. 5 **Vase carpet,** *seventeenth century. Wool.*
Amongst the flowers which form the major part of the decoration are three vases which give the carpet its name.
(Keir Collection, London.)

6

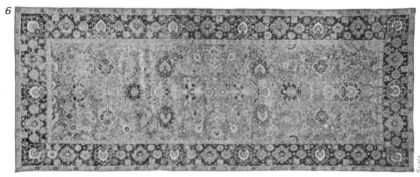

Fig. 6 *'Herat' or 'Isfahan' carpet,* seventeenth century. Wool.
Some of these carpets could have been made in India.
(Museo Bardini, Florence.)

7

8

9

10

early French gothic cathedrals.

Figure 2 shows an extremely fine silk carpet which belongs to a small group of which perhaps not more than ten have survived. The interplay of the rich colours, the restraint in design and the perfect proportions render this carpet exceptionally attractive.

For the Persians, many carpets not only represented, but also provided substitutes for, gardens. In the severity of Persian winters, and from the aridity of the deserts, they could be admired, and the brief spell of spring could be recalled and compared with the Paradise so beautifully described by the Prophet in the Koran.

Figure 10 shows a so-called garden carpet which is a perfect reproduction of a sixteenth-century Persian garden and is now the property of the Museum of Applied Arts, Vienna. Formerly it belonged to the celebrated Dr. A. Figdor, one of the greatest collectors of the century, who found it in a farmhouse in Upper Austria. The field is divided into six compartments which are separated by water canals, in which fishes swim. Each compartment represents a section of the garden, full of trees, birds and animals. The colour is red and the carpet is composed of nineteen thousand knots, eight hundred to every square inch. Among the few surviving sixteenth- to eighteenth-century garden carpets, this one takes a special place. The most celebrated garden carpet, however, is in the Prince of Wales Museum in Jaipur.

The nostalgic feeling for gardens and nature is expressed in the so-called 'vase' carpets (Fig. 5). These are longish, narrow carpets with flower decoration, and among them can be discerned one or two hidden vases. The colours used are usually blues or reds and the design of flowers is often most effective. Truly, these carpets are good substitutes for a garden.

'Polonaise' carpets were typical products of the period of Shah 'Abbas. During his reign, European art began to influence Persia and the 'Polonaise' carpets have a certain 'baroque' feeling. The name of these carpets originates from the 1878 Paris Exhibition when quite a few of those exhibited came from Poland. Beyond any doubt, they are Persian and most of them were produced between 1600 and 1660. Perhaps they were the results of the Persians' attempts to export more silk products to the West for they are made entirely of silk, inlaid with gold and silver threads. The colouring is delicate, subtle pastel shades and when in good condition they are incredibly beautiful (Fig. 8).

In the seventeenth century, Polonaise carpets were presented by the Shah to European rulers and princes. In Venice, at the San Marco Treasury, several are preserved which can be related to the Persian Ambassador's gifts between 1607 and 1622. The most famous 'Polonaise' carpet is perhaps the 'coronation' carpet in Denmark which has been used for the coronations of the Kings of Denmark since the seventeenth century.

Another carpet of the seventeenth century which is seen quite frequently is the so-called 'Herat' or 'Isfahan' carpet. These are often large and their fields contain elaborate, almost over-elaborate, designs with cloudbands, scrolls, palmettes and other plants. Their colouring is usually red and their border often in greens or blues. The knotting is rather coarse and there is no evidence that these carpets were in fact produced in either Herat or Isfahan. On the contrary, some of them were probably made in India, whence they were exported to Europe in fairly large quantities. Standing alone, these carpets are quite attractive; but putting a 'Herat' or 'Isfahan' side by side with a sixteenth-century Persian carpet, one cannot fail to notice the great difference between the two (Fig. 6).

Fig. 7 'Ardabil' carpet, Persia, 1539. Wool, 208 x 437 ins.
This 'Ardabil' carpet originally decorated the shrine of Shaykh Safi, ancestor of the Safawid dynasty. The central medallion is so delicately designed that it is reminiscent of a stained glass window.
(Victoria and Albert Museum, London.)

Fig. 8 'Polonaise' carpet, seventeenth century. Silk woven with silver and gold threads. 'Polonaise' carpets such as this, show the influence of European design which was filtering into Persia at this date.
(Keir Collection.)

Fig. 9 Diagram of a horizontal cross-section of a 'Polonaise' carpet.

Fig. 10 Garden carpet, sixteenth century. Wool.
The field is divided into six canals in which fish swim. The whole carpet is a reproduction of a Persian garden of that date.
(Museum of Applied Arts, Vienna.)

11

Oxford University Press

Fig. 11 Medallion carpet (fragment), 1550.
Wool, 77 x 82 ins.
(Formerly in the collection of Baron F. Hatvani, Budapest.)

MUSEUMS AND COLLECTIONS

Persian carpets and rugs may be seen at the following:

AUSTRIA
Vienna: Museum of Applied Arts

FRANCE
Paris: Musée des Arts Décoratifs
GERMANY
Berlin: Islamisches Museum
GREAT BRITAIN
London: Victoria and Albert Museum
HUNGARY
Budapest: Museum of Applied Art
IRAN
Teheran: National Museum
UNITED ARAB REPUBLIC
Cairo: Museum of Islamic Art
U.S.A.
New York: Metropolitan Museum of Art

FURTHER READING

Oriental Carpets by Kurt Erdmann (translated by Charles Grant Ellis), London, 1962.
Antique Rugs from the Near East by Bode and Kühnel (translated by Charles Grant Ellis), Berlin, 1958.
Survey of Persian Art ed. by A. Upham Pope, London, 1939.
History of Oriental Carpets before the Eighteenth Century by F. R. Martin, Vienna, 1908.

Islamic
Arms and Armour

John Wallace

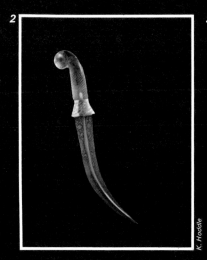

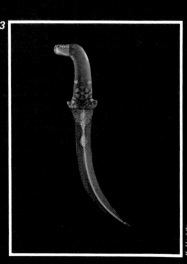

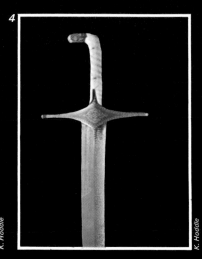

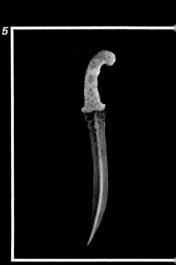

Fig. 1 *Persian soldiers in battle*,
detail, c.1548.
*From battle scenes in miniatures
we can learn much about Persian
arms and armour and the way in
which they were used.
(Victoria and Albert Museum,
London.)*

Fig. 2 *Dagger*, seventeenth
century. Length 13 ins.
*The hilt is of carved rock-crystal
and the blade is decorated with
gold.
(Victoria and Albert Museum.)*

Fig. 3 *Dagger*, seventeenth
century. Jade inlaid with silver,
length 13 ins.
*The curved blade for swords and
daggers came into vogue at the
beginning of the sixteenth
century.
(Victoria and Albert Museum.)*

Fig. 4 *Shamshir or sabre*,
sixteenth century. Watered steel
blade with an ivory grip, steel
mounts and gold inlay.
*The watered steel blade bears
Arabic texts from the Koran and
along the back is laid out the
genealogy of Shah Tahmasp
(1524–76) showing how he was
descended from Muhammad's
son-in-law, 'Ali.
(Victoria and Albert Museum.)*

Fig. 5 *Dagger*, seventeenth
century. Jade hilt with gold
piqué, length 13 ins.
(Victoria and Albert Museum.)

The West has always regarded Eastern warfare as strange and romantic but the Persians were formidable warriors whose chief concern was maximum efficiency

'He [Saladin] unsheathed his scimitar, a curved and narrow blade which glittered not like the swords of the Franks, but was, on the contrary, of a dull blue colour, marked with ten millions of meandering lines, which shewed just how anxiously the metal had been welded by the armourer . . . the Soldan . . . drew his scimitar across the cushion, applying the edge so dexterously, and with so little apparent effort, that the cushion seemed to fall asunder than to be divided by violence.'

from The Talisman, *by Sir Walter Scott.*

In this passage, Walter Scott was conceding to the conventional belief held in his time, that Crusaders' swords had straight blades, and the swords of Saracens were curved. In fact, existing examples of twelfth-century Persian swords show that there were few differences between the blades of Christendom and Islam at that period, the Persian blades being equally straight and broad, usually double-edged, and often channelled. The curved blade that we associate with the Near East did not appear until the end of the fourteenth century, and even then the curvature of the blade usually remained slight until the beginning of the sixteenth century, a moment in history which coincided with the beginning of the Safawid dynasty, and a subsequent two hundred years of relatively stable rule in Persia (Figs. 2, 3 and 5).

Take Scott's description of the Saracen's sword out of its supposed historical context and read Persian instead of Saracen, and it serves as a fairly accurate description of the weapon which evolved in Persia early in the sixteenth century, reaching its highest level of perfection through the sword-makers who flourished during the reign of Shah 'Abbas the Great. It highlights two major characteristics of the Persian sword. First, the particular way in which it was used: it was drawn across an object, thus bringing the whole length of the blade to bear on the stroke (its purpose and effect are paralleled in the oblique-edged blade of a guillotine). Since a Persian warrior habitually fought on horseback, he would grip the hilt squarely and deliver a stroke, usually backhand, at the full length of his arm without altering his grip. Throughout the stroke, he kept the blade at right angles to his arm. This mode of swordplay was the main contributory factor to an early development of a sword hilt markedly shorter than that of a European sword which, in use, often demanded that the blade and arm were almost in a straight line (Fig. 4). It is true that the hands of Eastern peoples are generally slightly smaller than those of Europeans, but this fact was a contributory factor to the shortness of grip on Persian swords, not the main one.

Since the shape of Persian swords remained unchanged, except in minor details, from the early sixteenth to the nineteenth centuries, collectors need to take a leaf out of the Japanese sword collector's book, and concentrate on points of quality rather than of style. Scott's 'millions of meandering lines' is a nicely non-technical description of the second main characteristic of a fine Persian sword – namely, the damascening on the blade. This term refers to the effect of a particular process in the forging of steel, where a high percentage of carbon is incorporated. Apart from giving the blade an unusual combination of hardness, toughness and resilience, the process brings out figurings on the surface, known to the Persians as *jawhar*, and to Europeans as damascening. The great tenth-century Persian poet Firdausi, who wrote the *Shahnama*, Persia's greatest national epic, frequently talked of 'watered steel' – an apt description of a blade with a strongly marked *jawhar*, and one frequently used in Europe for that particular metallurgical process. Incidentally, the word damascening alludes to an association of sword-making with Damascus which was hardly applicable during the two centuries with which we deal.

The steel for the best Persian blades almost always came from India, or Golconda as it was referred to by European travellers in Persia when remarking on sword manufacture. Persians themselves judge, categorise and value a sword by its *jawhar*. It was a Russian engineer, early in the last century, who found by experiment that it was the proportion of carbon present over and above the amount necessary to convert iron into steel that dictated the various patterns of the *jawhar*, which range in ascending order of excellence from parallel stripes, through wavy lines and mottled spots, to vertebrae or 'steps'. The best blades should also have a darkish background to the *jawhar*, grey, dark-brown or black, with an overall lustre. The ideal sword has a deep dark ground with a golden gloss and a *jawhar* of *chehel nardabán* ('forty steps'), sometimes called 'Muhammad's Ladder'.

Tabriz, Qazwin and Isfahan, centres for sword manufacture

Under the early Safawid monarchs, the main centres of sword manufacture were Tabriz, Qazwin and Isfahan. By the middle of the seventeenth century it appears from accounts left by European travellers, that Qum was the city where the best swords were being made, even though this was the period of the most famous of all Persian sword-smiths, Asadallah, who signed himself as 'of Isfahan' (Fig. 6).

It would be a fortunate collector indeed who discovered a Persian sword dating from earlier than the seventeenth century. And the finding of a seventeenth-century sword complete with signature and inscription becomes more unlikely as time goes on. Inscriptions, where they exist, are usually inlaid in gold, and could comprise the swordsmith's signature, and a statement about his royal patron; more usually, the statement would be something like 'Slave of the King of the Universe' [Allah]. Or there could be religious inscriptions, chiefly texts from the Koran, or statements of ownership or poetical quotations. Not uncommon is the magic square *buduh*, which consists of a square ruled into four, and with the Arabic letters B, D, U, H set into each quarter. There are many forgeries of signatures of well-known smiths – the great Asadallah probably had his signature forged during his own lifetime – but anyone with a feeling for good taste and workmanship should spot the clumsiness of most forgeries.

It is still possible to acquire pieces of armour from this period. Apart from the existing pieces of armour which are dated, we derive our chronological knowledge from Persian miniatures of which there are many thousands. A large number of these miniatures are illustrations for the *Shahnama* which, being a traditional epic, is full of battles. Consequently, many armed warriors are depicted and provide useful material for a reasonable date structure.

By the end of the fifteenth century, the elongated helmet with a long spike had already given way to a tall, conical helmet, often fluted and crowned with a spike or plume-holder. The bowl, decorated with engraved and gilt patterns, had a broad band extending around the rim, also ornamented or inscribed. From it hung ear-guards, and a mail aventail (curtain) that fell to the shoulders.

In the first half of the sixteenth century, the helmet still had what Stocklein, in the *Survey of Persian Art*, called a 'half-ogee section', where the point of the helmet was forged in one with the skull, and drawn out. By the seventeenth century, the Persian helmet had developed into the form it was to keep until the nineteenth century; a round bowl, with a platform into which screwed a long quadrangular spike, small plume tubes riveted on each side of the skull, and a movable nasal which, when lowered, gave some protection to the face against a sweeping sword-blow (Figs. 8 and 9). A mail aventail hung to the shoulders – clear of the face in miniatures but in practice extending low over the brow in a deep fringe which all but covered the wearer's eyes. The only fairly reliable way of telling a seventeenth-century helmet from later specimens is to check whether the aventail is of riveted rather than butted mail and to ascertain whether the decoration still retains a degree of simplicity and restraint.

Changing types of armour and shields

The lamellar body armour, which is so much in evidence in earlier miniatures, appears to have given way to mail – a reasonable assumption, even though any evidence for this through miniatures always seems to be obscured by rich and colourful coats. The armour covering the thigh, a vulnerable part of the body for a horseman, is usually depicted as rows of small horizontal plates set side by side, and joined by mail to a circular dished plate protecting the knee-cap (Fig. 7). Often this type of protection is extended to the instep.

Circular plates commonly appear in sixteenth-century miniatures on the outside of a coat. It has been pointed out that this is probably a convention representing part of a cuirass (body armour) similar to, or identical with, the well-known 'pot-lid' or 'janissary' cuirasses which were stored in their thousands at the Arsenal of St. Irene in Istanbul. These consist of large, circular, convex plates for the breast and back, with further horizontal and vertical pieces joined together with mail.

Certainly this kind of cuirass was not peculiar to the Turks, for a breastplate, richly gilt-engraved with Persian inscriptions, is in the Topkapi

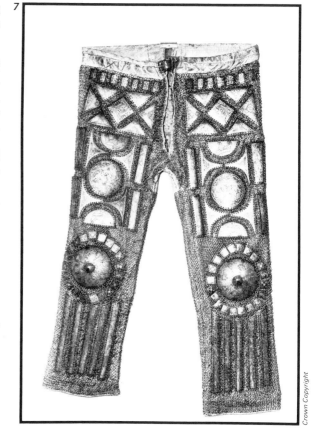

Crown Copyright

Saray Museum, Istanbul. There is evidence that these heavy cuirasses were lineal ancestors of the typical Persian *char aina* ('four mirrors') which evolved at the end of the sixteenth century and continued virtually unchanged in form right into the nineteenth century. Again, miniatures of the seventeenth century show only a single rectangular plate, when the *char aina* in fact consisted of four plates: two larger ones to cover the breast and back and two smaller ones with sections cut out to fit around the armpits. These latter are joined by straps or hinges over a mail shirt.

The characteristic tubular vambraces (armour for the forearm) which have the lower of their two hinged plates extending into a point to protect the elbows, made their appearance in the late fourteenth century. They are depicted constantly in Persian miniatures of the sixteenth and seventeenth centuries which feature armed men. By the end of the seventeenth century the short inner wrist plate is replaced by several steel splints connected by mail (Fig. 11).

A rare piece of defensive armour is the Persian cane shield constructed of willow or fig tree branches, bound in concentric rings with wool, silk or gold thread, and culminating in the centre with a steel boss. The design of this kind of shield often closely resembled the design found on carpets and other textiles of the period. In 1529, a Portuguese traveller reported that 'they (the Persians) bear shields of silk and cotton, so stout that no arrow can go through them'. It was possibly the wider use of firearms from the seventeenth century onwards that brought all-steel shields into greater favour.

The shape of the Persian circular steel shield, with its pronounced lip at the edge, may have had its origin in the hide shield of India and Central Asia. The edge is generally reinforced with a rim of iron or brass. There is no central boss, there being instead four small ones attached over the points

Museum Photo

Fig. 6 *'Damascus' blade (detail), 1660, showing the signature of Asadallah 'slave of Shah 'Abbas'. (Victoria and Albert Museum.)*

Fig. 7 **Battle trousers,** *late seventeenth century. Covered with mail and plates. The Persians were excellent horsemen and their cavalry was strong. Protective clothing for the legs and particularly the thighs was a necessity for mounted soldiers. (Royal Scottish Museum, Edinburgh.)*

Fig. 8 **Helmet,** *seventeenth century. Height 12 ins. Helmets were often fluted, as in this example. (Victoria and Albert Museum.)*

Fig. 9 **Helmet,** *sixteenth or seventeenth century. This was the type of helmet which gained popularity during the last years of the sixteenth century. The spike was now made separately and could be detached. (Private Collection.)*

Fig. 10 **Shield,** *late sixteenth century. Steel with gold decoration. (Victoria and Albert Museum.)*

Fig. 11 **Bazuband or Vambrace**, *1711. The vambrace protected the forearm.*
By the end of the seventeenth century the design of the vambrace had become refined. The inner wrist plate was replaced by several steel splints connected by mail.
(Royal Scottish Museum.)

Fig. 12 *One plate of a **char aina** ('four mirrors'), 1702.*
A char aina consisted of four plates, two larger ones to cover the breast and back and two smaller ones cut to fit round the armpits.
(Royal Scottish Museum.)

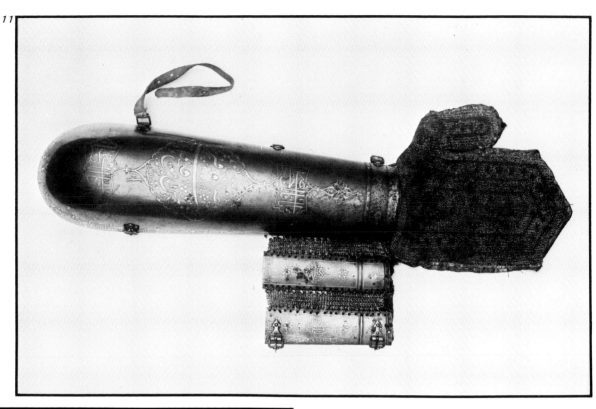

where the grip rings are riveted. The makers of this kind of shield lavished much care on its decoration, using all manner of techniques – damascening, chiselling, engraving and piercing.

The Persians were great archers, and perfected a short bow which could easily be fired from horseback. This bow was made of horn and wood, covered with birch bark, then lacquered and decorated with floral and animal motifs. Since it was a re-curved bow, it appears rather graceless when unstrung and therefore not a favourite with collectors; this could be one of the reasons why few bows of the sixteenth and seventeenth centuries have survived. One survivor worthy of special comment is a huge bow now on show in the Topkapi Saray Museum, Istanbul. It featured in a story related by the seventeenth-century Turkish historian Naima, where the only man capable of bending it was a woodcutter named Hosayn. The interest shown by the Sultan in this feat contributed to Hosayn's future fame and fortune, and subsequent elevation to the rank of Pasha.

MUSEUMS AND COLLECTIONS

Persian arms and armour may be seen at the following:

GREAT BRITAIN
Edinburgh: Royal Scottish Museum
London: British Museum
             Victoria and Albert Museum
             Wallace Collection
SWITZERLAND
Berne: Bernisches Historisches Museum
TURKEY
Istanbul: Topkapi Saray Museum
             Museum of the Janissaries
U.S.A.
New York: Metropolitan Museum of Art

FURTHER READING

Oriental Armour by H. Russell Robinson, London, 1967.
Survey of Persian Art ed. by A. Upham Pope, London, 1939, Vol. III, 'Arms and Armour' by Hans Stocklein.

Tom Scott

KINGDOM OF THE TSARS

Janis Sapiets

Russia in the 16th
and 17th Centuries

Fig. 1 (Frontispiece) *The Cathedral of St. Basil the Blessed*, *Moscow, built under the direction of Ivan the Terrible (1530–1584), mid-sixteenth century.*
The 'fairyland' architecture of St. Basil's Cathedral makes an astonishing impact on the Moscow skyline.

Fig. 2 *The Cathedral of St. Sophia*, *Novgorod, 1045–50. Iaroslav the Wise, son of the Duke of Vladimir, commissioned the building of St. Sophia. The predominant influence in the architecture is Byzantine.*

The Church, the Tsars and the Stroganovs were the major patrons of Russian art as the various regional schools came together to form a new national style until, with the accession of the Romanovs, Russian interest in the West was reawakened

The two centuries between 1500 and 1700 were marked by Russia's transformation from a weak federation of princedoms, torn and tortured by their Tartar overlords for nearly three hundred years, into a monolithic and mighty empire stretching from the White Sea to the Caspian and eastward from Novgorod to the Urals and beyond. The centre of Russia's culture and civilisation passed from the gay splendour of Kiev to the sombre

Political stability returned in 1613 with the election of Mikhail Romanov as Tsar but towards the end of the century the country was shaken by two further outbursts of violence: the religious schism in 1666–67, when the 'Old Believers' were led by the fiery and heroic Archpriest Avvakumand, and the Stepan Razin Rebellion of 1670–71.

The transitional and unsettled character of this period left a visible mark on the development of Russian art and architecture. There was great confusion of techniques and styles as the earlier Novgorod, Pskov and Suzdal' traditions merged into the new Muscovite style. This new style was formed by a combination of these regional elements of popular art with western influences. Thereafter (that is, from the seventeenth century onwards) the regional centres of art and culture such as Novgorod and Suzdal' diminished in importance in the face of the national and authoritative conception of art and architecture emanating from Moscow.

Throughout this period the Church remained the most influential patron of the arts. In icon

Victor Kennett

Novosti Press Agency

majesty of Moscow. The new power shifts were reflected in the change of the dynastic title. In the fourteenth century the ruler of Moscow was called the Grand Prince (*Velikii Kniaz'*) but by the end of the fifteenth century Ivan III of Moscow, who married the Byzantine princess, Sophia Paleologue, began to sign himself 'tsar' (a Slavonic corruption of the Latin *Caesar*). This change was formalised in 1546 by his grandson Ivan IV, called The Terrible, who became the first Russian sovereign to have himself crowned Tsar.

Russia's transition from her position as a vassal state of the Tartars to that of European power was accompanied by violent political and social upheavals. After Ivan the Terrible's death in 1584 and after the brief and ill-fated rule of Boris Godunov, the country was ravaged by a period of civil strife and foreign invasions. This became known as the *Smuta* (the Time of Troubles). Twice during this period the throne was occupied by pretenders who acquired power with the help of Poland.

painting there was a movement away from the clarity of composition and brilliance of colours typical of Novgorod, towards intricate decorative design accompanied by the subjugation of style to mystical and doctrinal themes. Traditional themes were often used together, and at times even western iconography was incorporated to form a highly complicated symbolic entity. A fine example of this can be seen in the icon representing *The Only-Begotten Son, the Word of God*, which expresses the concepts of the Creation, Redemption and the Last Judgement. It even includes the western image of the *pietà*.

The artist tried to squeeze as much as possible from life into a limited framework

Colour became subdued, flat and sometimes almost sombre. One of the most popular themes for the icon painter was the tragic life of St. John the

Fig. 3 *Portrait of Boris Godunov* (c.1551–1605), late sixteenth century.
Boris Godunov was elected Tsar in 1598. He had been Ivan the Terrible's favourite and chief member of the Regency during the minority of Tsar Fëdor Ivanovich, Ivan's successor. The details of his life are familiar to us through Pushkin's famous play, Boris Godunov. (State Historical Museum, Moscow.)

Fig. 4 *The Domes of the Annunciation Cathedral, Kremlin, 1482–90, enlarged by Ivan the Terrible, 1564. The onion-shaped domes are characteristic of ecclesiastical architecture in Russia.*

Baptist, prophet, martyr and forerunner of Christ, and the patron saint of Ivan the Terrible.

In the seventeenth century, once the *Smuta* was over, the decorative element in icon painting became even more pronounced, and colours regained their brilliance. A characteristic feature of seventeenth-century icon painting is the display of large ensembles with considerable attention paid to details of everyday life. Thus, the icon dated 1680 depicting the *Virgin of Tikhvin*, with twenty-four surrounding scenes depicting various miracles, shows the history of the province and of the construction of the monastery; the building of churches, visits of grand princes, landscapes – one has the impression that the artist tried to squeeze as much as possible from life into the limited framework of his painting.

One of the greatest repositories of icons and other *objets d'art* is the *Troitsa Lavra* (Trinity Monastery), Zagorsk, near Moscow. A most striking collection in the monastery includes a number of fifteenth- and sixteenth-century embroideries – hangings, icon cloths, shrouds, palls and

century onwards was towards a heavy and solemn style.

In architecture, too, the sixteenth and seventeenth centuries marked a period of gradual transition. Until the middle of this period Russian towns and cities were built almost entirely of wood, a matter of constant amazement to European travellers. Giles Fletcher, the English emissary to Moscow in 1588, reported 'The streets of their cities and towns instead of paving are planked with fir trees, planed and layed even close the one to the other. Their houses are of wood material without any lime or stone, built very close together with dents and notches at every corner, and so clasped together. Betwixt the trees or timber they thrust in mosse (whereof they gather plenty in the woods) to keep out the aire. . . .'

Wooden structures were dominant in Russian towns well into the nineteenth century. Until its last disastrous fire in 1812, Moscow itself was largely built of wood. But a new urban class was rising fast; well-to-do artisans and merchants determined to emulate the way of life of the nobility. One of the indications of great wealth was the possession of a palace or mansion built of stone.

For the vast majority of people, this remained no more than a dream. A very modest stone-built dwelling cost fifteen to twenty times more than a timber-built house. Besides, there was a great shortage of good master-builders and stone buildings were often badly constructed and were cold, damp and draughty, especially in winter. Living rooms were therefore made of wood until the end of the seventeenth century and even later, while stone structures were reserved for the reception chambers and the 'treasury rooms' in which valuables were stored.

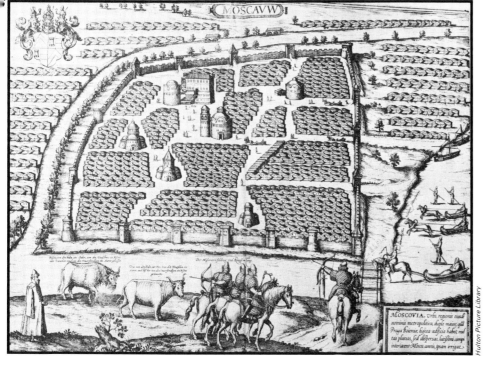

Fig. 5 *Topographical map of Moscow* from Braun and Hohenberg's Civitates Orbis Terrarum, *1573, engraved by Hoefnagel, 1573. The legendary date of the founding of Moscow is 1147 but it was not until the beginning of the fourteenth century that Moscow became the political and ecclesiastical capital of Russia, a position which it held until the founding of St. Petersburg in 1703.*

ecclesiastical vestments. One of the finest examples of this art is the icon cloth made in 1561 to the order of Princess Evfrosinia Staritskaia, the aunt of Ivan the Terrible. Evfrosinia, later put to death by her royal nephew, had a well-equipped workshop where the most skilled embroiderers of Moscow were employed. Another gift from the Staritskii family to *Troitsa Lavra* was a large shroud depicting the Lamentation which, on account of the incredible variety of stitches, creates the impression of a woven brocade. As with most works of art of this period, the embroideries display strong decorative elements.

Decorative carving was of a high standard. Every local centre had its own local craftsmen who carved crosses out of wood and other materials and who also made various objects in silver and gold for both ecclesiastical and domestic use, such as chalices, pendants, decorative book-covers, and icon mounts. Early examples of this art show a remarkable feeling for tasteful and restrained composition but the tendency from the sixteenth

The most illustrious of the privileged merchants were the Stroganovs

The wealthiest among the urban dwellers were the privileged merchants known as 'guests', the most influential members of the merchant class. The 'guests' traded in foreign countries on their own account but simultaneously fulfilled the functions of the tsar's official business agents. In return for their duties they were accorded a special status similar to that of the nobility.

The most illustrious of these merchants were the Stroganovs, who rose to fame in the sixteenth century and played the leading role in the conquest and commercial exploitation of Siberia. They not only set up trading posts along the Urals, but founded whole towns and villages. Through their efforts Perm', Velikii Ustiug and Sol'vychegodsk became, for a time, important commercial and cultural centres. The Stroganov palaces in Sol'vychegodsk and on the shores of the Kama in Novoe Usole were as magnificent as those of the Muscovite nobles and merchants.

The Stroganovs were also great patrons of the arts. The icons painted for them were the first examples of icons produced in quantity for private patrons. The exquisite draughtsmanship exhibited in these icons, their technical refinement and magnificent colours, reminiscent of the great Novgorod School of icon painting, earned their creators the name of Stroganov Masters. Their contribution to Russian art was unique; they provided art for the enjoyment of private individuals as distinct from the tsar's entourage and the Church, something which until that date was almost unknown.

The one characteristic feature in the interior of houses was the ornamental tiled fireplace. This was often splendidly designed to match the rest of the interior decoration. The bright colouring of the tiles compensated for the lack of light in the rooms and added liveliness to the interior.

Icons, in rich gold and silver mounts, were

Fig. 6 ***View of the Moscow Kremlin** from* The Travels of Olearius, *1696. Engraving. Olearius, a Western traveller in Muscovy, gives in his book a fascinating account of life in seventeenth-century Russia. This view of the Kremlin is not only a record of the impressive architecture but also serves as a catalogue of the various forms of criminal punishment to which Muscovite felons were sentenced.*

Fig. 7 ***Portrait of Tsar Aleksei Mikhailovich.***
The Romanov tsar, Aleksei Mikhailovich (1645–1676), was one of the first rulers in Russia to enjoy a Western way of life. He was particularly fond of the theatre, music and dancing.
(Collection of Count Bobrinskoi.)

Fig. 8 ***Izba,** or peasant's hut.*
Wood was a necessity in the life of every Russian. Izbas *were made on much the same plan as this for countless generations.*

another essential item in every home. 'Everyone has countless icons in the house' wrote a contemporary, Archdeacon Paul of Aleppo, 'not only inside but behind every door, even at the gates of the house, and this not only among the noblemen but even among the village peasants'.

Among the Moscow palaces and mansions of the nobles the most magnificent were those of the Princes Iusupov, Romanov and Golitsyn and of the *boiars* (noblemen) Miloslavskii and Troekurov. One can form some impression of the size of these buildings from the fact that households numbered about five hundred or more people, including several tailors and chefs and two or three score grooms.

Wooden architecture came into its own in church building

Wooden architecture had its most fascinating application in church building and this is where Russian architecture came into its own. The basic building technique consisted of laying down a frame of logs horizontally on a rectangular or polygonal plan with a roof made of flat planks laid on beams running lengthwise between the gables. This shape was common to all buildings, from a

peasant's hut (*izba*) to a church. The latter was distinguished only by the small bulbous dome on a tall drum placed over the central element. Out of this, other, sometimes very complex, shapes and structures were developed: octagonal churches with 'tent' roofs (pyramid-shaped), 'storeyed' churches with a number of shallow cubes piled on top of a cubical mass and 'cube' churches with flattened dome roofs, always crowned with a bulbous cupola. The pyramidical silhouette of the church surrounded by a cluster of peasants' huts remained a characteristic feature of the Russian landscape until after the October Revolution of 1917, and it has not quite disappeared even today.

The stone churches of the sixteenth and seventeenth centuries preserved and adopted many traditional elements of Russian architecture combining them with Western influences and skills. The influx into Moscow of foreign craftsmen in the fifteenth and sixteenth centuries was such that the city at times acquired the appearance of some prosperous Italian or Flemish town.

The Moscow Kremlin was reconstructed under Ivan III. The work was largely accomplished during his reign and was completed during the sixteenth century. Some of the most impressive Kremlin buildings from this period were erected under the supervision of the Italian architects Aristotle Fioravanti and Alevisio Novi. Ivan the

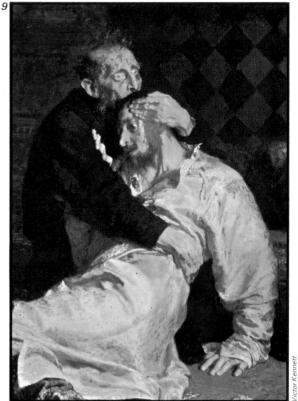

Fig. 9 **Ivan the Terrible holding his murdered son.**
Ivan the Terrible is said to have been driven mad by the death of his wife and son, Dimitrii. This madness took the form of violent fits of temper and in one of these rages he killed his other son, Ivan, in 1580.

Fig. 10 **The Church of St. Nicholas of the Weavers,**
Moscow, seventeenth century. St. Nicholas was built by the Weavers' Guild to commemorate their patron saint. It is of interest to note that it is one of the few Moscow churches in which services are still held.

Terrible added the finishing touch with the erection of the church dedicated to the protection and intercession of the Virgin, popularly known as the *Cathedral of St. Basil the Blessed*, with its richly coloured towers and cupolas. With its strange mixture of architectural styles it remains Moscow's most characteristic landmark.

The stage was set for Peter the Great and for a decisive break with the past

With the seventeenth century and the accession to the throne of the Romanov dynasty, Russia began to show more and more interest in the West. Aleksei Mikhailovich rode in a German coach, took his wife on hunting trips, went to see foreign entertainments and theatre performances and enjoyed music and dancing. The Tsar's favourite, *boiar* Matveev, whose wife was English, held receptions in his house which was furnished in a Western European style.

The stage was set for Peter the Great and for a decisive break with the past: in 1703 a new capital, St. Petersburg, was founded on the banks of the Neva and Moscow was no longer to dominate the art and architecture of Russia.

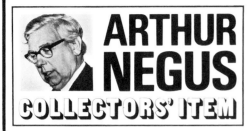

ARTHUR NEGUS COLLECTORS' ITEM

HORN

The word itself is instantly suggestive, either of red-bearded Vikings quaffing amid the smoking ruins of some East Coast Abbey, or of a quaint old lady with horn-rimmed spectacles, doing fine work at a lace-covered table. In fact, horn is one of the oldest forms of decoration.

Only in the eighteenth century did it lose its popularity; at this time when man chose to emphasise his remoteness from the animal, horn was seldom used, save as a decoration for hunting-knives and accoutrements.

In the Middle Ages, horn was an essential commodity, and the Gothic revivalists, in their attempts to recreate that age of faith, returned horn to the domestic purposes from which it had been ousted by the more practical pewter and silver.

In the later nineteenth century, horn drinking-mugs, platters and *objets* were familiar to the followers of William Morris. Horn was also used as a more refined form of decoration on crochet-hooks, pocket-knives and diary- or pencil-cases; this was in imitation of the seventeenth-century practice of combining horn with silver or gold in the decoration of cups, pistol butts, book-bindings and other essential items. The rediscovery of Scotland by the English gentry in Victoria's reign led to a new interest in horn as a relic of the Celtic past. Furniture was made incorporating antlers, for use in Scottish shooting-lodges, and the more remote passes of Central Europe were filled with English sportsmen in baggy tweeds held together by horn buttons. The longest-lived horn product was probably the hornbook, used regularly in school from the time of Augustine down to the early nineteenth century; these school-books, carrying the catechism and the Lord's Prayer, can still occasionally be found in country antique shops or bookshops.

Collecting Hints

You are most unlikely to find objects of great antiquity. Most of the medieval horn utensils were replaced by pewter or earthenware, and if you do come across a drinking-cup decorated with sea-serpents and Norse gods, it is more likely to be the property of John Ruskin than of Harald Blue-Tooth.

Where to Buy

Antique markets and jewellers' shops are the likeliest sources, as horn was often combined with precious metals.

Opposite: *Nefertiti,* Egyptian. Buffalo horn inlaid with silver. Price £3.87.

Above: Top: *Fan, 1850. Price £5. This piece illustrates how finely and delicately horn can be carved and pierced.* Bottom: *Moth brooch, 1900. Price, £14.*

Left: *Drinking-cup, eighteenth century. This fine example with its engraved pattern would fetch about £15.*

Below: Top left: *Cigar case, 1880. Price £3.50. This piece shows the use of lacquer on horn.* Top right: *Snuff mull, Scottish. Horn and silver. Price £20.* Below: *Cheese scoop. Horn and silver. Price £3.25.*

Abacus Antiques: K. Hoddle

Private Collection: K. Hoddle

Abacus Antiques: K. Hoddle

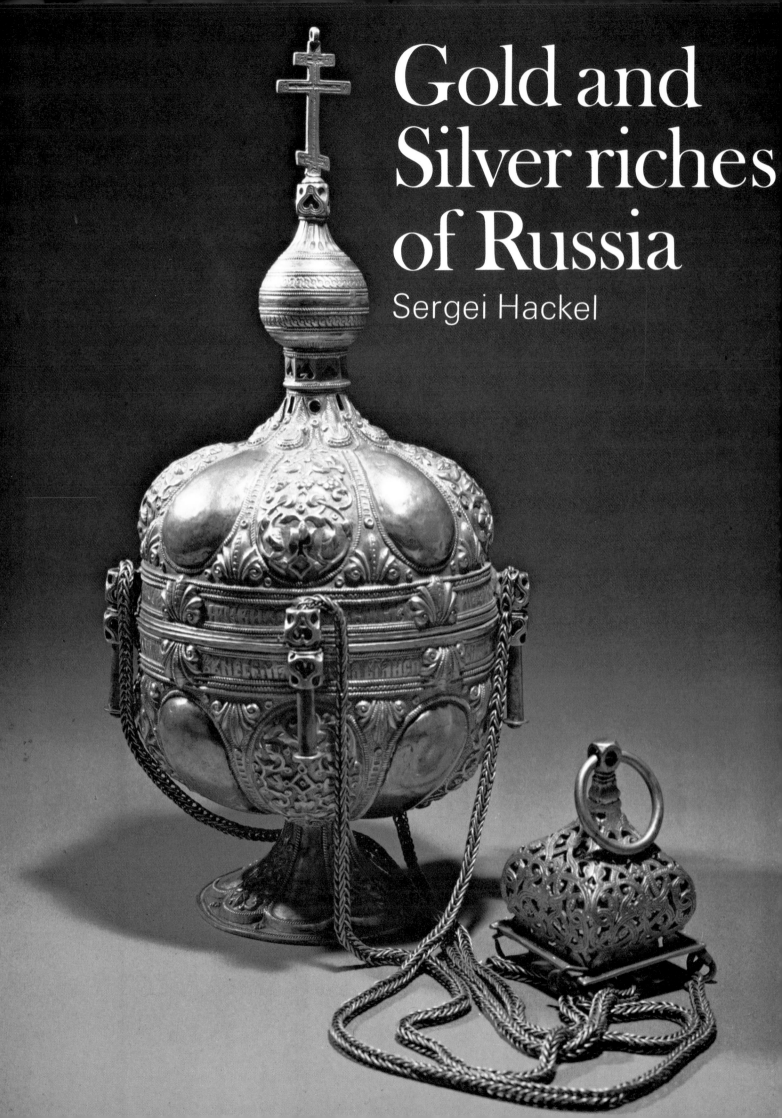

Gold and Silver riches of Russia

Sergei Hackel

As they emerged from the Time of Troubles, Russian metal-workers concentrated on the production of finely worked and elaborately decorated objects, both secular and ecclesiastical

For Russia, the sixteenth and seventeenth centuries are divided from each other by the so-called Time of Troubles, the *Smuta*, which followed the reign of Boris Godunov. It was a period of anarchy and violence, a time of bitterness, anguish and despair.

From the point of view of metal-ware, the *Smuta* meant an excessive and degrading concentration on military needs. Base metals were required primarily for guns and swords. Gold and silver were likewise perpetually in demand, both as booty and as pay for restless troops. Countless works of art

1514, the Muscovite ruler had gold- and silversmiths in his personal employ; and the influential Armoury workshops were established in the Kremlin by the middle of the century.

In the sixteenth century the Kremlin workshops were manned largely by Russians, though by the end of the century it was not uncommon for western craftsmen to be employed for a season or even longer. By contrast, the metals at their disposal, especially gold and silver, were almost invariably imported. For Russian prospectors had as yet discovered little, and exploited even less, of Russia's rich resources. Only a limited number of iron foundries were at work by the early seventeenth century. Copper and tin had to be imported throughout the sixteenth and seventeenth centuries. Silver was uncovered in the Urals only in 1667, and the serious working of Siberian gold was not to begin until 1745. Admittedly, there was a native source of gold and silver in the prehistoric burial hoards of the steppes; but even their looting began only late in the seventeenth century, and it was soon to be arrested (or, at least, exploited) by

Novosti Press Agency

Novosti Press Agency

Fig. 1 **Censer** from the Church of the Resurrection, Debra, 1674. Gold, with elaborate embossed decoration. This censer is in the form of a church, with egress for the incense through the 'windows'. (State Historical Museum, Moscow.)

Fig. 2 **Portable Icon** commissioned by Ivan Griazev, early seventeenth century. Tempera on wood mounted in silver and gold, decorated with pearls. The chased silver is decorated with enamel. (State Armoury Museum, Moscow.)

Fig. 3 **Bowl of the Tsar Aleksei Mikhailovich**, c.1629. Gold chased and decorated with polychrome enamel. The inscription states that it was presented to the Tsar in 1653 by the newly appointed Patriarch of Moscow, Nikon. (State Armoury Museum.)

were melted down to provide coinage while the disruption of social life as well as of the economy spelt unemployment for the surviving craftsmen. Only with the accession of the first Romanov in 1613 did new opportunities present themselves – to the craftsmen of Moscow, at least.

As a result of the *Smuta*, the art of sixteenth-century gold- and silversmiths has survived in comparatively few examples. This is all the more regrettable since surviving works indicate that it was the sixteenth century which saw the apogee of medieval Russian craftsmanship in jewellery and precious metals.

The inexorable rise of Muscovy among Russian principalities had culminated in the coronation of its Prince as Tsar of all Russia in 1547 and the recognition of its Bishop as Patriarch in 1589. Moscow's early sixteenth-century claim to be the 'Third Rome' in succession to the conquered Constantinople was thus rendered more convincing. But names were insufficient to impress all Russians, let alone foreign embassies. The visible glory, the trappings rather than the nomenclature of power, were needed. Consequently, from at least

Peter the Great.

In the sixteenth and seventeenth centuries, therefore, gold and silver were usually obtained from the unwanted objects of the past, from coinage or from foreign sources. And only at Court, in the great cathedrals, or in the best-endowed of monasteries, would gold and silver objects be found in any quantity.

The comparative rarity of metals helped to ensure their skilful exploitation. Though the sixteenth century decorated its metal-ware less generously than the seventeenth, few objects were left unadorned. And, with few exceptions, the techniques employed for their decoration and elaboration were the traditional ones, inherited from the Russian medieval past.

Niello, filigree and polychrome enamel were the three types of decoration most frequently applied to gold and silver. These techniques retained their popularity throughout the two centuries. Only in one respect did the sixteenth century differ from the seventeenth: in the course of the latter, filigree was no longer used as an independent ornament. It appeared only in conjunction with *cloisonné* enamel, for which it formed the frame.

For niello work, the required design was first engraved on the metal ground, then lowered by chasing. The channel thus created was filled with a black alloy and fired in a kiln to fuse it with the metal. The final product was then carefully polished to bring the pattern and the metal flush with one another. It was a technique that remained unchanged until the 1670s. The brilliant black of niello was used for outline drawings, decorative patterns, and for calligraphic ornaments.

While the brilliance of good niello work may impart an illusion of relief, filigree necessarily stands out from, and contrasts with, the background to which it is applied.

The gold and silver filigree of the sixteenth century is unmatched in its subtlety and grace. It enriches large sections of processional Gospel covers. It decorates the borders of portable icons and, on an even smaller scale, of ear-rings. Sometimes it has the organic vitality appropriate to its foliate patterns; at other times (especially in Novgorodian work) it is distributed in even, almost static patterns formed of hearts or simple spirals. At all times it has a distinctive appearance, and is

the century saw the belated introduction and growing popularity of painted enamel.

The chasing of gold and silver was undertaken throughout the period. It found particular favour in the seventeenth century, when some of the finest gold and silver objects were chased – the loving-cups of the aristocracy, for example or, towards the end of the century, the ornate chalices of Iaroslavl' and Nizhnii-Novgorod. In the virtual absence of sacred statuary (always discouraged by the Orthodox Church), and with no tradition of secular statuary until the eighteenth century, the Russian artist's nearest approach to three-dimensional representations was by way of chased relief. The expressive effigy of the Prince Dimitrii (now in the State Armoury Museum, Moscow), prepared for his tomb in 1630, is perhaps the finest example of this kind of work.

The casting of objects and ornaments in precious metal was undertaken comparatively rarely owing to the scarcity of the raw materials. The cast silver reliefs, such as adorn the Gospel cover of 1568 in the State Armoury Museum, are therefore of special interest. At the same time, it was normal and even necessary to cast objects in baser metals.

Fig. 4 *Endova, or jug,* by V. I. Streshnev, Moscow, 1644. Silver with niello decoration, diameter 11 ins.
The endova *is distinguished from the otherwise similar* bratina *(loving-cup) by its lip.*
(State Armoury Museum.)

4

Novosti Press Agency

5

Fig. 5 *Silver plated bowl* with coloured enamel decoration, Sol'vychegodsk, second half of the seventeenth century.
The pastoral scene in the base of the bowl and the surrounding floral decoration are typical of Sol'vychegodsk ware.
(State Armoury Museum.)

Fig. 6 *Liturgical hand cross,* from the Ipat'ev Monastery, Kostroma, 1562. Gold and silver ornamented with embossed figures, filigree, pearls, rubies and sapphires.
(State Armoury Museum.)

not easily confused with the contemporary productions of Hungarian, Venetian or Armenian workshops.

Even in the sixteenth century, despite its obvious popularity, filigree was not employed as the sole decoration for any given object – it was used to frame or to highlight such features as reliefs or plaques. But in the seventeenth century, when filigree became the handmaid of *cloisonné* enamel, its independence was altogether eroded.

The sixteenth century had preferred to use enamel over limited areas. And it had preferred muted and harmonious colour combinations, with a distinctive range of blues prominent in the spectrum. In the following century the use of enamel tended to increase in quantity and in intensity of colour. At times, indeed, the colours verged on the garish, though there is a rich dignity about the finest examples.

While the sixteenth century, as far as Russia is concerned, appears to have pioneered the application of enamel to raised surfaces, the seventeenth took this a stage further and developed a technique for enamelling chased metal. The last third of

6

Museum Photo

Fig. 7 **Three Bratinas.**
Left: *Seventeenth century.*
Engraved silver and parcel-gilt.
Inscribed 'The bratina of Abbot
Ignatii of the town of Serpukhov'.
Centre: *Engraved silver, with a*
cast foot. Inscribed 'The bratina
of the servant Nikon Ragozhin'.
Right: *Sixteenth century.*
Silver-gilt repoussé, engraved
and nielloed. Inscribed 'The cup
of the good man to drink from it
to your health praising God and
for the Tsar's health for many
years'. (Victoria and Albert
Museum, London.)

Fig. 8 **Beaker,** *seventeenth*
century. Silver-gilt.
(Victoria and Albert Museum.)

Museum Photo

The elaborate 'tabernacle' in the Dormition Cathedral of the Moscow Kremlin, for example, was cast in bronze by Dimitrii Sverchkov and his assistants in 1625. Richly ornamented bells and cannons were also cast in bronze.

Artistically of much less interest was the wrought iron work to be found in ornamental locks, window grilles and wall brackets. The objects made or decorated in these ways had forms that were controlled partly by their function, partly by tradition – a tradition that was essentially, though not exclusively, Byzantino-Russian until the mid-seventeenth century.

The development of metal-ware was influenced by function and tradition

Function and tradition both helped to determine the form of church metal-ware and plate. They determined the form of the generous chalice, with its almost hemispherical cup; or of the wide paten on a stand, with its rim to keep the offertory breads in place; or of the metal icon cover (*oklad*), the form of which was always defined by the painted icon beneath, though more and more it trespassed on the latter's space as time went on. Though there was a relentless tendency from the eve of the *Smuta* to the end of the seventeenth century to decorate an ever greater proportion of any given surface, and the earlier and more sophisticated balance between the object and its decorative accretions was no longer sought, the objects used in church tended to maintain their basic outlines. Indeed, there was even a deliberate reversion to essentials towards the end of the seventeenth century; in an age of over-elaborate decoration, and no doubt as a reaction to it, some Gospel and icon covers were produced whose smooth, beaten surfaces were adorned only by an occasional plaque or jewel.

Function and tradition also determined the development of secular metal-ware to a significant degree, though both were more susceptible to the

new influences at work in the seventeenth century, in the course of which, half a century before Peter the Great, profound changes in Russian social life were already taking place and paving the way for the eventual westernisation of the ruling classes.

During this period, of the two typically Russian drinking vessels, the *bratina* and the *kovsh*, one retained its form, the other lost it. The *bratina* was a loving-cup, often made in gold or silver, with a hemispherical base, no handles, and a wide, slightly concave rim, usually decorated with a convivial inscription or the owner's name in Slavonic lettering (Fig. 7). The rest of the exterior was decorated with ornamental (and increasingly complex) foliate and floral patterns.

The *kovsh* was an individual drinking-vessel (Fig. 9). Its stylised form was based on that of a floating water-bird – no doubt a traditional design in wood, which had been adapted for use in precious metal. Northern by origin (the earliest examples are from Novgorod), it had passed south to Moscow by the very end of the fifteenth century. There, during the second half of the following century, a delicate form of the *kovsh* developed, with a fluent, oval body, rising to a point at the tail and, at the other extremity, to a handle, subtly reminiscent of a bird's head. Unfortunately, towards the end of the seventeenth century, the addition of spherical supports (and sometimes even claws) to the base, and the distortion of neck and tail destroyed the traditional ornithological associations and made the *kovsh* into a different receptacle, even though the old name was retained. Meanwhile, other drinking vessels, like beakers (engraved or nielloed), were coming into fashion.

Only first grade silver was permitted to be used

Up until the early seventeenth century, hall-marks were not used. The earliest surviving Russian hallmarks date only from 1651–1652, when

Fig. 9 *Kovsh, or drinking-vessel,*
inscribed as a gift from Tsar
Mikhail to Ivan Kostiurin, Lord
of the Council, dated 1635.
Silver, engraved and parcel-gilt.
(Victoria and Albert Museum.)

Fig. 10 *Monomakh's Cap.*
Sixteenth century. Gold, with
jewels.
(State Armoury Museum.)

a double-headed eagle was introduced to designate Moscow. Until the eighteenth century, in the absence of provincial hallmarks, it is not always possible to determine the provenance of a work. It is even more difficult to make attributions to specific craftsmen, since as yet no personal marks were authorised or used. Nevertheless, an extremely strict control was exercised by the government over the quality of gold and silver, and not until 1684 was it permitted to work in less than first grade silver.

Moscow, the assayer's centre, was also the unchallenged centre of the gold- and silversmith's craft. The Kremlin workshops formed probably the most cosmopolitan, least tradition-bound and best endowed centre for the arts in late Muscovite Russia. But Moscow was not the only centre of

importance. In the sixteenth century, Novgorod still retained its integrity and something of its old significance. By the end of the following century, Iaroslavl' had developed its own distinctive style.

Of all the provincial centres Sol'vychegodsk was perhaps the most individual and the most uninhibited by precedent. Sol'vychegodsk gold- and silverware, produced under the aegis of the Stroganov family, had already attracted attention in the sixteenth century. But it was in the second half of the following century that Sol'vychegodsk came fully into its own with the production of a wide range of domestic and ecclesiastical objects, decorated with painted enamel. Here, as nowhere else in Muscovite Russia (possibly under Ukrainian influence), enamels were applied on a white enamelled ground in freely elaborated designs and cheerful colours. The bowls, boxes and cosmetic jars of Sol'vychegodsk, with their typical floral decoration, have an infectious *joie de vivre* about them (Fig. 5). The painted designs were often framed in borders of *cloisonné* enamel, with which the exteriors of many objects were also adorned.

Russia began to look to the West for guidance in the arts

The drawing on Sol'vychegodsk ware was in the Western European manner, the subject matter, as often as not, secular. In their technique, as in their style and subject matter, the masters of Sol'vychegodsk marked the end of one age and the beginning of another.

The formal inauguration of the new age was not to be delayed for long. As far as gold and silver are concerned, it took place on 21 October, 1700, with the promulgation of Peter the Great's decree on mandatory hallmarks. The transfer of the capital to St. Petersburg was soon to follow. The new capital, and the new Russia, were to look unequivocally to the West for guidance in the arts.

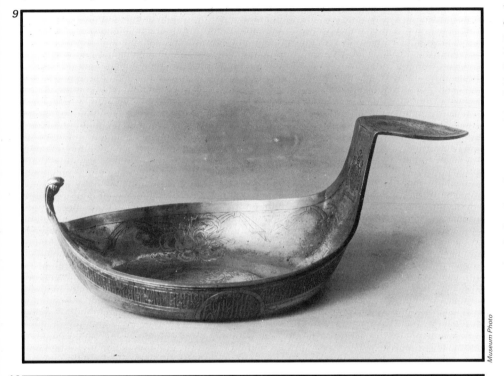

9

10

Museum Photo

Novosti Press Agency

MUSEUMS AND COLLECTIONS

Russian metal-work can be seen at the following:

RUSSIA
Leningrad: State Russian Museum
Moscow: State Armoury Museum, Kremlin
Novgorod: State Art History Museum

U.S.A.
Maryland: Walters Art Gallery, Baltimore
Washington   Dumbarton Oaks Museum
DC:

GREAT BRITAIN
London: Victoria and Albert Museum

FURTHER READING

Drevnerusskaya Melkaya Plastica XI–XVI vekov (Plastic Art of Old Russia XI–XVI centuries) by T. V. Nikolaeva, Moscow, 1968.

Russkoe Zolotoe i Serebrianoe delo XV–XX vekov (Russian Gold- and Silverware XV–XX centuries) by M. Postnikova-Loseva and others, Moscow, 1957.

Russkoe Khudozhestvennoe serebro XV–XIX vekov (Russian Artistic Silverware XV–XIX centuries) by M. Postnikova-Loseva, Moscow, 1959.

Images of God

Richard Temple

The Russian soul, the *ducha*, coupled with the rich intellectual and classical traditions of Athos and Constantinople, created the ambience in which icon painting first flourished.

It is a mistake to view Russian icon painting through the telescope of European history. How then should we try to understand icons? Perhaps the best way is to do so with no intellectual conceptions at all.

If we approach icons in the same way as we approach music – emotionally and instinctively – we may be well on the road to grasping what the painter intended. After all, the vast majority of Russians for whom icons were originally painted had no knowledge of cultural influences and transitions from one style and period to another, and yet the icon expressed for them a familiar language

Fig. 1 *The Evangelist St. Matthew, Moscow School, early sixteenth century. Tempera on wood, 21 x 17 ins. From the same source as the St. John (Fig. 6), St. Matthew is in the best tradition of sixteenth-century Russian painting. (Temple Gallery, London.)*

Fig. 2 **St. Paraskeva and Scenes from her Life**, *Russian late sixteenth century. Tempera on wood, 33 x 25 ins.*
One of the major female saints of the Orthodox Church, St. Paraskeva is worshipped as the patron of trade and the protector of all women.
(Temple Gallery.)

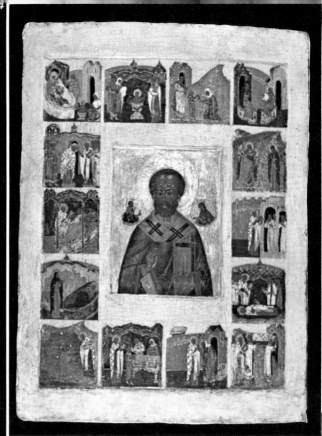

Fig. 3 **The Fiery Ascent of St. Elijah,** *North Russian School, c.1600. Tempera on wood, 32 x 36 ins.*
In the northern provinces a primitive, medieval style continued even into the seventeenth century whereas in the metropolitan centres such as Moscow a much more sophisticated style developed. This icon illustrates the naivety of the north Russian tradition.
(Temple Gallery.)

Fig. 4 **St. Nicholas and Scenes from his Life,** *Stroganov school, c.1600. Tempera on wood, 28 x 22 ins.*
The central panel is an icon of the late seventeenth century which has been inserted at a later date. The surrounding illustrations of scenes from the life of the saint are possibly from the workshop of Semeiko Borozdin.
(Temple Gallery.)

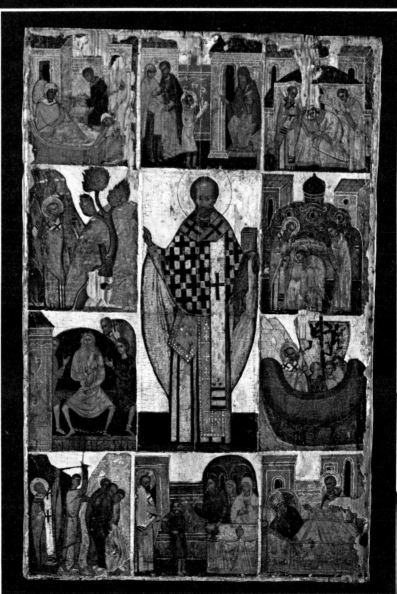

Fig. 5 **St. Nicholas of Zaraisk and Scenes from his Life,** *Russian, mid-sixteenth century. Tempera on wood, 38 x 25 ins.*
Not dissimilar to the Western European polyptych, this icon depicts St. Nicholas surrounded by small scenes showing the various miracles ascribed to him.
(Temple Gallery.)

in which the profound and the mysterious could be understood. But it is difficult for the Western mind, formed by the logic and realism of renaissance humanism, to enter the inner world of icons and the thoughts that produced them.

So, before looking at sixteenth- and seventeenth-century icons in any detail, a few generalisations must be made.

The great era of Russian icon painting runs from the Christianisation, or perhaps Byzantinisation, of Kiev in the tenth century, to the school of Dionisii in Moscow at the beginning of the sixteenth century. The superb art which continued to be produced throughout the sixteenth century depended for its momentum on the great schools

travelled from one place to another according to circumstance and need.

It is essential to understand that the Russian medieval painter, like his Byzantine and European brothers, was a servant of the church in the same way as were the builders and the clergy. Their work was traditional and functional, and, because the function was specifically ecclesiastical, liturgical. The majority of icon painters were monks, and icon painting was sometimes part of a special system of meditation and spiritual discipline. There is evidence of Hesychasm (from the Greek *hesychia*, quiet) in Russian monasteries. This is a system involving meditation, breathing exercises and constant repetition of a certain prayer which goes back to the desert fathers and the dawn of Christianity.

The concept of the icon painter, attentively and humbly searching for a special kind of spiritual perfection, is very different from the renaissance view of the artist. The icon painter never sought personal individuality or originality; he was content to serve within an ancient tradition whose spiritual aims had already been achieved and whose forms and imagery could not be improved upon but which needed only to be revivified.

Until the collapse of Constantinople in 1453, Russia was her intellectual and cultural dependant. Not until the reign of Peter the Great (1682–1725) did she transfer her allegiance to Europe. The two centuries lying between mark the period of gradual transition.

The centre of icon painting in Russia at the beginning of the sixteenth century was Moscow which, after the fall of Constantinople, had become the capital of Greek orthodoxy and was known as the 'Third Rome'. The last of the great schools was still active under Dionisii (1440–1509) and displays characteristics of the schools which preceded him: the brilliant, high-key colouring from Novgorod, and from Rublev the gentle rhythms, delicate drawing and diaphanous colours.

No icon by Dionisii exists outside Russia, but two icons showing many of the characteristics of his school are *The Evangelist St. John* (Fig. 6) and *The Evangelist St. Matthew* (Fig. 1). They can be fairly confidently dated to the beginning of the sixteenth century. We have no means by which we can know what relationship (if any) existed between the painter of these and Dionisii, and our speculations are based purely on style. There is nothing clumsy or primitive about them. On the contrary, they have a high degree of refinement and are brilliantly executed. Both compositions are conventional and can be found in Byzantine manuscript illuminations from the tenth century. Each Evangelist is seen writing his Gospel. St. John dictates to his secretary, Prochorus, on the island of Patmos; St. Matthew works alone indoors. But the painter was far from stifled by convention: he had as much freedom as a musician performing a set piece – the entire range of interpretation was open to him within the context of the formula and no two renderings were the same. The muted translucence of the colours was derived from Rublev, as were the voluminous but weightless figures. But these characteristics were beginning to be a little exaggerated; the entire icon had become an almost total abstraction.

Earlier icons have a certain rigidity and severity, but, after Rublev, a poignant sweetness which

6

A. C. Cooper

Fig. 6 *The Evangelist St. John, Moscow school, early sixteenth century. Tempera on wood, 21 x 17 ins.*
Originally forming part of a pair of royal doors, this icon of St. John dictating The Revelation *is in the style of the Dionisii school.*
(Temple Gallery.)

of the fifteenth century, which was possibly the climax of Russian art: Novgorod, Suzdal, Moscow and the school of Rublev. Other schools existed about which not so much is known and whose importance has not yet been fully assessed: Tver, Iaroslavl', Rostov, Vladimir, Dmitrov, Kirillov, Ustiug, Vologda. In all these schools the influence of Byzantine painting, both direct and indirect, must be noted. Without supporting historical evidence, it is usually impossible to identify the various regional schools with any precision. There was, in any case, a good deal of cross-influence and painters became universal in the sixteenth century characterises the style. No sentimentality, of course, no mundanities although they followed only too soon. At this point the icon still provided a vision of another world, where all-wise unearthly beings exist timelessly, casting no shadows and having no weight.

The same sweetness can be seen in the St. Nicholas series. These are also from the first half of the sixteenth century. They have a degree of naivety which suggests one of the provincial centres such as Rostov. The drawing is a little thicker and the figures do not have the mysterious elongation of the Dionisii style.

The rest of the sixteenth century continued to produce icons in a pure, unwesternised style. The dominating influence was always Rublev. But there is no evidence of an important workshop or *druzhina* such as that of Dionisii which was independent of the church. Icons like St. *Nicholas of Zaraisk and Scenes from his Life* (Fig. 5) were probably monastic works. The late sixteenth century is represented by St. *Paraskeva and Scenes from her Life* (Fig. 2). There was, as yet, no question of Western influence and the feeling was still medieval. However, the scale is smaller and figures and architecture have begun to lose their timelessness and monumentality. The episodes are less abstract in feeling and display a more illustrative and narrative character.

At this time a specific factor occurred which altered the subsequent course of icon painting. In 1598 the *Polyglot Bible* was published in five languages in Holland with a Dutch engraving at the head of every page. Many copies of this bible, with its profusion of baroque illustrations, found their way into Russia. Icon painters were fascinated; it was the first significant new influence for a hundred years and it came from Europe (Russian painting had always previously been self-generating or influenced by Constantinople). European influence was really disastrous for the true spirit of icon painting, which was thereafter confused. It resulted in several different styles: either a tasteless version of baroque religious art, or an academic and self-consciously 'correct' version of the old style. The 'true style' continued in the provinces where the medieval spirit remained in icons that were losing touch with any outside influence. They have great charm despite their somewhat crude execution (Fig. 3).

Also at the end of the sixteenth century, the Stroganov School made its appearance. This comprised a group of icon painters under the patronage not of the church but of the fabulously wealthy merchant family of Stroganov. This was highly significant and indicative of the new direction away from abstract and spiritual values and towards a realism and brilliance which, though it gave pleasure to the eye, lacked the inner force so characteristic of earlier icons.

An example of the earliest Stroganov school style is St. *Nicholas and Scenes from his Life* (Fig. 4) – the centre panel is later but the miniatures are typical. They can be fairly accurately dated to the year sixteen hundred. The quality of the painting and the technical finesse of its execution is high – higher, for instance, than the St. *Paraskeva* of a generation earlier. But the essential magic is wanting. The architecture and landscapes are still unreal but they lack conviction; we feel that the painter was paying lip-service to the old canon, his chief interest being to achieve a level of decorative brilliance.

Also in the seventeenth century there grew up the so-called *School of the Tsars*, whose style is similar to that of the Stroganov School; icon painters and copies of icons were interchangeable between the two groups. The Stroganov style, to use the general term for all fine miniature icons produced in Moscow in the seventeenth century, has always fascinated collectors both in the West and in Russia where high prices were paid for such works long before the 'discovery' of the medieval tradition at the end of the nineteenth century. There are several reasons for their popularity. Being products of fine craftsmanship rather than true art, they could be produced in large numbers; their jewel-like charm and finesse are essentially decorative; they have no deeply abstract qualities, make no demands on the intellect, and their small size and comparative modernity have ensured their preservation in good condition.

Icons of the Stroganov School proper are very rare; these are works which can be attributed to known painters (Borozdin, Sobolev, Perstikin and others), working specifically under the patronage of the Stroganov family, by inscriptions and dates (between 1596 and 1654). The border scenes on the St. *Nicholas* (Fig. 4) can be attributed to such a painter. Other paintings in the Stroganov style are designated to the school of the Tsars, the seventeenth century Moscow School, or the Baron's School; all these so-called schools were derivatives of the Stroganov School, and, in many cases, there were painters who worked in first one and then another of these workshops.

In the provinces, especially in the north, a primitive medieval style continued to exist; it was touched by neither European influences (Raphael, Guido Reni, and Dutch prints) nor by the 'virtuoso' style of the Stroganovs.

MUSEUMS AND COLLECTIONS
Russian icons may be seen at the following:

EIRE
Dublin: National Gallery of Ireland
FRANCE
Paris: Musée du Louvre
GERMANY
Recklinghausen: Ikonenmuseum
GREAT BRITAIN
London: Temple Gallery,
4 Yeoman's Row, S.W. 3
RUSSIA
Leningrad: State Russian Museum
Moscow: Tretiakov Gallery
Rublev Museum

FURTHER READING
Tretiakov Gallery Catalogues by V. I. Antonova, Moscow, 1969.
Korin Collection Catalogues by V. I. Antonova, Moscow, 1968.
Theophanes the Greek by V. Lazarev, Dresden, 1968.
Andrei Rublev and his School by V. Lazarev, Moscow, 1966.
Early Russian Paintings – Recent Discoveries by S. Iamshchikov, Moscow, 1966.
Icons by K. Onasch, London, 1963.
The Meaning of Icons by L. Ouspensky and V. Lossky, Olten, Switzerland, 1952.

1

K. Hoddle

Embroidery the Gentle Art

Ara de Korostovetz

Velvets, silks and fine brocades imported from all over the world were among the materials used by Russian women embroiderers in the manufacture of some of the most rich and sumptuous needlework ever produced

Christianity, introduced from Byzantium in the tenth century, brought to Russia church utensils, crosses, chalices, gospels and elaborate embroideries. This was the first instance of sophisticated needlework in Russia. Though a strong pagan tradition had existed previously, due to the frequent destruction of cities by fire and the Tartar Invasion, none of these early examples is extant. However, a chronicler of the period mentions in his annals that there was a school of embroidery in the Monastery of Ianchin in the eleventh century whose works were considered so fine that they were sent to the sacrosanct Mount Athos.

Who were the Russian women who executed these embroideries? Until the Tartar invasion, women had been entitled to dispose of their own property and mix freely with masculine company, but thereafter they led a secluded life, confined to the *Svetlitsa* (women's quarters) and were concerned only with their households and children. They filled the long hours making church embroideries and teaching their daughters and female household staff to do the same.

Their works were mainly of religious subjects: the Crucifixion, Lamentation and Descent from the Cross, the Virgin and Child and feast days and saints. They used home-woven and -spun materials, coarse flaxen linen and a kind of bunting made and dyed at home, which was used as a lining for fine quality materials. These elaborate and expensive materials came to Russia from East and West: Theodosia, Damascus, Florence, Spain, Arabia and Turkey; Venetian velvet, silk, and gold and silver brocades from Persia and China. The latter were used for the Tsar's and High Clergy's vestments, cuffs, mitres, *aer* (veil to cover paten and chalice), *inditia* (altar-cloth) and chasubles, and were heavily adorned with pearls, precious stones, and gold and silver threads. The Armoury Palace's books quote as many as 160,580 pearls weighing

fifty pounds, to be used for one vestment. Works such as these for tsars and patriarchs were hung on golden cords and displayed in the churches.

In order to execute these lavish embroideries, at least three workers were needed: one to design the pattern on paper; this, if approved, was executed in colour on the *kholst* (bunting) which was used as lining for the silk material or velvet on which the embroidery itself was to be done. The second worker embroidered with coloured silk threads and gold and silver (according to the taste and the financial position of the donor), a task that sometimes took several years. The third worker, the calligrapher, was entrusted with drawing an intricate design of lettering around the border – generally a prayer appropriate to the embroidery, or the name of the donor. This lettering, skilfully interwoven and executed in golden thread, involved an incredible variety of seams and stitches.

A very important factor, both religious and political, in the fourteenth century was the foundation of *Troitsa Lavra* (Trinity Monastery) by St. Sergii at what is now Zagorsk, near Moscow. He gave his blessing to the struggle against the Tartars and gathered monks around him, attracting princes, *boiars* (noblemen), patriarchs and influential people who made donations to his monastery. His popularity was so great that when he died 'all Moscow wept', and his coffin was covered with a *pokrov* (shroud) bearing his full-size effigy embroidered with great refinement and beauty (Figs. 1 and 4).

Two other interesting embroideries are kept in Zagorsk. They do not represent the usual embroidery subjects and are exceptional in that they commemorate two important royal events relating to the line of succession. Tsar Ivan III lost his first wife at an early age; his son, married to Elena of Moldavia, died soon afterwards, leaving a male who was proclaimed heir. The Tsar himself, who was still fairly young, married Sophia Paleologue, a scion of the Imperial Byzantine family. Though Constantinople had been devastated by the Turks, and the Paleologues were in exile, Russia was still infatuated with the idea of the former glory of the Byzantine Empire. Sophia realised this, and forcibly so, when she bore the Tsar a son. Both his wife and his daughter-in-law considered their respective sons to be the Tsar's lawful heir; so the struggle began. The Tsar was easily influenced by the one, and then by the other; one was in favour today, to

be disgraced tomorrow. Elena finally got the upper hand and her son, after a church service of great pomp, was again proclaimed heir.

She immediately ordered an embroidery to commemorate this event (Fig. 3). A long procession of High Church dignitaries carry the Icon of Our Lady; the Tsar, the newly proclaimed heir and his mother, Elena of Moldavia, form a group in the centre; Sophia Paleologue, though wearing the Imperial Byzantine Insignia, stands near the choir singers. Research has now established the exact date of this event: it was between nine in the morning and three in the afternoon that the procession moved from the Cathedral of the Ascension to the Cathedral of the Dormition; the day was Palm Sunday, 8 April, 1498.

Elena's victory was short-lived, however, for the very next year she and her son were sent to prison where they subsequently died. Soon afterwards, Sophia Paleologue's son was proclaimed Prince of Novgorod and heir to the Moscow throne. Sophia responded to this event by bequeathing a *pelena* (embroidered icon) to the *Troitsa Lavra*, with a suitable inscription in which she is referred to firstly as 'Tsarina of Tsargrad' (Empress of Constantinople) and only afterwards as 'Grand Duchess of Moscow'.

The epoch of the renowned mural and icon painter Dionisii and his two sons, who were second only to Rublev, inspired an embroidery executed in 1500 which is now in the Tretiakov Gallery, Moscow. It was found in the Volokolamsk Monastery and depicts in meticulous detail rarely illustrated scenes from the life of the Virgin, taken from the Apocrypha. The figures of the women who surround the resting St. Anne are slender, elongated and almost Hellenistic in their elegant movement.

The *omophorion* (clerical vestment) of the Patriarch Nikon, dated 1672, now in the State Art History Museum, Novgorod, is important because the name of the artist who executed the sketch for this embroidery is known: he was Mikhail Novgorodets and his work here, showing a panoramic view executed in silver and gold threads, faithfully depicts the architecture of the Novgorod Detinets and Moscow's Kremlin as they then were.

After Ivan the Terrible cruelly suppressed the Free City of Novgorod, which was a member of the Hanseatic League (a political and commercial league of Germanic towns), all the political power centred around the Tsar and the Patriarch in Moscow, and one or two rich families. One such family, the Stroganovs, left the conquered Novgorod and Sol'vychegodsk, where they had amassed fame and fortune, and moved to Moscow, becoming the Tsar's bankers. They brought with them their icon painters and embroiderers. So far, forty-eight donations made by this family have been discovered and attributed to their workshops. A peculiarity of the Stroganov family workshops was that their craftsmen signed their works, giving the date and the name of the donor, which now helps in the reconstruction of the Stroganov family-tree.

The Stroganov workshops flourished in the sixteenth century. One *pelena* dedicated to the memory of the murdered Tsarevich Dimitrii, possibly killed on the instruction of Boris Godunov, shows the moment when Dimitrii is falling, stabbed by the assassin's dagger. Another shroud, a full-

**Russian Textiles
and Embroidery**

Fig. 5 *Embroidered icon, worked
by the first wife of Ivan the
Terrible, Anastasia Romanovna,
sixteenth century.
(Suzdal' Museum.)*

Fig. 6 **The Lamentation** *(detail),
Staritskii School, 1561.
Embroidered in coloured silks,
gold and silver.
(Zagorsk.)*

Fig. 7 **Inditia,** *or altar-cloth,
Godunov School, 1601. Monastery
legend ascribes this work to
Ksenia, Boris Godunov's daughter.
(Zagorsk.)*

Fig. 8 **Sapega's Banner** *(detail),
Tsar's workshop, sixteenth
century.
The Tsar's embroiderers
produced not only liturgical and
commemorative embroideries
but also battle-dresses and
war-banners. This banner
represents the Archangel Michael
appearing to Joshua before the
Battle of Jericho.
(Tretiakov Gallery, Moscow.)*

size effigy of St. Sergii dated 1671, now in the
History and Art Museum, Zagorsk, is embroidered
with silver and gold threads, the finest quality
pearls marking the outlines (Fig. 1). It gives an
almost colourless impression, relating it to the gold
or silver *oklad* (metal used to cover an icon).
This was something new in embroidery.

The Tsar's workshops only worked to orders
given by the Tsar and his family. They produced
battle-dresses, church donations, vestments and
war-banners. One sixteenth-century example
known as the Sapega's Banner, now in the Tretiakov
Gallery, shows the Archangel Michael appearing to
Joshua before the Battle of Jericho (Fig. 8).

An unusual portable *iconostasis* (icon screen),
not painted but embroidered, is kept in the State
Russian Museum, Leningrad. It was ordered in
1592 by the devout Tsar Fëdor and his wife Irina,

to be taken on their pilgrimages. In later years
it travelled with Tsar Aleksei Mikhailovich on his
journeys and even later with Peter the Great.
In Alexander I's days it was given to the Winter
Palace Church and then to the Pensioner Soldiers'
Home in St. Petersburg, where it was badly
damaged by fire. What was left was transferred on to
green velvet (the previous base had been scarlet).
At this stage the faces of the saints were over-
painted with oil colours. It is now in the Moscow
Restoration Workshop, where attempts are being
made to salvage as much of the original work as
possible.

The Armoury Palace, Moscow, has a special
Equestrian Department with a remarkable
collection of the Tsar's boots, quivers, saddles,
caparisons (horses' trappings) and bridles – all of
which are lavishly embroidered with gold threads

and precious stones on leather (Fig. 9).

We have mentioned two embroidery workshops already, those of the Tsar and the Stroganov family. Who could compete with them in terms of finance and sophisticated taste?

Recently in Moscow it was discovered that a technique used by Andronikos Paleologue in 1300 for an embroidery in the church of St. Clement in Okhrida, was adopted by the Staritskii workshop. It consisted of the insertion of beige silk between the lining and the tissue on which the embroidery was to be executed corresponding to the areas where faces, hands and bodies were to be worked.

The Princess Staritskii's family, related to the Tsar Ivan the Terrible, was extremely rich and very ambitious. The Princess's mother even wanted

sonally ordered a *pelena* to be worked on red silk, decorated with pearls and golden plaques engraved with the faces of saints, to be hung under the famous icon of Rublev's *Trinity*. His daughter Ksenia is said to have executed an *inditia* (altar-cloth) in 1601 on silvery brocade with black velvet arabesques (Fig. 7), representing Christ enthroned, with his Mother and St. John standing beside, and two kneeling monks, St. Sergii and St. Nikon of Radonezh. Recent research has shown that the brocade for this altar-cloth was brought from either Spain or Florence and came from the same workshops as the material for the robe worn by Eleanora of Toledo (wife of Cosimo I de'Medici) in 1553, in the two portraits of her by Bronzino, (now in the Uffizi, Florence, and the Wallace Collection, London), and in which she was found buried when her coffin was opened in 1857. It is an example of the very high quality materials used four hundred years ago in Spain, Italy and in some Russian workshops.

One should not wonder that robes worn by people of high rank in Russia, attracted the attention of ambassadors or visiting foreign dignitaries; their chroniclers never forgot to mention the elaborate robes and vestments that they saw, or the profusion of pearls, brocades, gold sequins, stones, diamonds and furs of the Russian Court.

But what about the Russian peasantry? Could they develop a creative folk art? For the sixteenth- or seventeenth-century Russian, Moscow was the metropolis, but there was little connection between the capital and provincial towns, villages and hamlets. The peasant population used home-made, cheap, primitive materials and patterns which had been passed down from generation to generation. Unfortunately, wear and tear have denied us knowledge of all but a handful of the early examples of their work, but in the last few decades great and successful efforts have been made to revive this craft as folk art.

Novosti Press Agency

Artia K. Newberth

Fig. 9 **Quiver** *by Prokofii Andreev, 1673. Gold and silver embroidery on red morocco leather.*
Various of the Tsar's family emblems are depicted here and in the centre is an embroidered view of the Kremlin.
(Armoury Museum, Kremlin, Moscow.)

Fig. 10 **Pelena,** *or **embroidered icon,** Godunov workshop, 1593. Given by a member of the Godunov family to the Ipat'ev Monastery, the icon depicts three angels and biblical scenes.*
(Boris-Gleb Monastery, Moscow.)

to poison Ivan and proclaim her own son tsar. The plot was discovered and both she and her son were executed. Looking at some of the Staritskii's very fine works, such as *The Lamentation* with the tragic expression on the faces of Mary Magdalen and the Virgin, one feels that the Princess's mother had a premonition of what would happen to her (Fig. 6); but as long as she lived, she did her best to provide her workshop with rare samples, materials and embroideries.

She undoubtedly had contacts with the West. A sixteenth-century shroud which she bequeathed to the Pskov Pecherskii Cloister, employed Italian material. On another, dated 1540, the Mother of God is seated on a carved gothic bench, a style unknown at that date in Russia.

Another workshop belonged to the family of Boris Godunov during his short reign as Tsar. He per-

MUSEUMS AND COLLECTIONS

Russian embroidery may be seen at the following:

GREAT BRITAIN
London: Victoria and Albert Museum

RUSSIA
Leningrad: State Russian Museum
Novgorod: State Art History Museum
Moscow: State Tretiakov Gallery
Zagorsk: History and Art Museum

U.S.A.
New York: Metropolitan Museum of Art
Washington University of Washington Costume
D.C.: and Textile Study Centre

FURTHER READING

Art Treasures of Russia by M. V. Alpatov, London, 1968.
Drevnerusskoe shit'e by A. N. Svirin, Moscow, 1963.
'Old Russian Embroideries' by E. Tolmachoff in **The Needle and Bobbin Club Bulletin**, New York, 1947.
'Russian Ecclesiastical Embroidery' by Cyril Blunt in **The Connoisseur** Vol. 98, London, 1936.

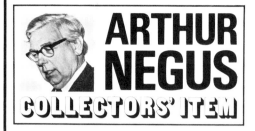

ARTHUR NEGUS
COLLECTORS' ITEM

PHOTOGRAPHIC FRAMES

Although the group portrait, whether of college, club or regiment, lent itself readily enough to framing in the conventional style, single portraits, particularly if they had sentimental value, looked impersonal in the plain wood or metal frames popular in the 1850s. Such photographs were generally too small to be placed in an elaborate frame of gilt plaster and some more suitable form of decoration had to be found. Queen Victoria used velvet to frame photographs of her children and that material, with its softness and hint of luxury, became universally popular for framing sweethearts and little ones. Many different kinds of wood were also used; beechwood for its softness and colour was popular in the 1860s, and maplewood recovered its pre-eminence at the end of the century. The Art Nouveau designers took up the plain silver frame whose chaste colouring and lines had been thought appropriate for portraits of the deceased, and transformed it into many graceful and fantastic designs. Sea-nymphs gazed piteously on the face of the dear departed and delicate, silvered clouds encompassed the beautiful Maud or Dorothy.

After the turn of the century, there were many kinds of fabric-covered frame. Covered in pale satin and ornamented with a sprinkling of gilt leaves, the beauties of the Edwardian era looked altogether more enticing than their sombre, stiffer predecessors.

Hints To Collectors
It is easy to pick up any number of frames made in this century, from Jarrold's debutante best to the strange, wooden monkey-puzzles of the twenties. It is not so easy, however, to find Victorian frames in a good state of repair. They are not objects which lend themselves easily to restoration, so if one is found it is almost certain to be original.

Opposite: **Silver frame,** c.1900. *Elaborately worked silver, backed with velvet, £22.*

Above: A group of frames, from the left: **Mosaic frame,** *Victorian,* £10. **Silver-plated frame,** *depicting Romeo and Juliet,* c.1910, £2.50. **Painted metal frame** *on metal stand, Victorian,* £5. **Silver frame,** *commemorating the coronation of George V, 1911,* £5.50

Below left: **Silver frame** *depicting a goose-girl, Birmingham, 1905, £24.*

Below right: A group of frames, from the left: **Oval diamanté frame,** *Edwardian, about £9.* **Green metal frame** *inlaid with pewter foliage, late nineteenth century, about £5.* **Velvet-covered boxwood frame** *of a shape derived from late medieval portrait frames, c.1860–70, about £8.*

Wooden Russia

John Stuart

Fig. 1 *Detail of the Iconostasis (icon screen) from the Trinity Cathedral, Ipat'ev Monastery, Kostroma, 1756–58.*
This heavy and sumptuous gilt-wood carving is a native re-working of the western Baroque. Western influence became an important factor in Russian art in the mid-seventeenth century and led to a certain confusion since it inevitably obscured the concepts and ideas for which the traditional Russian art had provided a lucid expression.

K. Hoddle

Fig. 2 *Church of the Dormition, Kondopoga, 1774.*
Churches were often constructed of wood. Here, the architectural shapes usually associated with Byzantine architecture, like the dome, manifest themselves in wood.

The forests of Russia provided the raw material from which the people constructed their basic necessities, both for their houses and for their churches

Fire was the proverbial curse of old Russia. Olearius, a seventeenth-century Western traveller in Muscovy, relates that 'not a month, nor even a week goes by without some house – or, if the wind is strong, whole streets – going up in smoke. Several nights while we were there we saw flames rising in three or four places at once'. Shortly before Olearius arrived in Moscow, a third of the city had been reduced to ashes, and two thousand people were homeless and living in tents.

Wooden Russia – such is the name used historically to describe the forest-clad Russian land where wood, so vulnerable to destruction by fire, provided the raw materials for so many of the people's basic needs.

The houses were of pine logs piled horizontally, one over the other, and fitted together by means of dovetailing ends, their roofs shingled and reinforced with bark. Even the streets were paved with logs to prevent the pedestrians from floundering in the thick mud.

Olearius also tells us that the Muscovites made use of a form of prefabricated house. He writes: 'Those whose houses were destroyed in a fire can quickly obtain new ones. Outside the "white" wall is a special market with many partly assembled houses. One can buy one of these and have it moved to a site at little expense.'

The designation 'Wooden Russia', like the other historical epithet, 'Holy Russia', conjures up many associations and images. When one thinks of the enormous girth of the great tree-trunks of the Russian forests, one remembers how they were hollowed out in ancient times to be used as boats in which the 'Russian Barbarians' sailed down the Dnieper to threaten the sacred, imperial city of Constantinople (called Tsargrad).

A chicken god was found near Moscow nailed up in a hen-coop

During the sixteenth and seventeenth centuries hollowed-out wooden tree-trunks were still used as baths, or as large receptacles in which, for instance, to ferment *kvas* (Russian rye beer).

'Your idols are wood', quotes the chronicler, writing of an encounter between the Christians and the followers of the old pagan religion. And when, during the tenth century, the wooden figure of Perun (the god of thunder and lightning) was hurled into the river Dnieper, worshippers followed the floating figure, calling upon it to 'dive out'.

Pagan belief lingered on in Russia. During the sixteenth century at least there were instances of the worship of Perun, and the fashioning of small and crude wooden figures and 'house goblins' has survived down to modern times. In 1927, a 'chicken god' was found near Moscow nailed up in a hen-coop. Such figures are commonly made from mis-

shapen pieces of wood, with the head carved from a tree-trunk and the neck fashioned from a branch.

From ancient times the Russians have been renowned as skilled joiners and carpenters. With only an axe, a knife and a rough plane, and not so much as a nail, they fashioned household utensils, and constructed their log-cabins and great soaring cathedrals.

The Tsar's country palace at Kolomenskoe, built during the seventeenth century and destroyed during the reign of Catherine the Great, shows old Russian secular architecture at its most developed and picturesque. It was a mighty complex of independent pavilions of different heights and sizes, linked by a labyrinth of external staircases and covered passageways. The greatest care was taken to equip it with different forms of roofing – tent-shapes, barrel-vaults, spires and structures recalling the *kikoshnik*, or woman's head-dress, adorned with gilt upper storeys of the private apartments and women's quarters.

The wood craftsman of the sixteenth century attached great importance to outline silhouette, whether he was working on a house or a wooden drinking-vessel. Such, for instance, are the

3

Fig. 3 *The tomb of St. Zosima, 1566. Wood carved in bas-relief.*
St. Zosima was the founder of the remote monastery of Solovki on an island situated in the White Sea.

K. Hoddle

traditional *chashi* (boat-shaped, swollen bowls) and the decorative friezes over doorways and on window surrounds. The simple patterns and shapes used to enliven the solid, tree-trunk supports all adhere to the basic tradition with which the carpenter was so familiar that his sense of proportion, volume and silhouette was infallible.

The sparse house-furnishings are related to principles of construction and architecture. The tables, their four sturdy legs supporting the wooden top, are heavy, solid structures with the same monumental and architectonic quality found in domestic buildings. Other objects, such as boxes, cupboards, icon shrines, and trunks, all show the

4

Fig. 4 **Kovsh or traditional drinking vessel**, *seventeenth century. Wood with painted floral decoration. (Author's Collection.)*

Fig. 5 **The Ante-room of the Church of the Dormition,** *Kondopoga, 1774. The ante-room served as a meeting place, centre for communal activities and a warm waiting room for those who had travelled long distances to attend services.*

5

same derivation. The apex of icon shrines, for instance, frequently terminates in a clump of cupolas, such as may be seen on wooden church architecture. The slanting lids of reading-desks recall the simple line of a roof-top. The analogy is particularly striking in the *analoi*, or icon stand, the wooden support upholding the small ledge, fulfilling the function of a structural column (Fig. 10).

The most common item of furnishing was the wooden bench. No house or church ante-chamber was without one. Indeed, they often formed an integral part of the architecture, set into the wall. Used for many purposes, the bench served as a bed and as a work-bench. On it, food was also prepared and laid out. Its position in a room was dictated by tradition. The place of honour was always in the 'beautiful corner', opposite the door, where the icons were massed together and lit by oil-lamps suspended on chains. Entering the room, the guest would first turn to this corner and pay his respects. And if, for some reason, he failed to see the icons, he would ask those present

where they were before so much as greeting anybody. Only then would he bow to the assembled company. In the grander houses, these benches were often carved with fretwork, incised with stylised animal heads, upholstered with leather or material and, occasionally, painted with polychrome decorations.

During the seventeenth century some furniture was imported from the West through the port of Archangel. Tables with 'pitcher' legs as well as high-backed chairs were introduced. And although the majority of Russians continued to sleep on a mattress laid over a bench or on a ledge constructed over the stove, the wealthier Muscovites became familiar, for the first time, with the bed.

In the city market-places many specimens of the carpenter's craft were to be found. There were sledges and the high curved wooden harnesses (*duga*) which had to be bent slowly into shape while the wood was malleable from prolonged immersion in water. There were also household implements, wooden buckets, carved plates, boxes of birch-bark

Fig. 6 **St. Paraskeva,** *fifteenth century. Polychrome wood. Stern and immobile, this figure is more closely related to icon painting than to a sculptural tradition. (Historical Museum, Kostroma.)*

and carved candlesticks.

Sometimes the salesmen came from afar. In the trading books of Ustiug we read under the year 1676 that 'Petr Petrovich Lobanov has arrived by boat bringing 6,100 wooden spoons, 36 salts and 35 drinking vessels of Birch' (Fig. 4).

Carpenters also showed much ingenuity and skill in the fashioning of chess-men, Easter eggs and icon shrines, as well as making an infinite variety of toys and dolls. The latter were popularly known as 'dumbs', a name they shared with the resident foreigners whose failure to communicate was a source of frustration to the Muscovites.

Wood was the raw material used for popular art

thanksgiving. The crest of the building soared sometimes to twice the required height over the internal chamber, sprouting into globular domes and crosses which made a bold pattern against the horizon (Fig. 2). Subsequently, wooden architecture inspired the construction of stone buildings, such as the church of St. Basil in Moscow, where features of wooden architecture are re-translated into stone.

In order to understand the nature of the inspiration which guided the Russians into fashioning wood for the creation of art, as opposed to popular craft, it is as well to remember that their faith taught them to look at everything in nature as a part of

Fig. 7 **Icon representing the Church,** *seventeenth century.*
This icon was made for orthodox Christians who refused to accept the liturgical innovations of the Patriarch Nikon. (Author's Collection.)

Fig. 8 **Detail from the interior of the church of Kolomenskoe,** *near Moscow, sixteenth century.*

as opposed to 'high' culture and was employed by the Russians for the re-working of Byzantine art at a popular level. Since wood is a versatile material, new patterns were evolved which, in their time, were to influence the more sophisticated art forms. In this way, traditional stone architecture, which had developed in the southern Mediterranean to meet the requirements of the Byzantine liturgy, was modified when wood became the building material. Climatic conditions and a response to the peculiar beauty of the Russian landscape did the rest.

The Russian artist raised his church like a paean of thanksgiving

As the internal ceiling of the churches was always low, there was no structural necessity to heighten the external outline of the building by raising the high-pitched roofs and cupolas so characteristic of Russian wooden churches. The Russian artist raised his church like a paean of

God's creation, which could participate in His plan for the universe and assume a new 'spiritual form'. Nature was to be reconstituted with a new meaning in the service of God.

As with all Byzantino-Russian culture, the finest pieces are of a religious significance. Even during the seventeenth century, when traditional Russian culture was being undermined by a new secular spirit emanating from the West, the wealthy continued to live in comparatively simple wooden houses, vying with one another only in the erection of splendid churches through which they expressed their appreciation of beauty.

Among the most interesting wood carvings of the sixteenth and seventeenth centuries are the Royal Gates – the central doors which give access through the icon screen to the altar (Fig. 1). Here again, the emphasis was upon expressive silhouette. When darkness fell, the lamps of the altar behind the closed doors outlined their decorative contours with a rim of light.

Often the artist reproduced in wood patterns

Fig. 9 **St. George slaying the
Dragon,** *early seventeenth
century. Icon carved in relief
and painted.
(Museum of Fine Arts, Archangel.)*

Fig. 10 **Analoi or Icon stand.**
*Wood.
This* analoi *is clearly derived
from architecture. It can be
compared with the structural
columns in Fig. 5.*

taken from another medium. On the doors, the precise, undulating rhythms of the decorative work are reminiscent of the motifs found on the sheets of silver *(basma)* fixed to the background of some icons. Not unlike strips of leather, they are at other times reminiscent of delicate lacework. Adding to the richness of the effect, the doors were generally picked out in two colours – red, over a background of gold.

Among the most intricate wood carvings are the small-scale reliefs of saints recalling the work of the jeweller. Executed in miniature, they were often mounted in silver and gold.

Another category of carvings, though rarer, is that of the full-length figures of saints, which are only occasionally free-standing. It is more common to find that the back is flat, or only superficially carved, since the figures were intended to stand against a painted background. They are, therefore, more like carvings in high relief than sculpture in the round, but what is most striking about Russian wood carving is its close dependence on the art of the icon (Fig. 6). And here it is of interest to note that the finest icons show the influence of Hellenistic (late Grecian) sculpture and its two-dimensional beauty. The Russian peasant-artist translated the two-dimensional language of the icon back into three dimensions, without in the least aspiring to capture the sense of movement and naturalism associated with Hellenistic sculpture. The figures are, in its other sense, quite literally 'wooden' –

rooted to the spot – with the folds of their garments sharp and angular. And just as though he were painting a panel icon, the sculptor coated the carving with a layer of gesso.

On other occasions, the wooden effigy of a saint would be laid on his tomb (Fig. 3). Such recumbent wooden figures were habitually covered with finely embroidered palls stitched with a further likeness of the saint. It is hardly surprising, therefore, that as the congregation approached the tomb to kiss the pall and worship at the shrine they frequently mistook the outline of the form under the draped pall for the actual body of the saint. Consequently, in 1722, the Holy Synod ordered the destruction of all three-dimensional wooden sculpture.

The seventeenth century was a period of transition

The seventeenth century was, for Russian art and indeed for Russian life, a period of transition characterised by a search for new forms. On the one hand, the Russian artist was technically brilliant, capable of achieving a number of effects at will. On the other, an exaggerated striving after trivial decorative effects indicated a certain decadence and a possible lack of genuine emotion.

It was the period of the breakdown of Byzantine culture in Russia, at least on the level of high art forms, and of a trend to seek inspiration in quite another concept of European culture, namely that of the Germano-Latin west. During this period decorative wood-carving often became heavier in style and more intricate. And although it was used by sculptors and craftsmen working in a western or pseudo-Byzantine style, it still continued to be an important medium for the expression of traditional Byzantino-Russian art down to modern times.

MUSEUMS AND COLLECTIONS

The following museums have collections of woodwork though only a small number of them are on permanent exhibition.

RUSSIA

Leningrad: State Russian Museum

Moscow: State Historical Museum
State Tretiakov Gallery
Church of the 'Laying of the Garments', Kremlin

Perm': Perm' State Art Gallery

FURTHER READING
Wooden Architecture by G. I. Mekhova, Moscow, 1966.
Etindi po Istovii Russkogo Iskusstva, Vol. I, Moscow, 1967.
Russian Wooden Sculpture, W. Pomerantsev, Moscow, 1967.
Drevnerusskaia Melkaia Plastika XI–XVI vekov (The Art of Carving in Old Russia, XI–XVI centuries) by T. V. Nikolaeva, Moscow, 1968.
The Travels of Olearius in Seventeenth Century Russia translated by S. H. Baron, Oxford, 1968.
Russkoe Dekorativnoe Iskusstvo, Vol. I, Moscow, 1962.

St Petersburg
A Window on the West

John Stuart

Fig. 1 **Catherine II** (1762–96) by
S. Torelli (1712–80), c.1765. Oil
on canvas.
Dressed in her coronation robes,
Catherine the Great is wearing
the Imperial Crown. It was made
by the Court jeweller, Jeremy
Posier, and was not completed
in time for the coronation. The
official portrait was therefore
postponed until 1765.
(State Russian Museum,
Leningrad.)

Fig. 2 **St. Petersburg,** now
called Leningrad, from the
river Neva.
Magnificently sited on an island
in the river, the Fortress and
Cathedral of St. Peter and
St. Paul is the last resting-place
of Peter the Great and his
descendants. Built by Trezzini
between 1714 and 1725, the
Cathedral reflects the Emperor's
delight with the steeples he had
seen in England and Holland.

3

Novosti Press Agency

4

Colin Jones

Peter the Great founded a new Russian capital on marshy wasteland, and his heirs embellished it with magnificent palaces and public buildings

One of the remarkable features of Russian history is that, unlike the history of other countries, its evolution lacks continuity. Russia's history falls into clearly defined periods, each with its own peculiar character. There is Kievan Russia, the Muscovite Tsardom, Tartar Russia, the Petersburg tradition and now Soviet Russia.

Although the period from the foundation of St. Petersburg, in 1703, to the fall of the monarchy, in 1917, forms such a historical entity, it is useful from a cultural point of view to divide the period into two sections. During the second half of this period, in the 1860s, the great reforms of Alexander II were implemented, reforms which led eventually to the emergence of a new modernised Russia.

The grand architect of the whole period was Peter the Great, acclaimed during his lifetime as the 'Father of the Fatherland', without regard to his august predecessors, St. Vladimir and Ivan the Great. The key to an understanding of the period is to be found in his grandiose creation – St. Petersburg, now Leningrad. The city, commemorating Peter's name in a foreign tongue, was erected at enormous cost in human lives on a remote marshy wasteland, the delta of a magnificent river, which Peter had only just wrested from the Swedes. The founding of St. Petersburg served on the one hand the practical purpose of providing Russia with an essential maritime outlet; on the other hand, it was a symbolic act, not unlike the founding of Constantinople. For this great new city was to provide, in the words of Pushkin, 'a window on the West', representing the new cultural and spiritual values of the westernised empire.

Through St. Petersburg the Russians were supposed to assimilate those still unfamiliar aspects of European culture. They were to be initiated into the pagan heritage of Greece and Rome as it had been transmitted to the Germano-Latin West by the Italian Renaissance. They were, further, to catch up on 'rationalism' and 'enlightenment'. Peter's adoption of the title of Emperor, in place of Tsar, signalled Russia's transformation from a theocratic state into an absolute monarchy on the lines of the most advanced western states. In the cultural sphere this meant that art, in this new period, was to lose its religious connotations and reflect the tastes of a secularised society.

The question of whether the reforms of Peter the Great had a detrimental effect on Russian life and culture was to become a burning issue during the nineteenth century. Even today, some historians refer to pre-Petrine Russia as a place where men lived 'in a thick fog of ignorance, bias and superstition, unenlightened by any effort on the part of church or government'. This view, expounded by advocates of westernisation, would have aroused nineteenth- or even twentieth-century Slavophiles to fury. But had Russia not been westernised by Peter, she would undoubtedly have succumbed to

Mansell Collection

Novosti Press Agency

Mansell Collection

Novosti Press Agency

of a literary tradition that was essentially Russian in its interpretation of western culture.

Peter's creation has not survived, despite its apparent vitality. The Petrine revolution anticipated that of the Bolsheviks by implementing a blueprint for a new society. Both revolutions have in common a profound hatred of traditional Russian values, coupled with a fanatical determination to ignore them in the shaping of a new society. Peter's revolution only affected the elite. Whilst founding a new empire, he had left the old one, only partially destroyed, in his wake.

From this period onwards, Russians lived on two completely different levels of consciousness. This rift between the westernised elite and the traditionalist, non-secularised masses, who were no more than the passive or hostile spectators of a 'revolution from above', widened with each successive generation. During the nineteenth century a significant number of the elite were overcome by a sense of guilt which resulted in an inability to fulfil their role as leaders of the new society; the tragedy was complete.

In 1741, when a coup brought Peter's daughter, Elizabeth, to the throne, a foreign observer described the architecture of St. Petersburg as 'a mixture of Italian, French and Dutch influence, with the latter predominating'. Elizabeth, however, who once considered the idea of marrying Louis XV, had a definite predilection for the scintillating splendour of the French court. Basically frivolous, she had an insatiable taste for entertainment and a love for masquerade and was reputed never to have worn the same dress twice. None the less, it was she who founded the Imperial Porcelain Factory, the Academy of Art and the Imperial theatres. She was also the first European ruler to abolish the death penalty. From this time, the theatre became a popular institution and many noble families maintained troupes of serf actors on their estates.

Architecture was, however, the most vital art form in Russia during the eighteenth and early nineteenth centuries. Throughout the twenty years of the Empress Elizabeth's reign, the erection of buildings was directed by Count B. F. Rastrelli (1700–71), the son of an Italian sculptor who came to Russia at the age of fifteen. Rastrelli built a number of graceful buildings in the rococo style. Not only the town houses built for the Stroganov and Vorontsov families, but the Anitchkov Palace, the Smolny, the Winter Palace and Tsar'skoe Selo were his creations. Built of brick covered with plaster, and originally brightly painted in strong primary colours picked out in gold, these buildings, which were to provide the setting for the apotheosis of the monarchy, epitomised the theatrical taste of Russia's Elizabethan era.

It was the monarchy which gave the guiding line to the arts through its patronage during the eighteenth and early nineteenth centuries. The artistic tastes of Catherine the Great (1762–96) were totally opposed to those of Elizabeth. If Peter could be termed a 'crowned Bolshevik', Catherine was a reigning intellectual – perhaps the most intellectual woman of the century in Russia. Discounting the work of her immediate predecessors, she looked upon herself as the heiress promoter of Peter's work. To give expression to this idea, she summoned the French sculptor Falconet to create a monumental sculpture in memory of Peter. The work which he executed is an effigy of

Fig. 3 **Palace of Pavlovsk** by C. Cameron (c.1740–1820), 1782–86.
Catherine II discovered an architect of genius in the Scottish Jacobite, Charles Cameron. Living much of his life in Italy, Cameron had made a special study of Greek and Roman monuments. Designed for Catherine's heir, the Grand Duke Paul, the superb palace of Pavlovsk was one of his greatest masterpieces.

Fig. 4 **Peter the Great** by E.-M. Falconet (1716–91), designed and cast 1766–78. Bronze.
This monumental sculpture conveys not only the dynamic and ruthless character of the founder of St. Petersburg, but also his role in the historical and cultural evolution of Russia.

Fig. 5 **Senate Square**, later called Peter the Great Square and, more recently, Decembrist Square. Engraving.

Fig. 6 **The Winter Palace** by Count B. F. Rastrelli (1700–71), 1754–62.
This brightly painted baroque building surmounted by dramatically gesturing figures epitomises the flamboyant character of the Empress Elizabeth.

the growing power of Sweden or Poland.

Peter the Great was, above all, a technocrat. Art and culture failed to claim his interest because he lacked the reflective turn of mind necessary for its appreciation. The only art which appears to have awakened his interest was that of seascapes, scale models and *trompe l'oeil*. His chief concern was to acquire practical knowledge, whether it involved surgery, ship-building, the construction of a fort or the circulation of a fish. Although artistically a philistine, Peter's activities were far from culturally barren.

Although art in Russia was largely the work of foreigners working in Russia and influenced by the Russian environment, Peter and his successors were keen that native Russians should also be trained in the artistic principles of Western Europe. Many of these artists achieved a complete mastery of their medium and should by rights now fill a worthy place in the story of eighteenth-century European culture. Thus, despite the lack of a native tradition in sculpture in the round, the peasant Shubin, sent by an aristocratic patron to study in France, produced work of a standard equal to that of his best western contemporaries. Levitsky (1735–82), Borovikovsky (1757–1822) and Rokotov (1730–1808) are among the noted portrait painters whose work recorded the process of assimilation of at least the trappings of western culture by Russian society. Rokotov, for instance, invites comparison with Gainsborough through his skilful delineation of character and impressionistic handling of print.

These artists, along with the architects and sculptors of the Petrine Empire, followed the canons of a universal European style, inspired by France; there was nothing specifically Russian about their work. The nineteenth-century thinker, Herzen, considered that the genius displayed in Pushkin's writings was the first creative response to Peter's revolution. Pushkin laid the foundation

St. Petersburg

Fig. 7 *A Perspective View of Petersburg, the Capital of Russia* from G. H. Millar's New & Universal System of Geography, 1782. Engraving.

Mansell Collection

THE RULERS OF RUSSIA
Peter the Great 1682–1725
Catherine I 1725–27
Peter II 1727–30
Anna 1730–40
Ivan VI 1740–41
Elizabeth 1741–62
Peter III 1762
Catherine the Great 1762–96
Paul I 1796–1801
Alexander I 1801–25
Nicholas I 1825–55
Alexander II 1855–81
Alexander III 1881–94
Nicholas II 1894–1917

Peter which dominates the landscape of the capital. The bronze horseman is seen with his outstretched hand triumphantly pointing towards the West. An enormous granite boulder, dragged cross-country from Finland, forms the base, which bears the simple legend: 'To Peter I from Catherine II'.

It is not for the conduct of her internal policy that Catherine is remembered as 'the Great', for she not only failed to find any positive solution to many of the serious problems which beset her, but also had to face a major rebellion. She was great by virtue of her foreign policy and on the strength of her untiring intellectual activity and patronage of the arts, which brought great prestige, both to herself and to the Empire.

The *Nakaz*, the proposed new legal code which incorporated many 'advanced sentiments' borrowed from the latest western philosophical treatises, appeared in the West in twenty-six editions. Although virtually no one in Russia knew what it contained, it caused Catherine to be acclaimed as the 'mirror of enlightenment'. Voltaire wrote to her that the code would give her more glory than ten victories on the Danube. Catherine was also responsible for the building of the old Imperial Hermitage, designed as an annexe to the Winter Palace, and she was the first Russian sovereign to develop a discriminating eye for western painting.

Catherine was fortunate in securing the services of a French architect working in St. Petersburg, Vallin de la Mothe (in Russia 1759–75) to whom she entrusted the construction of the old Hermitage and the Imperial Academy. Another talented architect, Antonio Rinaldi (1709–90), built the marble palace and the small country residence of Gatchina as a present for Catherine's favourite, Grigori Orlov. The German architect Velten (1730–1801), was responsible for the construction of the severe and dignified granite quays which line the network of canals and the river-front.

Although Catherine was the first sovereign to make use of native Russian architects, the two names which figure most prominently during her reign are those of the Scotsman Cameron (c.1740–1820) and the Italian Quarenghi (1744–1817). Charles Cameron, whom Catherine described in

her letters as a 'Jacobite by profession', recommended himself to her as an expert on Palladio and the editor of a treatise on Roman baths. He designed the austerely beautiful Cameron Gallery at Tsar'skoe Selo which contrasts strongly with the Elizabethan rococo which adjoins it. He also redesigned Catherine's private apartments, making use of precious materials such as agate and silver, and used coloured felt cut-outs laid under glass and Wedgwood cameos to achieve the right decorative effects. Cameron also designed the palace of Pavlovsk, an architectural gem built for her son and heir, the future Paul I and his discerning wife, Maria Fedorovna.

Giacomo Quarenghi, who worked in Russia for nearly forty years, was a pure classicist who had made a profound study of Roman architecture and the Palladian style. His work is simple, powerful and serene. Whereas Cameron's genius was best served working on small-scale palaces or pleasure pavilions sited in landscaped parks, Quarenghi excelled in the designing of magnificent public buildings. The State bank, the Academy of Sciences, the Women's Institute, the Hermitage Theatre and the Alexander Palace are all his work, as also are the redesigned marble gallery and throne-room of the Winter Palace.

After the brief, uneasy reign of the insane Emperor Paul I, the accession of Catherine's favourite grandson, Alexander I, gave a new direction to artistic taste and architecture in particular. Broad minded, intelligent and charming, Alexander appeared to his contemporaries as a 'young Apollo'. A passionate builder, he personally supervised and approved all plans for the new constructions in the capital, with the help of the first permanent planning commission. Alexander's taste is epitomised by the Empire style. The Russian version of this style assimilated the new trends emanating from France, while retaining the aristocratic flavour which had characterised European culture prior to the French Revolution. The Empire style in Russia was the final stage in the evolution of classical forms. Catherine's architect, Quarenghi, far from falling out of fashion, continued to work until his death in 1817. Having its roots in the classicism of Catherine, the architecture of Alexander I and of his successor Nicholas I, characterised as the 'sublimation of the idea of a military and bureaucratic empire', remained the official style up to the death of Nicholas in 1855. Classicism and neo-Classicism therefore reigned supreme in Russia for a period of a hundred years, during which more buildings of distinction were erected in St. Petersburg than in any other capital city. Consequently, not only does St. Petersburg present a remarkably organic unity of appearance but, due to the munificence of imperial patronage, it is perhaps the most outstanding monument to Classicism in Europe.

In the early nineteenth century, the neo-classical tradition gradually became a native Russian, as well as an international style. The magnificent architecture of Thomon, Zakharov and Rossi was reinterpreted by architects of provincial towns and inspired the gentry in the construction of their more modest country houses. To this day, the main squares and monuments of provincial towns are marked by the classical heritage, and even the simplest country house boasts a portico of pillars which enlivens its façade.

The Uses of Malachite in Russia

G. Bernard Hughes

Fig. 1 **Peasant dance**, *Russian, nineteenth century. Malachite base with gilt-bronze figures. After about 1760, malachite became a favourite collectors' item. Flat platforms often edged with strips of silver-gilt were popular as a support for lively, boldly modelled figures in native Russian costume. (Private Collection.)*

Fig. 2 **Urn on pedestal**, *Russian, c.1810. Malachite with gilt-bronze mounts. Made for the Grand Duchess Olga as part of her dowry on her marriage to Frederick I, King of Württemberg, this magnificent urn was formerly in the Imperial collection at Tsar'skoe Selo. Malachite tazze and urns were particularly popular pieces early in the nineteenth century, and were made in a variety of shapes and sizes. Bands of ornamental ormolu were used to conceal the joints between plinth, stem and saucer. (S. J. Phillips Ltd. and H. Blairman and Sons, London.)*

Emerald green and delicately veined malachite, originally mined in the Ural mountains, was not only used as a veneer but was also found ideal for many decorative and practical purposes

The brilliant Malachite Hall, one of the one thousand and fifty rooms in Leningrad's Winter Palace, is perhaps the most spectacular apartment in Russia (Fig. 5). Columns, fireplaces, furniture, cabinets, clocks, candelabra, all display the smooth emerald green surfaces and handsome veining of malachite, enriched with ormolu moulded in high relief and exquisitely chased.

Malachite is a stalagmitic form of green carbonate of copper, compact in texture, displaying a silky lustre when polished; the concentric veinings on a single piece show several shades of green known as *foncée, ordinaire, claire* and *pale*, with intermediate variations. Malachite is softer than marble, but very much heavier and, because of a brittleness that verges on fragility, is more difficult to work.

The richest deposits of fine Russian malachite lie over the copper mines of Nizhnii Tagil on the Siberian side of the Ural Mountains. Masses of malachite occur in openings between garnet rock and limestone.

Slices of malachite were applied as a veneer over strong ornamental foundations of copper or iron and occasionally, as a more expensive process, over marble or stone. The essential was to use a material with a level surface and free of any danger of warping, which might cause the small malachite units to crack or become detached. Ormolu decoration cast in bold relief was cemented over this veneer, the contrast in colours being richly elegant.

The cost of malachite at the mine-head in the early nineteenth century was about fifteen shillings a pound. This cost was doubled by the workshop process of sawing it into slices which reduced its weight by half; weight was further lessened to about four ounces before the slices were shaped, fitted, cemented into position and polished. Thus, the final cost was about £3 per pound, a square foot of veneer utilising about two and a half pounds of malachite. The prepared slices were small and thousands might be incorporated into a single masterpiece.

Of the several workshops in St. Petersburg devoted to the design and manufacture of malachite ware, the most important were those operated by M. M. Demidoff, owner of the Nizhnii Tagil copper-mine. From about 1840 the undertaking was managed by L. Leopold Joffrian who had invented a machine capable of trimming the edges of thin slices of malachite, following the natural curves of

3

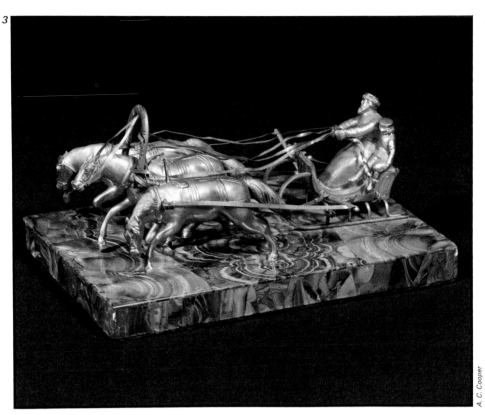

4

A. C. Cooper

Fig. 3 **Troika**, *Russian,
nineteenth century. Malachite
base with gilt-bronze figures.
This beautifully veined malachite
base supports a troika, the
traditional Russian sleigh drawn
by three horses running abreast.
(Private Collection.)*

Fig. 4 **Table**, *Russian, early
nineteenth century. Wooden
veneer with ormolu mounts and
malachite top.
Given to the first Duke of
Wellington in 1814 by Alexander I
on his arrival in England, this
superb table is typical of the
luxurious uses to which malachite
was put at that period.
(Wellington Museum, London.)*

Fig. 5 **The Malachite Hall** *in the
Winter Palace, Leningrad, early
nineteenth century.
Perhaps the most spectacular
apartment in Russia, this Hall has
columns, fireplaces, furniture,
clocks and candelabra of
malachite enriched with ormolu.*

Fig. 6 **A Large Vase, in
Malachite. Russia.** *Page 193
from the Great Exhibition:
Official Descriptive and
Illustrated Catalogue, London,
1851. Engraving by Jarvis.
M. M. Demidoff's collection of
Malachite was awarded a prize
at the Great Exhibition for its
'rare beauty and rich
magnificence'.
(Victoria and Albert Museum,
London.)*

the veining. Harmonious patterns were then produced such as had been impossible with the earlier straight-edged veneers. This stylistic improvement, costly in labour, was not perfected until about 1845, when craftsmen had become more experienced.

The malachite slices, cut to shape and size, were arranged in jigsaw fashion with the natural markings displayed to their finest advantage. The edges were machined by a pair of copper cutting wheels rotating at great speed. These shaped the edges dovetail fashion, each unit being recessed into the edge of its neighbour. The malachite slices were then veneered to the shaped foundation by means of cement and the surface levelled by sanding and polishing to a high lustre with a thin paste of tin oxide applied with a chamois pad. So meticulously was the work accomplished that joints fitted with supreme accuracy and were almost invisible, although in some instances a thick dark line might be left to accentuate highlights. Malachite and other colourful hard stones were polished in factories established for this purpose; the Imperial Polishing Manufactories at Kolyvan, Tomsk, and Ekaterinburg, Perm.

Small spaces left at the corners between slices were filled with a malachite *breccia* – the Italian term for a cement that becomes stone hard very quickly. *Breccia* was mixed with fragments of malachite in a tint matching the surrounding slices. This formed an agreeable breaking of the veining and vastly improved its radiance.

Malachite veneer was little known in Britain outside royal palaces and a few stately homes, until the Great Exhibition in 1851. Here Demidoff displayed a collection of malachite notable for its splendour. The Exhibition jury awarded him a gold medal, commenting that his malachite veneer 'attained a degree of beauty and rich magnificence rarely seen in this country'. Outstanding was a pair of vast double doors which hung in a framework constructed of copper covered with malachite a quarter of an inch thick – an unusual thickness – discreetly

embellished with highly polished ormolu mouldings and mountings in high relief. Thirty men had been engaged in cutting, fitting, finishing and polishing the malachite alone, working day and night from May Day 1850 until May 1851 when the doors were despatched to London. They were the subject of a full-page engraving in the Exhibition Catalogue. Engraved too, also in full-page size, was Demidoff's drawing-room fireplace designed in the curvaceous manner typical of early Victorian design, and several gigantic vases on truncated columns ranging in height from six to twelve feet. There was a noble vase with a capacious, near-spherical bowl, its stem in the form of a smaller sphere resting on a diminutive ball which was based on an expansive circular foot; it was lavishly enriched with fruiting vine motifs in ormolu (Fig. 6).

At the Great Exhibition following the display of Demidoff's vast collection of malachite, rooms furnished entirely in this medium became fashionable, but their contents for the most part have now been dispersed. Much gilding was used in rococo wall and ceiling ornament to harmonise with lavishly applied ormolu, and wall-sconces and chandeliers were of sparkling cut glass.

Demidoff's chairs in the contemporaneous French style are shown to have been oval-backed with deeply upholstered seats, with frames of hammered copper concealed beneath wide, flat panels of malachite sunk within rims of ormolu and ornately garnished on back, legs and feet and leg joints with clear-cut mouldings in high relief ormolu. The catalogue lists large and small round tables, oval and square writing-desks, the flat tops of which were veneered with malachite displaying to spectacular advantage its handsome veining and gorgeous green brilliance; they were all widely bordered with ormolu (Fig. 4).

Malachite *tazze*, wine-coolers, perfume-burners and mantelpiece vases were counted as modish presents from the 1850s onwards. *Tazze* were made in numerous deep and shallow saucer shapes. The

Novosti Press Agency

joints between plinth, stem and saucer were concealed beneath rings of ornamental ormolu, and a pair of elaborate handles were fitted including handsomely modelled dancing bears, winged dragons, rampant lions and heraldic dolphins, all heavily gilded and brilliantly polished (Fig. 2).

The showy veined green malachite was found ideal for many decorative and semi-useful furnishings. Malachite frames for overmantel mirrors became fashionable; an obelisk for the shelf might be set with a clock or engraved with a commemorative inscription. Siberian malachite was used for veneering clock-cases, sets of desk equipment, jewel-cabinets, dressing-cases, toilet-table sets and other articles all purely geometrical in outline.

Small ornaments in malachite had been acquired by the discriminating purchaser from about 1760. Typical was the low flat platform edged with a flat strip of gilt-silver, and supporting several lively, boldly modelled figures in native Russian costumes. These were either in solid silver, often gilt, or in ormolu. Groups of Russian dancers (Fig. 1), peasants, craftsmen and dancing bears have been noted. Paperweights and letter-pressers were on the European market throughout the period 1815 to the 1850s. These are differentiated in the Exhibition catalogue, the latter being used for weighting the wafers then used for sealing letters. Pedestals for supporting portrait busts carved in marbles of contrasting colours were always in demand.

Green malachite jewellery set in gold formed a gaudy contrast with the rather dull-coloured costume of the period, being particularly fashionable during the reigns of George IV and William IV but continuing into the 1840s. This included bracelets, brooches, ear-rings, finger-rings and garter-fasteners. The malachite was sliced into thin plaques and might depend wholly upon its own beauty of colour and figuring for ornament, or might be lightly carved with cameo designs.

Russian malachite was used exclusively until the discovery of large deposits in the copper regions of southern Australia. These were worked by a few Parisian gem-stone operators in the late nineteenth century, but, since they lacked the machine for trimming the edges of slices, the joints were straight, saw-cut as by the original method but with rather more finesse; joints were virtually invisible. In the twentieth century malachite from Rhodesia, the Belgian Congo and Arizona has been used.

MUSEUMS AND COLLECTIONS

Russian malachite may be seen at the following:

GREAT BRITAIN

London:	British Museum
	Geological Museum
	Victoria and Albert Museum

RUSSIA

| Leningrad: | State Hermitage Museum |
| Moscow: | State Kremlin Museum |

U.S.A.

| New York: | American Museum of Natural History |
| | Metropolitan Museum of Art |

FURTHER READING

The World of Jewel Stones by Michael Weinstein, London, 1959.
Official Descriptive and Illustrated Catalogue of the Exhibition of 1851, Vol. III, London, 1851.

K. Hoddle

ARTHUR NEGUS COLLECTORS' ITEM

Above: Obverse and reverse sides of the medal 'Corn Monopoly, a nation's curse', struck by J. Taylor of Birmingham in the 1830s. Worn as a protest badge, it bears a small hole in the rim. Made of white metal, it is worth about £4.

VICTORIAN COMMEMORATIVE MEDALS

Until late in the eighteenth century medallions were not commonplace. Presentation pieces were made but not in large numbers, although improvements in minting techniques made it possible to produce medals cheaply at the beginning of the nineteenth century.
Issued to celebrate the passing of parliamentary Bills — or to protest against them — to honour royalty, visiting foreign dignitaries, politicians, statesmen, reformers and even engineering and building achievements, these medals reflected diverse aspects of political and social life.

Collecting Hints

Generally speaking, the heyday of the commemorative medal was the first half of the nineteenth century; this is when they were most popular and when the best medals were made. Later in the century the designs tended to become fussy and over-ornate although technically the standard remained high.
One sometimes comes across a medal with a small hole bored in the rim. This enabled the owner to wear it on his coat as a protest or campaign badge.
It is interesting to note that with these medals one does not come across the problem of faking as one does with coins. There are, however, contemporary copies which are usually much coarser than the originals but, because they were never made to deceive, they are easily distinguishable.

Names To Look For:

Webb, who produced his best works between 1800 and 1820. As the first popular medallist he became known as the 'Father of the Victoria Medal'. His work can be identified without difficulty as it was usually struck in very high relief and in a neo-classical style.
J. Taylor, who was probably the greatest provincial medallist. Working in Birmingham in the 1830s and 40s, he too had a distinctive style. He tended to select genre incidents and paid close attention to detail, particularly in his narratives, for example in the medal *Corn Monopoly, a Nation's Curse* (far left).
The Wyon Family, who made medals throughout the nineteenth century. Leonard and William Wyon are perhaps the best known, but other members of the family were also fine craftsmen. They were undoubtedly the finest medallists of the age.

Where To Buy

Any coin dealer will be able to show a prospective buyer a range of Victorian medals. They are usually obtainable at coin fairs held regularly in all parts of the country.

Prices

White metal medals are the cheapest. The prices range from about £1–£5. Bronze medals are a little more expensive, selling for anything between £1 and £20, or even £30 for an exceptionally rare specimen. The price range is to a great extent dependent on condition. A medal that is badly rubbed or worn is worth less than the same medal in mint condition.

Opposite: Medallion commemorating the visit of Napoleon III and the Empress Eugenie to London, 1855, by B. Wyon. Bronze. In mint condition it would fetch about £12.

Below left: Medal commemorating the abolition of the Slave Trade by J. Webb, 1807. Bronze. It depicts Wilberforce, 'Friend of Africa'. £7–£12.

Below right: Art Union of London medal celebrating the painter William Hogarth, by L. Wyon. 1848. Bronze. Worth between £7 and £12.

The Imperial Glass Factory

Malcolm Burgess

From the late seventeenth century Russia followed western styles and fashions in the manufacture of glass and, on occasion, seriously rivalled the best that the west produced

The development of a glass industry in Russia was a slow and uncertain process. It was not until the late seventeenth century that a Swedish master of artillery named Koyet received the Tsar's permission to establish and run a glass manufactory for a space of fifteen years at the village of Dukhanino, near Moscow. Foreign craftsmen were sought out to work at the Dukhaninsky Zavod. The new enterprise, however, could not turn out sufficient glassware to meet the needs of both the Court and the aristocracy.

A second factory was accordingly set up in 1668 pertaining solely to the Tsar Aleksei Mikhailovich on land belonging to his summer residence at Izmaylovo. The Tsar personally controlled the works in which he took a great interest. Two craftsmen from the Dukhaninsky factory, Boris Ivanov and Grigory Vasil'yev, were appointed master glaziers. Venetian glass-blowers were also summoned.

The Izmaylovo factory produced jugs, dishes, plates, vases, goblets, tumblers and wineglasses as well as vessels now gone out of use: vessels for the apothecary, inkpots, candlesticks, lamps and ecclesiastical fittings. These were made of plain or decorated glass, transparent or opaque glass or lead glass. In 1671, Aleksei Mikhailovich richly rewarded his master gilder, Dmitry Stepanov, for his high quality output which 'has extended the renown of Russia'; standards were excellent, but it

Fig. 1 **Mug,** Imperial or Bakhmet'yev Glass Factory, c.1814. Milky glass, hand-painted with gold. In imitation of porcelain, this opaque white mug is painted with a caricature of Napoleon I. The meaning of the inscription is that Napoleon failed to make the Russians dance to his tune, and was forced instead to dance to theirs.

Fig. 2 From the left:
Inscribed glass, Imperial or Bakhmet'yev Glass Factory, c.1814. Diamond-cut clear glass with a gilt rim, set with an opaque-white oval inscribed in Russian 'Paris Taken 19 March, 1814'; height 6⅞ ins.
Rummer, Imperial or Bakhmet'yev Glass Factory, early nineteenth century. Diamond-cut clear glass with a gilt rim, set with a circular medallion bearing the portrait of Count Platov (1751–1818) in sepia enamels; height 5½ ins.
Platov was the Cossack commander during the campaign of 1812–14. He helped to defeat the French at Laon in 1813, captured Nemours in 1814 and entered Paris with the Allies in the same year. He was made a Count by Alexander I in 1812.
Crystal glass, Imperial or Bakhmet'yev Glass Factory, early nineteenth century. Diamond-cut glass with a gilt rim and grisaille portrait of Count Wittgenstein (1769–1843); height 6⅞ ins.
Count Wittgenstein was a Russian general who served in the 1807 campaign against Napoleon. He was defeated by the French in 1813 and relieved of his command, but was reinstated for the campaign of 1814.
(Sotheby and Co., London.)

is possible that they did not quite compare with the best products from Western Europe.

Such was the position of the glass industry in Russia at the opening of the eighteenth century. The Dukhaninsky factory held the monopoly of glass-making, while the remaining two glass-works were Crown property, under the Tsar himself.

The Dukhaninsky and Izmailovsky glassworks were closed down at the beginning of the eighteenth century when Peter the Great decided to move his capital to St. Petersburg.

Peter the Great devoted particular attention to the production of glass within his Empire, and shared the views put forward by his celebrated economist, Ivan Pososhkov, who vehemently protested against importing foreign glassware and proclaimed the necessity of native manufactories for glass. 'We may export glass to them', he pronounced, 'but not they to us'. In 1705 a glass-works was established on the Vorob'yov (Sparrow Hills) near Moscow, staffed initially by English glass-workers, later to be replaced by native workers. This factory started producing mirror-glass panels after the latest methods used in France.

Since the position of St. Petersburg had been consolidated by Russian force of arms in 1714, the Tsar decided to transfer the Vorob'yov glass-works to his new capital. Despite the wastage and complications involved in removing the fittings, a manufactory was established about sixty miles from the city on the banks of the river Luga. The factory was set up in two places: near the town of Yamburg (now Kingisepp), where glass mirrors and table-ware went into production, and at the village of Zhabino, some twelve miles along the Luga, where production was concentrated on glass panes for windows. The extensive forests around the Luga guaranteed supplies of fuel and charcoal for the smelting process.

The Yamburg factory was controlled by Peter the Great's powerful favourite, Prince Menshikov. Soon the glassworks were providing massive glass mirrors in cut-crystal frames, phials and jars for chemical solutions, optical glass and lenses of superior quality, hour-glasses and hookahs for export to the Orient. Also in production were the lanterns for the street-lighting which illumined Moscow's gloomy streets from 1730. On the death of Catherine I in 1727, Menshikov was exiled and his property confiscated. In 1735 both factories were taken over by the Crown. The Yamburg glassworks was transferred to St. Petersburg, while the Zhabino factory was moved to the southern shore of Lake Ladoga.

Throughout the 1730s, during the reign of the Empress Anna Ioannovna (1730–40), the Zhabino factory continued the production of window panes on the remote shores of the lake. The Yamburg branch, however, profited from the advantages of metropolitan life. The St. Petersburg Crystal Factory, as it was now officially designated, also owned a spacious warehouse for storing finished products and for general sale. This department store was situated on the Nevsky Prospect close by the Lutheran Church.

The St. Petersburg Glass Factory went on producing glass until its closure in the early 1770s. From that time onwards, glass for the Court was made at a factory near Schlüsselburg (now Petro-krepost') supervised by master craftsmen from the St. Petersburg works. The Naz'ya factory was founded in the 1750s and was honoured in the summer of 1765 with a visit by Catherine the Great. Only window glass was produced at first, until from 1770, other glassware was put into production, under the director Lilienthale. In 1777 the factory was let to Prince Potyomkin; after his death in 1792, the government took over the glassworks and incorporated it into the Imperial State Porcelain Factory.

Sperryn's Ltd.

Fig. 3 *The Battle of Poltava by Mikhail Vasil'yevich Lomonosov (1711–65), made at the Ust'-Ruditskaya Fabrika, 1763–64. Smal'ta (thick coloured glass) mosaic.*
This detail from one of Lomonosov's most magnificent and renowned mosaics shows Peter the Great defeating the Swedes at Poltava in 1709. (Academy of Sciences, Leningrad.)

Fig. 4 *Crystal dessert-plate, one of a pair from the Imperial Glass Factory, c.1812. Clear glass cut with strawberry diamonds, the centre amber-flashed, engraved with a scene inscribed in Russian: 'Everyone Taking Up Arms – 1812'; diameter 9½ ins. (Sotheby's.)*

Fig. 5 *Glass, Imperial or Bakhmet'yev Glass Factory, early nineteenth century. Clear glass cut with prisms and set with an oval medallion of opaque-white glass, which is painted in pale enamels with the winged figure of Victory and the towns passed through by the Russians during the campaign against Napoleon from Berlin to Bordeaux; height 5⅛ ins. (Sotheby's.)*

Fig. 6 *Glass, Imperial or Bakhmet'yev Glass Factory, early nineteenth century. Clear glass set with an opaque-white glass panel bearing a grisaille portrait of Count Platov (see Fig. 2); height 5⅛ ins. (Sotheby's.)*

Fig. 7 Left: *Small decanter and stopper, Imperial or Bakhmet'yev Glass Factory. Clear glass cut, gilt and set with an opaque-white medallion painted in sepia enamels with a scene of a Chinese man at a table; height 5½ ins.*
Right: *Rummer, Imperial or Bakhmet'yev Glass Factory, c.1814. Diamond-cut clear glass with a gilt rim, set with an opaque-white medallion bearing the gilt monogram of Alexander I and the Russian inscription: 'Russian Flags Raised on the Walls of Paris, 19th March, 1814'; height 5⅛ ins. (Sotheby's.)*

Fine quality glass in the second half of the eighteenth century was also being produced at the privately run works of the merchants Mal'tsov and the glazier Bakhmet'yev. In the mid-eighteenth century, the Mal'tsov combine established two factories. A third factory arose in 1792; it became the focus of the Mal'tsov enterprises, attaining its zenith in the middle of the nineteenth century with a complement of eight hundred workers. The Bakhmet'yev factory was opened at the beginning of the 1760s; during the Pugachev rebellion the factory, equipped with seven kilns, was wrecked. In 1775 it was restored and thereafter flourished. By the 1790s, the Bakhmet'yevs already owned three factories – for crystal, flat glass panels and everyday glassware. In 1802, manufactured wares amounted to some forty-five thousand roubles, at that time a very considerable sum.

In the second half of the eighteenth century, there were four large centres for the production of glass in Russia. Yet in spite of a decree from the senate in 1744, which required factories to impress their marks on all products, few signatures are found nowadays and consequently it is difficult to date or attribute any of the pieces which have survived.

A decorated and painted creamy-white opaline glass

In the latter years of the eighteenth century, thanks to M. V. Lomonosov's brilliant achievements in the preparation of coloured glass at Ust'-Ruditse, Russian factories were able to introduce a decorated and painted creamy-white opaline glass. Mikhail Vasil'yevich Lomonosov (1711–65), chemist, engineer and scholar, had been granted permission by the Empress Elizabeth Petrovna in 1753 to embark on a fresh venture, the making of mosaics at a well-endowed factory fairly close to St. Petersburg. At this works, known as the Ust'-Ruditskaya Fabrika, Lomonosov concocted a new material –smal'ta (thick coloured glass)–from which he produced mosaics, pendants, intaglios, medallions, brooches and beads, as well as table-services and toilet- and writing-sets of multi-coloured glass. Lomonosov's mosaic pictures of the Russian sovereigns and nobility, which were made to be framed and to hang on the wall, display a dazzling virtuosity. Among many superb portraits, *The Battle of Poltava* (Fig. 3) executed 1763–64, stands out as a masterpiece. In May 1764, Lomonosov was elected an Honorary Member of the Academy of Sciences at Bologna for his distinguished work in the field of glass.

The plain cut glass fashionable in the mid-eighteenth century eventually gave way to new designs. Coloured glassware was centred at Naz'ya and Potyomkin's Ozerki factory. When it was made 'Imperial' at the end of the eighteenth century the factory became the main centre for the production of glass in Russia and it remained so until the middle of the nineteenth century. Judging from the terms laid down in the agreement of 1777, which has been preserved, this factory turned out icicle-drops, lustres, baluster-stems and crystal attachments for all light-fittings.

Russian cut-glass chandeliers, girandoles and candelabra are celebrated for their elegance and beauty; an infinite variety of designs was evolved by Russian craftsmen. Many examples have survived from the eighteenth century and may be found throughout the capitals of Europe. In the last half of the eighteenth century, the general shape of the lustre fittings began to change. A series of circlets arrayed in tiers decreasing in circumference towards the apex, to which were attached pendants of cut glass, no longer in the form of oak leaves, but of icicles or tear-shaped drops, signified the swing to the neo-classical style.

The last third of the eighteenth century saw the customary ground and engraved glass yield to a decorated variety of glassware. Both plain and coloured, as well as the milky-white opaline glass, were now painted – silver and gold on the coloured products, gold on the plain with the addition of white and purple enamel, while the opaline was covered with polychrome patterns similar to porcelain. The rococo treatment of St. Petersburg glass was replaced by a classical, restrained design of ribbons, chaplets and acanthus leaves. Decanters and wineglasses were also turned out in some quantity. Their shapes conformed to prevailing fashion, but as time went by the wineglasses were given slimmer faceted stems supporting a conical bowl.

Not much coloured glass has been preserved. The blue variety has survived the best, followed by the violet and then the ruby. The green is very rare, but a lovely emerald shade may sometimes be found. Flasks, tumblers, decanters and wineglasses are fairly numerous. The earliest dated piece in the State Hermitage Museum is a deep-blue glass vase with cylindrical body surmounted by a lid adorned with a dove. The rectangular base is signed and dated in gold 'J.P. Burg, 1786'. Signed and dated wares from a later period come from the Bakhmet'yev factory.

St. Petersburg workshops made richly ornamented coloured, silvered and gilt glass

Coloured glass, generally ornamented in silver or gold, was more often than not purpose-made, since surviving examples carry an escutcheon, motto or monogram contained in a cartouche bordered with a floral garland. These pieces seem to have been issued by the St. Petersburg *ateliers* rather than by provincial workshops, judging by the style of decoration. During the eighteenth century, the St. Petersburg factory favoured compactly garlanded roses and other flowers, whilst the Bakhmet'yev and other glassworks preferred looser wreaths of long or narrow leaves. The decoration of glass and porcelain was often similar, which was not surprising since the State Glass Factory had been amalgamated with the State Porcelain Factory in 1792. Few signed pieces have been preserved from the Bakhmet'yev factory so that assessing the provenance of Russian glassware is a difficult task.

Plain glassware was also being manufactured in the latter part of the eighteenth century, some of it rather crude in quality, with an engraved pattern or a gold band round the rims of bottles and glasses. Higher quality products were rarely engraved or cut, relying simply upon a gold decorative pattern for effect. Dating may be surmised with reference to equivalent decorative styles on

Victor Kennett

Sperryn's Ltd.

Sperryn's Ltd.

Sperryn's Ltd.

Sperryn's Ltd.

porcelain.

A decorated milky-white opaline glass was much in evidence from the second half of the eighteenth century. Some examples have painted miniatures on them and friezes made up of a series of large blooms upon a black or gold ground, reminiscent of the work produced by the Imperial State Factory. Such wares must therefore derive from St. Petersburg. The decoration, however, is not always of the best. Basic motifs are often separate flowers, particularly roses or small nosegays scattered over the surface; garlands and bandeaux appear frequently. Genre scenes portraying cavaliers and ladies in a landscape setting were popular, as also were rococo scrolls.

The semi-opalescence of this creamy-white glass distinguishes it from the opaline produced by the Imperial State Porcelain Factory. With light passing through it, the body takes on a pinky-yellow tinge while in reflected light the glass appears very pale blue.

White opaline glass adorned Catherine's favourite rooms

The glass factories in Russia were kept particularly busy towards the end of the eighteenth century dealing with orders for the decorative glass panels which were inserted into Charles Cameron's Pompeian *ensembles* at the Palace of Tsar'skoe Selo. The St. Petersburg glassworks during the 1780s were turning out slabs and colonnettes of both coloured and white opaline glass to adorn Catherine the Great's boudoir and her favourite 'snuff-box', as she called the adjoining room. The Empress' bedroom walls were inlaid with medallions of Wedgwood Jasper ware and panels of milky-white glass set between gilt-bronze mounts, and with chased ormolu appliqué designs. Slender columns of purple glass were adorned with capitals and bases of bronze. The 'snuff-box' was panelled with opalescent white glass and gilt ornaments, its doors framed in columns of sapphire glass. *En suite* with Cameron's decor is a card-table with square legs of transparent blue cut glass. The top has borders inlaid with slips of dark-blue glass terminated at each of the four corners by white glass rectangles. The table is finished in gilt bronze and, like the walls, the glass strips are mounted on silver foil.

At the end of the eighteenth century, lead-glass was popular. It was used for the obelisks, icicle-drops and cut-glass pendants of chandeliers and lustres. Heavier and with more depth, the lead-glass enhanced the sparkle of plain glass. By 1800, coloured glass gave way to plain crystal which was then faceted and cut in a diamond pattern to reveal every radiant, glittering colour of the rainbow. After 1825, however, there was a decline in the quality of Russian diamond-cut glass.

The Imperial State Factory continued to execute a wide variety of wares throughout the nineteenth century. A library was installed; students were enrolled for classes in drawing and grammar, after which they entered the workshops receiving seventy-five roubles per annum, and those who were successful received a further education at the Mining School. The general standard of design nevertheless became more eclectic and self-conscious from the second quarter of the nineteenth century.

Giraudon

Novosti Press Agency

RUSSIAN PORCELAIN

Malcolm Burgess

Fig. 1 **Sugar bowl or écuelle**,
*with matching saucer and spoon,
Russian, late eighteenth century.
Monograms were a favourite
decorative device on Russian
porcelain. These pieces bear
that of Catherine II.
(Musée des Arts Décoratifs,
Paris.)*

Fig. 2 **Plate** *from the famous
Gur'yevsky Service (1809–17),
Imperial Porcelain Factory,
St. Petersburg, 1814–17.
(Palace of Pavlovsk,
near Leningrad.)*

Fig. 3 **Tartar archer** *after
J. Kaendler and P. Reinicke of
the Meissen factory in Germany,
Popov Factory, Moscow, 1810.
(Dashwood Collection,
West Wycombe Park,
Buckinghamshire.)*

Fig. 4 **Plate** *from the service
made for the Order of
St. Alexander Nevsky,
commissioned by Catherine II
in 1777, by F. Y. Gardner, 1780.
(Sotheby and Co., London.)*

Intrigue and technical failures inhibited the development of Russian porcelain until Imperial patronage and improving skills produced work of the highest quality

During the first decade of the eighteenth century, the premier factory for hard-paste porcelain was established in Dresden under the auspices of the German chemist Johann Friedrich Böttger (born 1682). This is important for the historian of Russian porcelain since Böttger's methods, triumphs and even his personality were influential to the development later of Russian porcelain.

Efforts to organise the manufacture of porcelain in Russia had first been made in the reign of Peter the Great; the Tsar himself was an admirer of faience and a keen collector. In 1718, the Dutch master-potter Eggbrecht, the owner of a small faience manufactory in Dresden, was invited to Russia, but his stay produced nothing remarkable. By order of the Tsar, a Russian agent abroad, Yury Kologrivy, tried to discover the secrets of the Meissen factory, but he was unsuccessful. Another agent, Andrey Kursin, managed to purchase the secret from a certain Chinese porcelain-master, but since the Chinaman failed to reveal an

essential element to Kursin he was unsuccessful in his endeavours despite an Imperial decree to start up a factory near St. Petersburg.

Although the foundation of a porcelain manufactory had made no headway under Peter the Great, it did not prevent the Tsar's daughter, the Empress Elizabeth, from embarking upon the actual establishment of a factory. In 1743, Russian troops were directed to Stockholm under the command of General Keyt to bolster up the Swedish Crown. Also resident there was the Russian diplomat Baron N. A. Korf. To both these gentlemen, foreign specialists offered their services. It was an excellent opportunity for adventurers to find service in Russia, and there was truth in the proverb: 'Whoever wants his bread provided without stirring his hand should come to Russia'.

Since 1729, the adventurer Conrad Hunger, self-titled 'Master of Porcelain', who had worked in Vienna (1717), Venice (1719) and Dresden (1727) as a gilder, had been living in Sweden. In Dresden, Hunger had gained the confidence of Böttger, then manager of the Meissen factory, from whom he had succeeded in extracting the secret of porcelain on an occasion when the manager was drunk. Hunger approached Korf and secret negotiations were initiated, with Korf meantime unaware that he was being double-crossed and that Hunger had also been invited to Sweden to found a porcelain manufactory being thus in debt to the Swedish government. As a result, on 1 February, 1744, Baron Korf concluded a contract with Hunger for the

A. C. Cooper

4

R. Todd-White

foundation in St. Petersburg of a manufactory for faience and hard-paste porcelain. Finally, by Imperial command, Keyt received Hunger on a warship and transported him to Revel, the General in no way suspecting the bogus arcanist.

The Russian government was obliged to pay dearly for Hunger – nearly five thousand roubles. The Empress Elizabeth, eagerly awaiting the novelty of Russian porcelain, appointed Baron Ivan Antonovich Cherkasov, then President of the Cabinet, as official supervisor of Russian ceramics. Cherkasov directed Hunger to St. Petersburg and engaged the Swiss architect Trezzini to prepare a suitable apartment for Hunger and to show him where significant china-clay deposits were to be found inside Russia.

Hunger was soon revealed as a complete charlatan; he had only a slight acquaintance with various crafts and his knowledge of porcelain was minimal. In September 1744, on the pretext of searching for kaolin around Moscow, he secretly retired to bed for three whole weeks. The fine quality clay in the Gzhel'sk area, used by Grebensh- chikov at his factory, and still in production throughout the nineteenth century and today, was considered to be the appropriate raw material for the proposed porcelain. Hunger requested the Empress to have a model medallion designed, from which he could make a porcelain plaque. A pottery was established in Trezzini's brickworks on a marshy bank of the Neva on the exact site of the present State Porcelain Factory named in 1925 after M. V. Lomonosov. The results were a dismal failure. All that Hunger was able to produce, in spite of his 'experience', was one imperfect little pot. Cherkasov, already suspicious and irritated by Hunger's manner, made a personal visit to the factory, which he found in a deplorable condition.

Hunger was forced to admit his incompetence and on 10 November, 1748, an official decree deprived him of his position at the Imperial Porcelain Factory, where he was replaced by his exceptional assistant Dmitri Vinogradov.

Vinogradov set about remedying the state of affairs. He had already written an eight-page memorandum on the manufacture of porcelain in 1745, and he now worked unceasingly at the potteries. He mixed the pigments, reconstructed the kilns, experimented with varying tempera- tures and composed the receipts for enamel and

A. C. Cooper

Fig. 5 *Tea-vendor with samovar
and cup*, mark of Alexander I,
Imperial Porcelain Factory,
St. Petersburg, c.1810.
(Dashwood Collection.)

Fig. 6 *Dinner-service* made for
Nicholas I and used at the
coronation of the Tsars, Imperial
Porcelain Factory, St. Petersburg,
nineteenth century.
(Christie, Manson and
Woods Ltd., London.)

Fig. 7 Russian porcelain marks:
the top three are of Gardner,
c.1765–1891; the next of the
Popov factory, Moscow,
c.1800–72; two eagles of the
Imperial Porcelain Factory,
St. Petersburg, 1741–62; the
mark of Catherine II, 1762–96.

Fig. 8 *Young woman* by
Gardner, Moscow, late
eighteenth or nineteenth century.
Height 8½ ins. (Sotheby's.)

Fig. 9 *Pastry-seller* by Gardner,
Moscow, late eighteenth or
nineteenth century.
Height 8 ins. (Sotheby's.)

7

porcelain. First small, then more ambitious pieces
were produced in an ever-increasing flow. A set-
back occurred in 1751 when he failed to provide
a piece commissioned in honour of the Empress'
Name Day. He had given way to an old enemy – the
bottle. By 1752, the master craftsman had become
so skilled that attempts were made at firing
miniature porcelain statuettes. St. Petersburg
came to be recognised as a rival to Meissen. Vinogradov died in 1758; he was succeeded by a master
from Meissen, Johann Gottfried Müller.

Russian porcelain of the mid-eighteenth century
is unsophisticated but it has an appealing fresh-
ness, exuberant colour and elegant form. Chinese
and Meissen wares served as models but were
never slavishly copied. Tea- and coffee-pots of
simple design made an early appearance but these
later became more sophisticated. Sculptured
decoration in the shape of garlands and flowers in
bas-relief or berries and roses on the lids of basins
and cups was also produced. Such ornament
developed into more complicated patterns with the
increase in new techniques. Fretted plates and
pierced baskets were made with appliqué mouldings of flowers, butterflies and other insects.

From 1752 the figurines, about six inches high,
included several engaging negroes. There was a man
dressed in a long kaftan with feathered head-
dress *à l'indienne*, a woman seated in a skirt with
a necklace and a kind of Cuban kerchief twisted
around her head, a pair of gesticulating men in
loin-cloths and another one in tunic and turban.
Other figures are a soldier warming himself, an
archer (Fig. 3) and an assortment of gentlemen
in oriental garb influenced by the vogue for
Chinoiserie. Although these latter are of better
quality, they do not possess the same charm.

At first, plates, flower-pots and vases were usually
coloured in a single tone – purple, green or gold.
Other articles were adorned with simple bouquets
or landscapes in black. Methods of ornamentation
later became more diverse – a background of white
or gold with a colourful posy of flowers, views of
feasting peasants or decorations of armorial
bearings (Fig. 1) were popular.

The Imperial State Porcelain factory had
engaged an expert staff and by 1756 the total
complement was seventy workers. All in all, it was a

fine creation which Catherine II inherited from
Vinogradov. N. Voinov had been appointed as
successor, and by Imperial decree on 29 January,
1762, the factory was removed from the control of
the President of the Cabinet and transferred to the
jurisdiction of the Senate. The new director was
the redoubtable M. V. Lomonosov (1711–65).

Officially re-established, the Imperial State
Porcelain Factory continued to turn out superb
ceramics. The celebrated Orlovsky Service, a
dressing table collection comprising morning-tea-
set, cutlery, looking-glass and receptacles for
brooches, pins, powder and cosmetics, was ordered
from the factory by Catherine II and presented to
her favourite Count Grigori Orlov. This service is
in dark-blue and gold, decorated with *amoretti*
curiously transitional in style, combining the styles
of the late Baroque and the then fashionable
Rococo and presaging the coming neo-Classicism.

In 1779, the sculptor Jean-Dominique Rachette
was invited to join the State Porcelain Factory.
Rachette was a brilliant artist; he was elected an
Academician in 1785 and appointed Professor at the
Academy of Sciences in 1800. His work may be
seen on many examples of Russian porcelain. A
famous set of porcelain still surviving is the
Gur'yevsky Service, named after Count Gur'yev,
President of the Cabinet in 1809, who commissioned it (Fig. 2). This service was designed mainly
by S. S. Pimenov in the Empire style. The colours
are deep Etruscan red and gold painted with views
of St. Petersburg, military and genre scenes and
vignettes taken from the work of the English artist
D. A. Atkinson (1775–1831).

The mark used in the time of the Empress
Elizabeth and Peter III was the Imperial two-
headed eagle, although other marks are also found.
During the reigns of Catherine II and Paul I, the
Sovereign's monogram was used often with the
addition of initials representing *Pridvornaya
Kontora* (Crown office). From the eighteenth
century onwards, the porcelain carried the escutcheon of St. Petersburg: two crossed anchors,
sceptre with crown above and the date.

The progress made by the Imperial State Porcelain
Factory, and increasing public demand for luxury
products, soon encouraged private individuals to
establish factories in Russia. One of the first

entrepreneurs to achieve renown was Francis Yakovlevich Gardner, an experienced business man who founded a porcelain manufactory at the village of Verbilki, near Moscow. Little is known of Gardner before his arrival in Russia in 1746 but it seems that, after having made his fortune in a Moscow banking-office, he decided to invest in a porcelain factory rather than return home to Aberdeen. Gardner received a permit on 21 February, 1766, from the Department of Manufacturers to set up his factory and started work the following year.

Early Gardner porcelain does not compare with the cool whiteness of Meissen nor the purity of the St. Petersburg factory, but it does show a lovely off-white hue more reminiscent of Chinese export products. Catherine II extended her patronage and commissioned Gardner to make grand services ornamented with ribbons, badges and stars of the leading Imperial Orders of chivalry, for use on the annual gala occasions held in the Winter Palace in honour of the Knights of the Orders. The St. Alexander Nevsky service, commissioned in 1777, is a triumph of the decorators art, the rich crimson of the moiré ribbon being particularly spectacular (Fig. 4). This was followed by the St. George service (1777), which includes an intriguing diversity of shapes, and the St. Andrey-Pervozvanny service (1780), remarkable for the ingenious variation of chain and ribbon. Gardner manufactured all kinds of porcelain (Figs. 8 and 9) and delightful little 'dolls', as they were called, in biscuit. Eight hundred of these were made in 1770.

Gardner's porcelain 'could be compared in fineness with any other foreign ware'

The neo-classical movement influenced designs, but the spirit was decidedly Russian. There were portraits of heroes of the Great Patriotic War and other models. G. F. Müller, visiting the Gardner factory in 1799, declared that the porcelain 'could be compared in fineness with any other foreign ware'. In 1814, the Gardner factory was awarded three medals and the first place for quality. It was made a Company in 1857. Until its takeover by the firm of Kuznetsov in 1892, the Gardner factory was held to be the foremost privately-managed factory in Russia. The mark on early Gardner porcelain is shown in Figure 7, being in over-glaze purple. The size of the mark varies: the more square the shape, the earlier the piece. From the 1770s to the beginning of the nineteenth century, the English letter 'G', in light or deep blue under-glaze, is more usual. Crossed swords with a star are also found towards the end of the century, sometimes with the star omitted. In the first quarter of the nineteenth century, the letter 'G' still appears, but becomes more like the number '6' in style. After this, the name Gardner appears in Russian characters on both porcelain and faience, with the arms of Moscow and, after 1850, the name. From the time of Alexander II (1855–81), the Russian double-headed eagle surmounts the arms of Moscow encircled with a band on which is inscribed the words 'Fabrik Gardner v Moskve'.

Besides Gardner's factory, another private concern was set up by Aleksei Ivanovich Bakhmet'yev in the second half of the eighteenth century. This enterprise suffered during the Pugachev rebellion in 1774 and its subsequent fate is unknown.

Just before 1800, there were already a number of private porcelain factories functioning in Russia. Of these, the Kievo-Mezhigorskaya Fabrika at Kiev was the most famous. Founded in 1798, its wares were decorated with relief flowers and foliage and adorned with pictures of peasants in national costume. The mark for this manufactory was the word 'Kiev', although on some pieces the Imperial eagle crowned, or the crown dove, may be found. In 1806, a heavy import duty was placed on foreign porcelain, so that an impetus was given to home-produced porcelain. Among the native enterprises which arose as a result, mention should be made of the porcelain manufactory started by Carl Melli in 1806 at the village of Gorbunov, near Moscow, which was bought in 1811 by the Moscow merchant A. G. Popov, and continued in operation until the mid-nineteenth century. The best products of this factory appeared between 1811 and the year of Popov's death in 1850.

In 1818 N. S. Kudinov set up a factory at the village of Lystsovo, near Moscow, and produced a fine quality porcelain until its closure in 1885, exporting in quantity to Persia and the East. Strong colours and a decoration of floral sprays characterise the output of this factory.

Finally, the porcelain manufactory of Prince Nikolay Borosovich Yusupov, established in 1814 at the village of Arkhangel'skoe, produced a high quality porcelain until Yusupov's death in 1831. Yusupov had replaced Prince Vyazemsky as Director-General of the Imperial State Porcelain Factory in 1792, and the standard of design and craftsmanship improved during his administration. At Arkhangel'skoe, a talented Frenchman named Lambert, from Sèvres, was imported to decorate the wares with portraits of celebrities, views and scenes from the 1812 campaign. The pieces are signed in under-glaze gold with the name *Arkhangel'skoe* in Russian letters or in the French form of *Archangeski*. Occasionally, Lambert's name or monogram is placed near this title.

Many of these private manufactories suffered severely from the Napoleonic invasion of 1812, and some were unable to recover. Gardner himself incurred losses amounting to seventy-three thousand roubles. Not only were his shop, warehouse and town mansion on the Basmannaya burned out, but his entire stock of china-clay was completely dissipated. Ironically, Russian porcelain had by this time acquired a universal reputation.

MUSEUMS AND COLLECTIONS
Russian porcelain and glass may be seen at the following:
GREAT BRITAIN
London:	British Museum
	Victoria and Albert Museum
U.S.A.	
Washington D.C.:	Hillwood (Ross Collection)
U.S.S.R.	
Leningrad:	State Hermitage Museum
	State Russian Museum

FURTHER READING
Russian Porcelains by Marvin C. Ross, London, 1969.
'Russian Ceramics' by C. G. E. Bunt, in **Apollo**, October 1929.

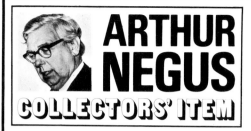

ARTHUR NEGUS
COLLECTORS' ITEM

PINCUSHIONS

Pincushions were an essential ornament to every Victorian boudoir. Placed on work- or dressing-tables, decorative pincushions were used to hold pins for the hair, for hats and later for scarves and ties. Ornamental pins did not become popular until the second half of the nineteenth century, when changes in hair-styles and increasingly elaborate hats gave pins a practical as well as a purely decorative function.

Pincushions were a perfect vehicle for Victorian sentimentality. They were made in the form of birds, animals, shoes and even tiny figures of milkmaids or dancers. Birds were widely used because the presence of large numbers of coloured pins gave the effect of plumage. One very popular shape was the heart, often decorated with some insipid phrase picked out in white glass beads or coloured sequins. The casing or base of the cushion was usually made of finely worked silver or brass, and the cushion itself was covered in velvet, silk or tapestry. Pincushions were often given as presents between young ladies, and they were also offered as souvenirs of events, such as the marriage of the Prince of Wales or Royal Jubilees.

Hints To Collectors

One of the hazards of collecting any fabric-covered article is that the fabric itself wears

less well than the object. This is particularly true of pincushions, for the silk fibres from which the covering was usually made are vulnerable to the effects of repeated pin-pricking. Some collectors prefer to restore pincushions to their pristine state, using modern fabrics to re-cover the cushion itself.

Where To Buy

There is no shop which specialises in pincushions. Some dealers keep examples to decorate Victorian work-tables or boxes.

Prices

Prices range between £5 and £8 for richly beaded examples or those with silver or brass figures, and from 50 pence to £1 for simple cushions.

Top: **Pincushion** in the form of an owl, made of pewter, with coloured glass eyes. Birds were widely used in the 1850s and '60s. £5.15.
Velvet pincushion of simple design, ornamented with glass beads, c.1875. £2.50.
Crocodile pincushion made of white metal. Bizarre designs of this sort were made throughout the last half of the nineteenth century. £1.50.

Centre: **Brass pig**, the most popular of the wide range of animals used as pincushions, c.1900. £5.15.
State coach possibly made at the time of King Edward VII's coronation in 1902. The coach also contains a tape-measure. £8.
Running hare, made of brass and with the cushion covered with fur, c.1890. £8.

Below: **Silver slipper**, typical of the designs common at the turn of the century. £5.
Circular silver pincushion, the most common and least picturesque of many designs produced c.1870. £5.
Porcelain figure. Figures of this kind were made in the 1860s, but became less popular later in the century. £2.50.
Silver swan, the most decorative of the many bird figures made as pincushion holders, c.1880. £10.

Opposite: **Heart-shaped pincushions** were extremely popular in the last half of the nineteenth century. This example is heavily worked with glass beads. £10.

ROYAL ARTILLERY

THE JEWELS OF RUSSIA

Charlotte Gere

Influenced by the East, Russian jewellers aped French designs using fabulous stones that were almost barbaric to western eyes

Accounts of Russia written by English travellers in the eighteenth and nineteenth centuries rarely fail to mention the ostentatious luxury of aristocratic life in this remote and, to Western Europeans, virtually unknown country. A feature which struck them most forcibly was the lavish use of jewellery on every possible occasion. This magnificent outward show often concealed the scanty provision, even in the wealthiest households, of such fundamental household necessities as furniture, linen and crockery. Nevertheless, whatever deficiencies existed in the basic domestic equipment, the jewellery owned by the Imperial family, members of the nobility and even the prosperous merchants was truly remarkable.

The Russians, half oriental as they were, had a passion for precious stones. They made use of flawless diamonds of enormous size, rubies, emeralds and sapphires of fine colour, often left uncut in the eastern manner; turquoises, pearls and elaborately worked precious metals. Men as well as women wore jewellery to a far greater extent than was usual even in the European courts of the eighteenth century. A court official or high-ranking army officer might wear several Orders set with precious stones, a medallion portrait of the Empress surrounded with diamonds, as well as epaulettes or shoulder-knots and a jewelled sword-hilt and sword-knot.

The women's jewellery was even more magnificent and most pieces were of enormous size. For court functions the upper part of the dress was often entirely covered with jewellery, mainly diamonds; in the eighteenth and early nineteenth centuries, jewellery as such was subordinated to the embroidery of precious stones which covered the dresses and which consisted of yards of diamond flowers with borders *en rivière* strung on cat-gut, imitating brocade ribbon with matching bows or bouquets of flowers.

Peter the Great (1682–1725) opened up Russia to the West and started the flow of foreign artistic influence which was to permeate Russian decorative art for the next hundred and fifty years, but even in the period of intensive, indeed forcible, Westernisation the influence of European taste hardly extended beyond the aristocratic and moneyed circles of Moscow and St. Petersburg. In the provinces the indigenous Asiatic-Russian culture remained largely unaffected, especially in dress and personal ornaments. People clung so much to traditional regional distinctions that even as late as the 1880s, when peasant costume was becoming a curiosity in most parts of Europe, it was possible to tell by her dress from which region, or even village, a Russian woman came. These traditions were preserved by the 'Russian revival' in the mid-nineteenth century, which recreated a fashion for neo-Byzantine enamelling, niello decoration, and elaborations of peasant jewellery, for example the necklace made by Fabergé for the Empress Alexandra for the *Bal Costume Russe* in 1896.

From the early eighteenth century onwards, the Russian Court had established strong cultural links with France. The Empress Elizabeth, Peter the Great's daughter, who came to the throne in 1741, promoted French taste and fashion and continued to import Continental craftsmen to teach the Russians modern techniques. Only twenty years before Elizabeth's accession, Russian jewellery had been made in a style abandoned in France and in most of the rest of Europe soon after the middle of the seventeenth century. The coming of foreign craftsmen revolutionised its appearance.

Catherine the Great was aged fifteen in 1745 when she came to Russia from her native Germany to marry Elizabeth's nephew and heir, the ill-fated Peter III, and so her taste, so characteristically Russian in its extravagance, was formed in Russia largely under Elizabeth's influence. Although she shared Elizabeth's taste for sumptuous rococo jewellery, she also admired the more severe neo-classical style. Much of the Imperial jewellery had always come from abroad, and many pieces were made by foreign craftsmen working in St. Petersburg and Moscow. These men were employed to teach the secrets of their trade to the native goldsmiths and jewellers, and it seems legitimate to count as Russian those pieces made in Russia for Russian customers, even if the actual execution was by a Frenchman, an Italian or a Swiss.

The *cachet* attached to French-made jewellery was such that nobody would admit to having anything else. Moscow-made articles were continually disparaged in fashionable circles, and by the 1760s foreign influence had so modernised Russian jewellery that it was nearly indistinguishable from contemporary French or English work. Mid-eighteenth-century aigrettes and bouquets made from the enormous stones demanded by Russian taste were flung together in a parody of currently fashionable rococo design; clumsily asymmetrical and top-heavy, their unwieldy appearance suggests that they were made by Russian craftsmen.

Jewellery made for Elizabeth in the later years of her reign, and for Catherine after her accession, shows the refinement produced by contact with Western Europe. Elizabeth's court jeweller was a Swiss, Jeremy Posier, who came to Russia as a child

in 1729; Catherine's own jeweller when she was Grand Duchess was an Italian, Bernardi, but later she too employed Posier, and possibly also his fellow-countryman, L. Duval.

Catherine the Great came to the throne in 1762, and a new Imperial Crown was ordered from Posier for her coronation, but it was not completed in time. The complex design of the Imperial Crown, made of the inevitable large stones, displays a symmetry and refinement of technique which had been largely lacking in the jewellery made for Elizabeth. Catherine's generous nature and lavish taste combined to make her gifts of jewellery exceedingly valuable; they could, in fact, represent discreet gifts of money, since it was accepted that the diamond settings of the Orders and miniatures could be replaced with paste and the stones sold.

The 'award-portraits' and similar 'dames-à-portrait' were miniatures of the Empress framed in diamonds surmounted by a crown; they were given to court officials and to the *dames au portrait* (maids of honour) who also wore the Empress' cipher with the crown in diamonds when in attendance. Rings or boxes set with diamond-surrounded miniatures were given to visiting diplomats and other distinguished foreigners. A peculiarity of these gifts was that the miniature was covered with a thin diamond pane in place of the usual crystal or glass. Martha Wilmot recorded in her *Journals*: 'Count Alexis Orloff . . . wears the Empress' picture set in diamonds of enormous size and instead of a Glass, 'tis a single diamond which covers the portrait'. These *pichère* diamonds, as well as other stones and pieces of jewellery, were supplied by the English court jewellers, Rundell and Bridge, who found it worth maintaining an agent in St. Petersburg for the convenience of such a good customer.

By the mid-nineteenth century, Russian jewellery, though still extravagant by the standards of countries with less abundant natural resources, shed the savage magnificence that characterised the earlier work. The 'tasteful' jewellery shown by the court jeweller, W. Bolin, at the Great Exhibition in 1851 would not have looked out of place on the French stand.

Apart from the peculiarities of Russian taste which distinguish the Imperial jewellery from contemporary Continental work, there was more of the old Russian decorative tradition in the jewellery owned by prosperous merchants and peasants. Traditional jewellery was mostly made either of enamelled gold set with coloured stones or of pearls and beads strung in patterns of swags and fringes. The use of diamonds was so widespread in Russia that Martha Wilmot concluded that they must be much cheaper than in England, but she found on enquiry that they cost about the same.

The fact that peasant wet-nurses employed by aristocratic families were required to wear unbreakable necklaces, presumably made from the abundant Siberian stones – amethysts, topaz, malachite, lapis-lazuli, agate, jasper and chalcedony – suggests that much peasant jewellery was made of glass in the form of 'French' pearls or coloured Venetian-style beads. Martha Wilmot describes the effect of this jewellery when worn, in a letter written in 1803: 'I saw for the first time a proper Merchant's wife . . . she was array'd in a Jacket and petticoat of Damask brocaded richly with Gold, stomacher distinct and chiefly compos'd of pearls, a plaited

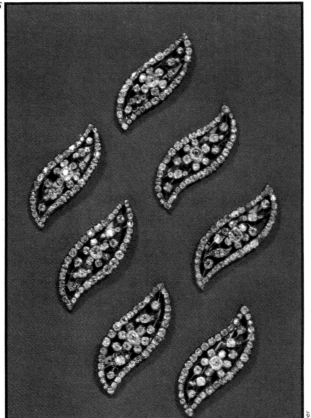

A. C. Cooper

Museum Photo

A. C. Cooper

Fig. 4 **Russian nuptial crown,**
from the Imperial Treasury.
Used for marriages of members of
the Imperial family, this crown
was assembled from diamonds
from Catherine's treasury which
were sewn on strips of velvet.
(Christie, Manson and Woods
Ltd., London.)

Fig. 5 **Cane-handle,** *Russian,*
late eighteenth century. Ivory,
the escutcheon engraved with the
arms of the Seymour-Conway
family, possibly acquired in 1827.
(By permission of the Trustees of
the Wallace Collection, London.)

Fig. 6 **Part of a set of forty-six**
shuttle-shaped dress ornaments,
c.1780–90. Set with diamonds
and marked with the monogram
LD or LP and the inventory
number 1764 of the Imperial
Treasury.
(Victoria and Albert Museum.)

Fig. 7 **Crown-shaped brooch,**
Russian, mid-eighteenth century.
Set with rose-cut diamonds
of Imperial provenance.
(Christie's.)

Fig. 8 Left: **Rococo diamond**
spray, *Russian, mid-eighteenth*
century. Right: **Diamond and**
emerald ornament, *Russian, late*
eighteenth century.
(Christie's.)

border of pearls as if it was muslin form'd the front of her cap, while a building scarcely half a yard high compos'd of pearls and diamonds completed the headdress. On her neck were twenty rows of Pearl, and on her Massy arms hung twelve rows (for I reckon'd them) by way of bracelets'.

By the middle of the nineteenth century, the old traditions of design and technique were revived in an attempt to counteract the enfeebling effect on Russian decorative art of dependence on French artistic influences. Although many cultivated Russians continued to adopt French fashions throughout the nineteenth century, more jewellery was made in the Old Russian style, using such enamelling techniques as champlevé and *cloisonné*, and the traditional Russian *skan* in which filigree patterns are applied to a metal base and some or all of the interstices filled with enamel colours. Painted enamels in the seventeenth-century style, the best of which use seven colours, were also used for small pieces of jewellery. These techniques, as well as the fashionable *tour-à-guillocher* (engine-turned) enamel and the complicated work in coloured gold based on the French eighteenth-century *quatre-couleurs* formula, show to greater advantage on the larger surfaces of cigarette boxes, Easter eggs and other ornamental objects. By the 1870s, the way was prepared for the popular success of Carl Fabergé, one of the few Russian jewellers whose work is widely known outside Russia.

The firm of Fabergé was founded in 1842 by Gustav Fabergé (1814–93), traditionally said to be descended from the Württemberg goldsmith Farberger, who worked for Catherine the Great. He retired in 1860 when his son Peter Carl (1846–1920) was still a child, and two years before the birth of another son, Agathon. Carl took over the firm in 1870, and in 1882 he was joined by Agathon. In the same year, he took the important decision to specialise in the production of *objets de vertu*. These were made of relatively inexpensive materials, especially the indigenous Siberian stones, combined with precious metals and enamel, but always of the finest possible workmanship (Figs. 1 and 3). He was immediately successful, winning a medal at the Pan-Russian Exhibition (1882). Two years later his first Easter egg was made, and presented to the Empress Maria Fedorovna.

Unlike most jewellery firms where the identity of individual craftsmen is concealed, Fabergé operated a 'workmaster' system by which objects were marked with the maker's initials. The firm's chief jeweller was August Wilhelm Holmstrom (b.1829 in Helsinki). The production of fashionable jewellery occupied a minor place in the firm's total output, but the pieces are distinguished by the fine workmanship for which it was famous.

The firm's great success at the Centennial Exhibition in Paris in 1900 greatly enhanced Fabergé's reputation outside Russia, and this year marked the beginning of the period when the Russian debt to French inspiration in the decorative arts was to be repaid with interest. ☙

MUSEUMS AND COLLECTIONS
Russian jewellery may be seen at the following:
GREAT BRITAIN:
London: Victoria and Albert Museum
Luton, Bedfordshire: Luton Hoo

FURTHER READING
A History of the Crown Jewels of Europe by Lord Twining, London, 1960.
Handbook of the Lilian Thomas Pratt Collection: Russian Imperial Jewels by Parker Lesley, Richmond, Virginia, 1960.
The Russian Journals of Martha and Catherine Wilmot, 1803–08, London, 1934.

Two Centuries of Russian Furniture

Mary Chamot

Although much fine furniture was imported from Western Europe the ship-builders of St. Petersburg were not deterred from turning their skills to the craft and creating an indigenous style

Fig. 1 **Armchair**, *Russian, early nineteenth century. Carved cherrywood.*
The back splat of this elegant armchair is carved in the form of swans, a favourite Russian motif at the time.
(Ross Collection, Hillwood, Washington D.C.)

Photo Hublitz

Very little has been written about Russian furniture, even in the country of its origin, and few examples can be found in the West; yet it is a subject well worth investigating. Woodwork has always been the major craft practised in Russia and Russian joiners made full use of their great skill when they were required to produce elegant pieces in a new style.

Furniture of a Western origin was first introduced into Russia on a large scale after Peter the Great returned from his European tour in 1698. The Emperor's preference was for everything Dutch: the small brick palace of Monplaisir in Peterhof, where he lived while his new capital of St. Petersburg was being built, was designed entirely in the Dutch style. The house contained wall-panelling, high-backed chairs and brass chandeliers, Dutch pictures hung on the walls and Dutch tiles lined the kitchen.

Peter forced the nobility to abandon their old-fashioned homes in Moscow and build themselves new houses in St. Petersburg, which had to be furnished in the latest Western style. Obviously, it was not possible to import sufficient foreign furniture to supply the needs of an entire new city. Russian craftsmen had to be trained to copy the foreign models and this they did with great success. Large numbers of ship-builders were brought down from the north and settled in the suburb of Okhta to begin work on the construction of the new Russian navy; this involved carving elaborate figure-heads and other ornaments as well as making the interior fittings and furnishings of the ships. When their initial task was completed, they were employed in making domestic and church furniture. A magnificent example of the latter is the screen (iconostasis) of the church of St. Peter and St. Paul in the Fortress. The craftsmen were all serfs and had been trained from boyhood to manipulate wood, hence the ease with which they could be switched from one job to another.

In the reign of the Empress Elizabeth (1741–61), the fashion for Rococo, more suitable for Rastrelli's splendid palaces, gradually replaced the earlier Dutch style. Foreign furniture continued to be imported and the French Ambassador arranged for whole shiploads to be brought to Russia and sold to the Court and its entourage. But the supply was never enough to meet the demand. Catherine the Great recalled that when she first came to Russia to marry the heir apparent in 1745, there was so little furniture available in the palaces that beds, chairs and tables had to accompany her on her travels, not only to her country palaces, but even to Moscow.

In the mid-eighteenth century, highly ornamental and richly carved and gilt furniture was produced in Russia, displaying exaggerations of French designs similar to those found in Germany and other countries where the prevailing style was imitated. In general, the tendency in Russia was to use less marquetry and bronze than the best French cabinet-makers employed, and the effect of ormolu was more often suggested by gilding the carved wood. One remarkable piece of marquetry that should be mentioned is a table-top at Kuskovo, the Sheremetiev estate near Moscow. It represents a

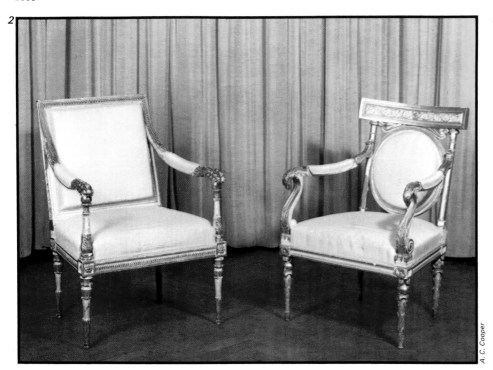

bird's-eye view of the house as it looked in about 1780–90, with a carriage driving up to the porch and the small clipped trees vanishing in perspective behind the house towards the orangery at the end of the vista.

The most important period of Russian furniture extends from the reign of Catherine the Great (1762–96), through that of her son, Paul I, and of her grandson Alexander I (1801–25). These monarchs and their wives took a great interest in the furnishing of their palaces; they employed famous architects, both Russian and foreign, and the style of each reign has a very distinctive character.

Catherine was fortunate in obtaining the services of Charles Cameron (c.1740–1820), who, like his contemporary Robert Adam, designed not only the structure itself, but every detail for the furnishing and decoration of the palaces which he built or altered for Catherine. These comprise the Gallery

which still bears his name, the Agate Pavilion and the suite of rooms he redecorated for her in Rastrelli's Palace, all in Tsar'skoe Selo (now Pushkin) and the Palace at Pavlovsk, built for her son Paul and later completed by Brenna, Voronikhin and Rossi. Cameron's arrival in Russia in about 1778 contributed to the change of taste from Rococo to a more classical style, and this is clearly reflected in the furniture of the last quarter of the century. The French Revolution of 1789 was another factor in turning the Empress' attention away from France to the more restrained design prevalent in England.

Furniture in the earlier period was carved with restless ornament, painted and gilt; by the late eighteenth century, it was more often made of polished mahogany or of other woods stained and polished to imitate mahogany since it was expensive to import. This transition is well illustrated by pieces in a private collection in London (Fig. 2). An

Fig. 2 Left: **Armchair** in the French style with claw-shaped arms, Russian, 1770–80. Painted, gilt wood.
Right: **Armchair** with arms terminating in eagles' heads on fluted supports springing from acanthus leaves, Russian, c.1785–90. Carved, painted and gilt wood. Probably made for Prince Kurakin, this chair illustrates the transition which took place in Russian cabinet-making around 1780.
(Private Collection.)

Fig. 3 **Secretaire**, Russian, 1810–20. Karelian birch. Of classical design with flat surfaces and bronze mounts, this desk was given by the Empress Alexandra to her niece.
(Luton Hoo, Luton, Bedfordshire.)

Fig. 4 **Settee and two chairs**, Russian, c.1800. Karelian birch. Probably made for Arkhangel'skoe, a magnificent country house near Moscow, this set has the severity of form typical of the period of Paul I. Native woods were often used, and a popular veneer was Karelian birch, which has a beautiful golden sheen.
(Private Collection.)

armchair of the 1770s, painted in white and gold, has arms carved in the form of claws. A pair of armchairs in the same collection, dating from about a decade later, have arms ending in eagles' heads resting on fluted supports, springing from acanthus leaves. A panel across the back is carved with a meander pattern giving the whole a simpler and more classical appearance. The Sheraton and Hepplewhite type of chair was reproduced with many variations of the splat with either upright or transverse bars, trellis patterns and even gothic tracery; chairs with lyre- or shield-shaped backs were very popular. The more elaborately carved furniture was decorated with swans, griffons and snakes. After Napoleon's campaign in Egypt, sphinxes and Egyptian heads began to appear in furniture and in architectural decoration.

Neo-Classicism dominated Russian taste for a long time. It produced the finest example of town-planning in St. Petersburg and influenced furniture design throughout the nineteenth century, when copies and imitations of the earlier neo-classical furniture continued to be produced in large quantities. The most severely classical period was the short reign of Paul I, when ornament was reduced to a minimum and became strictly geometric in form.

Sometimes the marble seats of antiquity were reproduced in wood. A typical example is the settee in the same private collection in London; it has no ornament except for a cylinder resting on each arm. It is very similar to one still at Arkhangel'skoe, near Moscow, the magnificent country house which once belonged to the Galitzines and later to the Yusupovs and is now a much frequented museum. Four Karelian birch chairs in the same collection probably also came from Arkhangel'skoe and similar ones are now in the Historical Museum, Moscow. Karelian birch is a beautiful golden wood with a variety of grains and burr, obtained from the roots of the tree, and capable of taking a fine polish. These chairs have smooth, slightly curved backs with a small anthemion motif carved in the centre (Fig. 4).

Many of the great land-owners in Russia trained their serfs to be excellent cabinet-makers, who could not only copy a given model faithfully, but were able also to introduce variations of their own, or their master's, invention. The result was that each country house had suites of furniture of distinctive design especially made for it and found nowhere else. Native woods also helped to distinguish Russian furniture from foreign manufacture. A very popular veneer was provided by the Karelian birch, which is said to have been first used for furniture by Prince Meshchersky in the 1770s. It continued to be extremely fashionable during the next half-century, at the time when satinwood was used for similar purposes in England. A certain amount of mahogany was also used in Russia, generally as a very thin veneer, as well as pine, lime, cherry, sycamore, ash, poplar and oak. Painting and gilding were used sparingly after the eighteenth century and bronze mounts very little other than in palaces.

After the Napoleonic Wars, Russians became more closely acquainted with Western life and styles of furniture. Russia's huge military contribution to the overthrow of Napoleon meant that a large number of Russians had an unexpected opportunity to view the West at close quarters. Furniture began to be designed more for comfort than for display, and simple, smooth surfaces replaced the former ornamented ones. Every Russian home had its round table where the family would assemble for interminable talk and tea-drinking; many additional forms of furniture became available, such as desks, corner cupboards, day-beds, dressing-tables, card-tables and sideboards.

A type of furniture peculiar to Russia was made at the Armoury works in Tula. This was constructed of steel enriched with cut-steel, gilt-copper, brass and sometimes silver. This technique had been used for ornamental arms and was applied to chairs, tables, beds, candlesticks, inkstands and a variety of smaller objects. These were often given as presents by the Court to foreign embassies and Eastern rulers and turn up occasionally in London, but it is not always easy to distinguish them from the similar products of Matthew Boulton of Birmingham. A fireplace with vase-shaped ornaments and a perfume-burner, in the Victoria and Albert Museum, London, is an excellent example of Tula work. It was probably the gift of Princess Dashkov to Martha Wilmot, who went to Russia in 1802. Another piece of exceptionally fine workmanship is the dressing-table with mirror, candlesticks, vases, a chair and a foot-stool in Maria Fedorovna's dressing-room in the Palace of Pavlovsk. It was made in Tula by the armourer Simon Samarin in 1788 and is decorated with thousands of minute pieces of steel cut to imitate diamonds.

In the reign of Alexander I, the work at Tula was discouraged; presents sent for the Tsar's coronation were returned with a message recommending the craftsmen to concentrate their efforts on the production of arms. Since there was no longer a demand for ornamental arms, the skill displayed in the earlier pieces was gradually lost. Later, in the reign of Nicholas I, small objects of daily use were made again and some were shown in 1829 in the first industrial exhibition in St. Petersburg.

MUSEUMS AND COLLECTIONS
Russian furniture may be seen at the following:
GREAT BRITAIN
London: Victoria and Albert Museum
Luton, Bedfordshire: Luton Hoo
U.S.A.
Washington D.C.: Hillwood (Ross Collection)
U.S.S.R.
Leningrad: Museum Palace of Lomonosov
Museum Palace of Pavlovsk
Museum Palace of Petrodvorets
Museum Palace in Pushkin
State Hermitage Museum
State Russian Museum
Moscow: Arkhangel'skoe
Kuskovo
Ostankino
State Historical Museum

FURTHER READING
The Art and Artists of Russia by Richard Hare, London, 1965.
World Furniture, ed. by Helena Hayward, London, 1965.
'The Romance of a Fireplace' by Charles Oman in **Apollo**, June, 1961.

1

2

A. C. Cooper

Sotheby Photo

3

Domestic Silverware in Russia

Ian Venture

Ian Venture

Fig. 1 **Beaker**, *Moscow, 1833.*
Silver-gilt.
The decoration of the figures of
the Muses is inspired by Greek
mythology. The mark is visible
below the rim at the left.
(Sotheby and Co., London.)

Fig. 2 **Beaker** *by Fedor Ruckert,*
Moscow, nineteenth century.
Silver-gilt and enamel, painted
with a view of Fabergé's Moscow
workshop.
(Sotheby's.)

Fig. 3 **Bell-push** *from the*
Fabergé workshop, marked 'IP'
for the workmaster, Julius
Alexandrovich Rappoport,
nineteenth century. Silver
decorated in the Louis XVI style
with garlands.
(Sotheby's.)

Russian silver design, heavy and crude by western standards, yielded slowly to the inventiveness and skill of Fabergé and Hahn

During the last two hundred years Russia has achieved no important breakthrough in the decorative arts, in contrast to other European countries. Although Russia had its own traditions in art, much of the sophisticated craftsmanship was obtained from foreign craftsmen who settled in Russia.

Because of its enormous population Russia did not have a period of prosperity comparable with most of western Europe, where increasing wealth led to patronage of the arts on a large scale. The hallmarking of silver was not introduced into Russia until 1700, at which time the two main areas for the manufacture of silver and gold articles were Moscow and St. Petersburg. A characteristic of Russian marks is the presence of the date in full and the town-mark or the initials of the assay master.

Slavonic coding was used until the early eighteenth century, and both Moscow and St. Petersburg used the Imperial double-headed eagle with slight variations as their town-mark until 1740, when Moscow changed its mark to St. George and the Dragon and St. Petersburg changed its mark to the crossed anchors. These two centres seem to have produced the greatest proportion of Russian silver.

The most prominent silversmith in Russia was Carl Fabergé. His workshops became so famous, by the third quarter of the nineteenth century, that naturally many other goldsmiths and silversmiths attempted to copy the fashionable objects produced by him. Unfortunately none of these imitators achieved either Fabergé's fame or the quality of craftsmanship which his objects possess.

One of the most famous of Fabergé's competitors was the German-born Carl Carlovich Hahn, whose work was patronised by the Tsar and Tsarina and other members of the Imperial family during the closing years of the nineteenth century. His most important commission was the coronation diadem of the last Tsarina, Alexandra Fedorovna. Hahn

Fig. 4 *Tea- and coffee-service from the Fabergé workshop, Moscow, nineteenth century. Silver with* repoussé *decoration in the Old Russian style which was used only rarely by Fabergé. (Sotheby's.)*

Fig. 5 *Three-piece tea-service by Maria Semenova, Moscow, nineteenth century. Silver with* cloisonné *enamel-work inspired by the Art Nouveau movement. Maria Semenova produced silver and enamel-work of a far higher quality than many other Russian silversmiths. (Sotheby's.)*

Moscow rather than in the more cosmopolitan St. Petersburg. Ovtchinnokov, one of the most original and productive of these silversmiths working in the pan-Slavic style, eventually founded a business in St. Petersburg, but most of his work continued to be carried out in Moscow. Fabergé was also known to have made articles in this Old Russian style (Fig. 4).

Concurrently with the gothic revival which influenced Europe at the end of the eighteenth century, native enthusiasm for early Russian styles became more marked. Catherine the Great was the first to encourage this, as her palace near Moscow demonstrates with its seventeenth-century decoration carried out by Kaiakov between 1775 and 1782.

During the early part of the nineteenth century, old motifs were used in silver, gold and porcelain items produced during the reign of Nicholas I (1825–55), and these bizarre adaptations lasted until 1882, when they received a fresh impetus.

The Pan-Russian Exhibitions in Moscow in 1882 and in Nizhnii Novgorod in 1896, in which silver and works of art were shown, were visited by Tsar Nicholas II and Tsarina Alexandra. This sign of Imperial approval, on the eve of the Tsar's visit to Paris in 1896, led to an increased interest in this form of Russian art.

Pavel Ovtchinnokov was the first silversmith to utilise the old techniques of enamelling in his silverwork, such as champlevé and *plique-à-jour,* and he founded a school for training students in all methods of enamelling and metalcraft. Khlebnikov was also noted for his silver and enamel work (Figs. 6 and 8) and he received many commissions from Fabergé himself. Maria Semenova produced silver and enamel pieces (Fig. 5), her work being of a higher standard than that of many silversmiths of her time, who chose merely to supply what Russian popular taste demanded, with little thought for design, individuality or quality.

Another popular technique adopted by the Russian silversmiths was niello work, in which an alloy of lead, silver, copper and sulphur was used as an enamel to cover an engraved surface; the technique was Roman in origin and was re-introduced as a form of decoration in the seventeenth century. It did not, however, become popular in Russia until the end of the eighteenth century and it was then used on small items, such as snuff-boxes, belt-fastenings and tableware.

Pavel Ovtchinnikov founded a firm of silversmiths in Moscow in 1851 and by 1872 his workshops were sufficiently well established and the quality of their output sufficiently well recognised for him to be granted an Imperial warrant. Because of the great success of this venture, a further branch was opened in St. Petersburg in 1875 under the directorship of the founder's son, Michael Pavelovski.

While Ovtchinnikov's and Khlebnikov's silver designs bore a very close similarity to the old Russian styles, Fedor Ruckert on the other hand based his designs more on those of the sixteenth century, at the same time incorporating Art Nouveau styles. In his own workshop, in which he employed as many as forty workmen, he also made pieces for Fabergé's firm (Fig. 2).

Sazykov, another firm which made objects mainly in silver, many of them for religious use, also produced items decorated with enamel. This firm

also made fine silver, gold and enamel boxes and silver *rizas* (icon-covers).

Other well-known makers of the late nineteenth century included Britzin, Ovtchinnokov, Khlebnikov, Sazkov, Maria Semenova and Ruckert. Many of these silversmiths worked almost entirely in the traditional or Old Russian style and they often incorporated enamel into their artistic designs. Britzin originally worked for Fabergé, from whom he learned the techniques of goldsmith's work before establishing his own workshop.

In contrast to Fabergé and some of his competitors, there arose during the last half of the nineteenth century a less sophisticated group of artists related to the pan-Slavic movement, who revived old forms, motifs and techniques adapting them to suit the fashion of the day. This form of art did not arouse very much interest among art historians until recent years, when such articles became fashionable throughout Europe and America, resulting in the payment of high prices for items which had long been regarded as practically worthless. This type of work was carried out in

Sperryn's Ltd.

Sperryn's Ltd.

Sperryn's Ltd.

Fig. 6 **Desk-set** *by Khlebnikov, nineteenth century. Silver-gilt decorated with* cloisonné *enamel, foliage and birds in the Art Nouveau style.*
(Sotheby's.)

Fig. 7 **Kovsh** *(traditional drinking-vessel), marked 'IP', probably for Julius Alexandrovich Rappoport, nineteenth century. Silver with* cloisonné *enamel.*
(Sotheby's.)

Fig. 8 **Casket** *by Khlebnikov, nineteenth century. Silver with champlevé enamel motifs in the Old Russian style.*
(Sotheby's.)

was started by Pavel Fedorovich Sazykov in 1793 and existed until the end of the nineteenth century. Although the firm itself was well known, most of the objects produced were of fairly simple style.

The designs for most of the silver produced were copied from various sources. A number of the bucolic designs and shapes which were adapted for use on silver survived with little change for many centuries. The most popular was the *kovsh*, a flat-based drinking-vessel applied at one end with a handle and widely used from the sixteenth century onwards (Fig. 7). Although the earlier examples were less elaborate and had deeper bowls, the general shape remained the same; these objects were often enriched with *cloisonné* enamel and set with *cabochon*-cut stones.

Carl Fabergé, best known for his Easter eggs and costly *bijouterie*, also produced many objects in silver. His designs in the main were not inspired by the pan-Slavic movement, but were based rather on German and French tastes (Fig. 3). Carl Fabergé and his brother, Agathon, spent their early years studying in Dresden, where the Green Vaults Museum had a great fascination for them; much of Fabergé's early work reflects this influence. He also spent much time in Paris and his work often has close affinities with French styles of the eighteenth and nineteenth centuries; he produced pastiches of French designs which in many cases are very close to the originals. Fabergé was a pioneer of the international Art Nouveau movement, which swept Europe during the last decade of the nineteenth century. His work also represents the best in Russian craftsmanship.

MUSEUMS AND COLLECTIONS

Russian silver may be seen at the following:

GREAT BRITAIN
Luton, Bedfordshire: Luton Hoo
London: Victoria and Albert Museum

RUSSIA
Moscow: State Kremlin Museum

FURTHER READING

The Art and Artists of Russia by Richard Hare, London, 1965.
The Art of Carl Fabergé by A. Kenneth Snowman, London, 1962.
Peter Carl Fabergé – His Life and Work by H. C. Bainbridge, London, 1949.

SCOTTISH DOMESTIC ARCHITECTURE

John Hunt

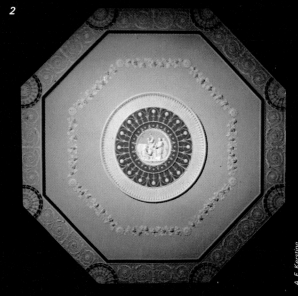

Fig. 1 *Charles, first Earl of Hopetoun* by David Allan (1744–96). (*Marquis of Linlithgow Collection.*)

Fig. 2 *Music-room ceiling* at Mellerstain, Berwickshire, designed by Robert Adam (1728–92), 1770s.

Fig. 3 *Culzean Castle*, Ayrshire, by R. Adam, 1777–92.

Catherine Cruft

Catherine Cruft

The grim austerity of baronial keeps, constructed by builders rather than architects, finally gave way to the comfort and refinement of Palladian villas

The emergence of the country house in Scotland is closely bound up with the nation's history. The need for castles or fortified houses persisted longer than in England, and it was well into the seventeenth century before greater political stability began to be reflected in less austere architecture. Only after the Restoration in 1660 was there a wholehearted break away from medieval styles and customs.

In Scotland, as elsewhere, the development of architecture depended upon patronage. Scottish patrons were the lairds, who, from the mid-seventeenth century, when they were no longer involved in repelling invaders, had more time and energy to devote to the improvement of their lands and to the modernisation of their houses. Outstanding among such lairds was David, second Earl of Wemyss, who made his own plans. Wemyss Castle, on the Fife coast of the Firth of Forth, had been the home of the Wemyss family for many generations; in 1670, Lord Wemyss set about turning the castle into an agreeable country house. The additions consisted of an L-shaped building attached to the west side of the castle providing three storeys of well-proportioned rooms, mostly overlooking the sea. Robert Mylne, Master Mason to Charles II, was employed to supervise the work.

The first Scottish architect – as opposed to inventive laird or supervisor – was William Bruce. During Charles II's reign he was created a baronet and later appointed Overseer of the Royal Works, a post which he held until he fell from favour in 1678. He was also a politician and in 1666 was appointed to a commission on witch-hunting.

William Bruce – the instigator of Scottish classical architecture

Bruce introduced a classical style to Scotland, thereby performing for Scotland a similar function to that of Inigo Jones in England some fifty years earlier. Bruce's use of classical ideas and the professional skill of his designs set him apart from contemporary master masons. He not only worked for other people but he also had the means and opportunity to work for himself, and in 1685 began building himself a masterly house at Kinross. It incorporates a central block slightly recessed from its flanking wings; fluted Corinthian pilasters frame each section and the interplay of vertical and horizontal proportions is most successful. The high, hipped roof, distinctly Continental in flavour, rises from a strong cornice which intriguingly helps to conceal the presence of attic windows. Inside the house a saloon, which was designed after the manner of the Double Cube Room at Wilton, occupies the centre of the first floor and the attic storey.

Bruce also planned the grounds and gardens, the fame of which was widespread before their completion; they suggest that Bruce was well aware of

Scottish Architecture

Fig. 4 **Kinross House** by William Bruce (died 1710), 1685–91. The east front of the house was designed by Bruce for his own use. It is positioned on the shores of Loch Leven, set in gardens which he also planned himself. Bruce was the first Scottish house-builder who deserves the name of architect, and he introduced Classicism to Scotland. His designs for Kinross incorporate a saloon based on the Double Cube Room at Wilton.

Fig. 5 **Duninald Castle**, Angus, by Gillespie Graham (c.1777–1855), 1819–32. Graham's gothic architecture was more scholarly and authentically medieval than that of his contemporaries. In Scotland the gothic style persisted in church architecture until the late seventeenth century; not long afterwards the gothic revival in secular architecture began.

Fig. 6 **Duff House**, Banff, by William Adam (1689–1748) c.1730–40. William Adam was the father of Robert and the three other Adam brothers. His first major commission was that of enlarging Hopetoun – his designs were reworked by John and Robert Adam – and some of his ideas for it were used here.

Fig. 7 **Cairness House**, Aberdeenshire, by James Playfair (died 1794), 1791–97. Cairness is a bold, rather stark example of the Classicism in Scotland made popular by the Adam family, but with an unusual combination of Greek, Roman and Egyptian elements. The interior is mainly decorated in the Greek idiom, and there is one Egyptian room ornamented with hieroglyphs.

Fig. 8 **Wemyss Castle**, Fife. Renovations to the castle were begun by the owner David, second Earl of Wemyss, in conjunction with Robert Mylne, (1633–1710) in 1670. Mylne, Master Mason to Charles II, supervised the carrying out of Lord Wemyss' plans; no genuine architect was employed.

the growing need to establish a relationship between house and grounds as was the custom in France. Whether or not he collected ideas on his visit to France in 1663, is a matter for speculation. On the east side of the house, the vista leads to the ruined buildings of Loch Leven Castle on the island where Mary Queen of Scots was imprisoned.

Towards the end of his career Bruce built Hopetoun House in West Lothian. Although only the centre block of the west front of the house as it stands today is by him, it was his largest work. The strong rustication of the façade is something more commonly associated with the work of James Gibbs and the English Palladian architects, but the high roof and the ogee pediment in the centre are identifiable as the work of Bruce influenced by French models. Lord Hopetoun subsequently commissioned Bruce's pupil and clerk of works, William Adam, to redesign the east front of the house. Bruce's house stands forward firmly from the flanking wings and screen walls which belong to the William Adam reconstruction. The fact that

Hopetoun House involved both Bruce and the Adam family, makes it an important link between two periods of architectural style.

The most important architect directly to follow Bruce was James Smith who, in 1683, was appointed to Bruce's former post as Overseer of the Royal Works. Smith had helped to superintend the work at Kinross and among his own best-known projects is Yester, East Lothian, which he designed in collaboration with William Adam for the second Marquis of Tweeddale. The main elevation of Yester was clearly inspired by Kinross, and the additional Palladian element in the design of its portico is entirely in keeping with the ideas of the early eighteenth century.

Of the country house architects in Scotland during the first half of the eighteenth century, William Adam is the one who stands out from the rest. Regarded by some as an abler architect for external designs than his better known son, Robert, William Adam's work is an important link between the post-Restoration classical architecture of Bruce and Smith, and the lighter neo-Classicism exemplified in the second half of the century by Robert Adam. Scotland has a special claim on the Adam family; William was born in Kirkcaldy in 1689, and in 1728 he was appointed Surveyor of the King's Works as a tribute to his skills. Although much of his source material was derived from Vanbrugh and other contemporaries, such as Kent and Gibbs, he maintained an independence of outlook and a degree of strength in his work which made it a natural sequel in Scotland to the restrained and dignified Classicism of Bruce and Smith.

Lord Hopetoun's commission to William Adam to work on the east front at Hopetoun appealed to Adam's sense of occasion. The design which he began in 1721 resulted in the massive façade which greets the visitor as he approaches the house from South Queensferry. It was left to Robert Adam to complete the work for the next Earl because progress was slow and both the original architect and the first patron had died before the house was finished.

On a much smaller scale, Sir John Clerk of Penicuik, enlisted William Adam's help in the design of Mavisbank in Midlothian. This house has a strong Palladian influence in its main pediment and fenestration and in the precise

have the most far-reaching effect because it was to him that Robert Adam owed the opportunity to spend four years in Italy from 1754. This visit gave Robert Adam the inspiration for much of his celebrated plasterwork and ideas for his colour schemes. He was essentially out to please his patrons and his Italian journal suggests that he was a considerable social climber. One of his last commissions was from Thomas Hog to build a house at Newliston, West Lothian, close to the site of an older house no longer in fashion. The restrained elegance and simplicity of the elevation of Newliston epitomises Adam in his mature period (the wings were added in 1831). The interior shows an economy of decoration that suggests that his patron kept a stern eye on expenditure, and the result is an elegant house with the minimum of extravagance.

Lightness of touch and elegance of design

Like other architects of the late eighteenth century, Robert Adam was aware of the romantic influence that inspired Georgian Gothic, which he used in his elaborate plans for Culzean Castle

Fig. 9 **Design for Melville House**, *Fife, by James Smith (c.1646–1731), 1697–1701. Smith, one of the master masons who worked on the rebuilding of Holyroodhouse, was married to the daughter of Robert Mylne (see Figure 8). He redesigned Traquair House, Peeblesshire, and was the architect of Yester House, East Lothian. Of this house he claimed, 'there is not a more Convenient Dwelling house nor any better built in North Brittain'. (Register House, Edinburgh.)*

Fig. 10. **Stracathro**, *Angus, by Archibald Simpson (1796–1847), 1827–30. Simpson was a nineteenth-century Classicist. The interior of Stracathro is grandly decorated with marble and painted imitations of marble.*

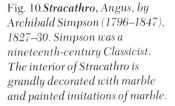

Fig. 11 **Chatelherault**, *Lanarkshire, by William Adam, c.1732. This is a building in what were the grounds of Hamilton Palace, now destroyed. The four pavilions frame a central gateway which led to a walled garden.*

geometrical design. Only his patron held back Adam from the greater freedoms that he later exhibited at The Drum, built a few miles away for Lord Somerville.

Further evidence of William Adam's versatility is shown in Chatelherault, a garden building associated with Hamilton Palace in Lanarkshire (now demolished), built for the fifth Duke of Hamilton in about 1732. This building was constructed to frame the entrance to the gardens and here Adam used prominent keystones and cornerstones strongly reminiscent of Gibbs. It exemplifies his robust method of treatment.

The Earl of Hopetoun may be regarded as the patron whose influence on architecture was to

for the tenth Earl of Cassilis. The Castle sits in a dramatic position which would have appealed to Wagner, on the cliffs of the Ayrshire coast. The exterior of Culzean may not be wholly satisfactory, but the interior shows Adam at his most fluent in the treatment of space and in his use of plasterwork. The oval staircase and the round drawing-room portray this genius.

Later architects who worked in Scotland up to 1830, before the aversion to classical order became prevalent, owed much to Robert Adam. It is a tribute to his skill that the lightness of touch and elegance of his designs, particularly of interiors, had such popularity in so stern an environment as Scotland.

Mauchline and Other Wooden Boxes

E. H. and E. R. Pinto

Fig. 1 **Lid of a tea-chest**, probably by G. Meekison of Montrose, c.1800–10. Sycamore with pen-and-ink and brush-work decoration, height 5½ ins., length 12 ins., width 6 ins. In this tea-chest the hinges on the exterior are rendered invisible by the decorative network of pen lines; the lids of the three tea-caddies inside also have integral hinges. (Birmingham Museum and Art Gallery. Pinto Collection.)

Souvenir boxes and trinkets, decorated with ferns, tartans and tributes to Robert Burns, were a major Scottish craft

The distinctive and highly decorative boxes and other small woodware made in nineteenth-century Scotland have lately become known as Mauchline woodware. Mauchline was only one of several small Ayrshire towns or villages in which the ware was made. The craft originated in east Scotland and spread across to the west. Admittedly, the remarkably inventive Smith family of Mauchline, in their several generations, contributed most to the range of objects made and to the varieties of finishes employed, and they converted a local craft into a world-wide business. They were also so ingenious, hard-working and enterprising that they survived long after most of their competitors had succumbed. In total, their output probably far exceeded that of all their competitors combined.

The story begins at Alyth, Perthshire, where James Sandy lived – a bed-ridden, legless, mechanical genius. He built a work-bench round his bed and, with a few tools, made musical instruments, chiming clocks, telescopes and some early electrical devices. His life (1766–1819) spanned the peak of the snuff-taking vogue, and his

Figs. 2, 3 and 4 **The Solway snuff-box,** dated 1823. Sycamore lined with lead foil, with pen-and-ink decoration, height 1⅝ ins., length 4 ins., width 2½ ins.
The story of the Maryport/Newcastle Canal project is told on the front (Fig. 2), back and sides of the box. J. Grierson, the donor of the box, is attempting to persuade James Holmes, a partner in the Douglas and Isle of Man Bank – hence the three-legged Arms of Man in the centre panel – to back the scheme to connect the 'British Ocean' to the Solway Firth. It also bears a tribute to the Scottish poet Robert Burns (1759–96). The lid (Fig. 4) shows 'The Ayrshire Bard', the cottage on the left is his birth-place, and he was buried in the graveyard of Alloway Kirk, on the right. The Burns mausoleum and a facsimile of the poet's signature appear on the base (Fig. 3).
(Birmingham Museum and Art Gallery. Pinto Collection.)

Figs. 5 and 6 **Burns snuff-boxes,** probably Glasgow, c.1850. Deeply carved sycamore. Traditionally ascribed to a blind craftsman, these snuff-boxes pay homage to Robert Burns.
(Birmingham Museum and Art Gallery. Pinto Collection.)

Fig. 7 **Transfer wares,** nineteenth century. The box with printed paper decoration commemorates Queen Victoria's Jubilee of 1887. The other objects are transfer ware, probably made by the firm of W. and A. Smith, with topographical decoration.
(Birmingham Museum and Art Gallery. Pinto Collection.)

Fig. 8 **Fern-pattern ware,** probably made by the firm of W. and A. Smith, Mauchline, late nineteenth and early twentieth centuries.
(Birmingham Museum and Art Gallery. Pinto Collection.)

2

3

4

inventive brain was challenged by the inefficiency of circular, lipped, wooden snuff-boxes with loose lids. Owing to the tendency of wood to absorb moisture, the lids of such boxes are apt to bind in wet weather and fall off when dry. Gold and silver hinged snuff-boxes were only for the wealthy, so Sandy designed an air-tight wooden snuff-box with an integral wooden hinge of superior standardised form which worked efficiently under all conditions. Wooden snuff-boxes with integral wooden hinges were made on the Continent, and possibly in Scotland, too, in the eighteenth century, but all were hand-made and they varied considerably in craftsmanship and effectiveness. Sandy designed tools which cheapened the process, and he also ensured that every hinge was alike – and mechanically perfect.

At nearby Laurencekirk lived Charles Stiven (1753–1820), a maker of high-class, sycamore snuff-boxes and tea-caddies with metal foil linings. He must have been acquainted with Sandy, but whether he bought his secret of the perfect hinge, or worked it out independently, is unknown. However, Stiven was using the hinge on what was already known as the Laurencekirk box as early as 1807.

At this point in the narrative, there appeared

Lord Gardenstone, an eccentric but philanthropic Scottish peer. Lord Gardenstone, a snuff addict who visited Spa at frequent intervals for his health, was much impressed with the wide range of hand-painted wooden keepsakes made there. At Spa in 1787, he 'engaged a Mr. Charles Brixhe, painter, to go to Laurencekirk, on a plan to introduce and establish his art of painting on wood, which is elegantly practised in this place'. Brixhe came, settled in Laurencekirk, and practised, and presumably taught, the art of box-painting.

The introduction of hand-painting or pen-and-ink work, on which the early reputation of Scottish woodware was founded before the famous hinge enhanced it, should, therefore, be credited to Lord Gardenstone who, until his death in 1793, was a good friend to Stiven and to Laurencekirk. Stiven's craftsmanship in Scottish box-making and finishing was never excelled, and his firm, which held the royal warrant, continued until about 1868. Stiven's boxes made before 1819 are unmarked, but after that, some were stamped 'Stiven & Son', or 'Stiven & Sons'. About 1807, the secret of the hinge leaked out and travelled across Scotland to Ayrshire, where the main development of the trade occurred.

William Crawford of Old Cumnock was probably

6

the first of the Ayrshire box-makers who made hand-painted or pen-and-ink work decorated snuff-boxes with integral wood hinges. The tale of how Crawford obtained the secret is controversial and involved, as are also the stories of how the secret eventually became known to many nearby small towns and villages. Among the box painters who eventually achieved fame were Daniel Macnee, Horatio M'Culloch and William Leighton Leitch.

By 1830 snuff-taking was declining and the erstwhile secret of the hinge was known to numerous makers who had sprung up in Cumnock and in nearby Auchinleck, Catrine and Mauchline; consequently prices were being cut and some fifty Scottish box-makers were now looking for fresh lines to augment their range of souvenirs, fresh finishes to attract the public and lower costs. As competition increased many makers fell by the roadside, but the range of objects increased and gradually came to embrace all the small objects associated with sewing, knitting, writing and postage, as well as money-boxes, trinket-boxes, pincushions, whist-markers and a host of other small, useful objects, decoratively finished.

The Smith family, makers of razor-hones and strops, moved into the field of decorated wooden boxes

Although some of the objects were made from various trees associated with historical places, or personages such as Burns or Scott, the most widely used wood for all objects in all finishes was sycamore, usually described in Scotland as plane, a mild, creamy-coloured wood which grows to perfection in Britain and can be obtained remarkably free from defects (Figs. 2, 3 and 4). When well seasoned, it is singularly free from warping and shrinkage – qualities essential where the integral wooden hinge is involved. The hinge had half its knuckles cut into the back edge of the lid, and half into the top edge of the box. The knuckles were drilled through their length and a brass pin was inserted. The pin, cut $\frac{1}{4}$ in. shorter than the length of the box, had a $\frac{1}{8}$ in. long plug inserted and glued in each end, concealing and imprisoning it.

The Smith family, established in Mauchline as stonemasons in the eighteenth century, also built up a reputation with their Water of Ayr razor-hones (whetstones). Hones needed strops, with wooden backings and handles, which took the Smiths into the woodworking industry. The brothers William (1795–1847) and Andrew (1797–1867) founded W. & A. Smith's boxworks; they and their direct descendants developed an enterprise whose products were sold not only throughout the United Kingdom and in Western Europe, but eventually also in North America, Australia and India. The early trade of the Smiths' boxworks was in the expensive hand-painted and pen-and-ink decorated snuff-boxes which, according to the type of varnish used, is said to have entailed anything from fifteen to thirty coats, followed by polishing with ground flint.

Transfer ware, with local views of places where it was to be sold at home and abroad (Fig. 7), was the Smiths' first attempt to produce inexpensive souvenirs which imitated mechanically certain effects produced by pen-and-ink work. Although

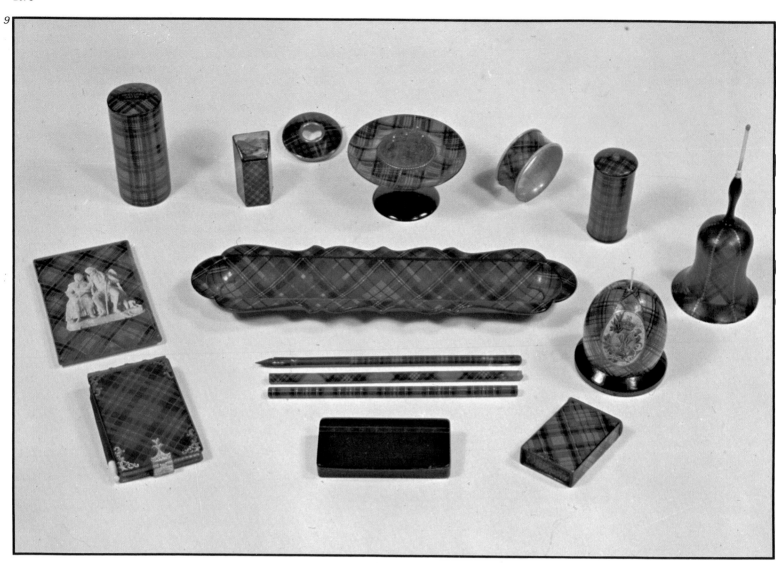

Fig. 9 **Tartan ware**, *probably by the firm of W. and A. Smith, nineteenth century. Tartan wares were first produced in the 1820s. The early ones were hand decorated, but a mechanical process was soon invented. (Birmingham Museum and Art Gallery. Pinto Collection.)*

transfers of the royal arms of William IV on Smith razor-strops date from 1832, the date when they received the royal warrant, the main flow of transfer ware commenced about 1845, reached its zenith between 1860 and 1900 and continued on a diminishing scale until fire destroyed much of the works in 1933.

Various names which appear on Smiths' transfer ware are invariably those of shops which sold it. The engraved plates for transfer work, and certain components, were made in Birmingham where the Smiths established a warehouse and showroom in 1829; a little later, they added there a factory with a stoving plant under the control of Andrew Smith's son, William, an inventive genius. Towards the end of the nineteenth century, retaliation for the Smiths' Continental invasion brought woodware decorated with foreign copies of British scenes into this country.

Tartan ware (Fig. 9) was produced by various Scottish makers in the 1820s and at first was an expensive hand-process, but William Smith II soon invented a remarkable multiple pen machine, which applied lines and colours mechanically. Early tartan patterns were applied direct to the wood, but before long mechanically printed tartan paper was glued to the wood. Where the paper joint occurred, the wood was painted black, so that it should not show as natural sycamore would have done. Sometimes joints were marked with a wavy, tooled, gold line. The Smiths printed or transferred the names of clan tartans in gold on their various products, which they continued making

after the nineteenth century ended. Their later tartan ware is inferior to the earlier.

From about 1875, the Smiths added fern-patterned products to their range. Ferns from the Isle of Arran were pinned on the boxes; brown paint was then spattered around them and the ferns were removed, leaving their silhouette on the natural sycamore. After rubbing down, the whole object was varnished. Soon, in order to cheapen the work, a paper covering printed with fern-pattern was used; towards the end of the nineteenth century, fern-pattern transfers or photographic labels were used as centrepieces on tartan backgrounds.

MUSEUMS AND COLLECTIONS

Scottish decorative woodware may be seen at the following:

Birmingham: Birmingham Museum and Art Gallery. Pinto Collection
Blair Atholl: Blair Castle
Edinburgh: National Museum of Antiquities of Scotland
The Museum Gallery

FURTHER READING

'Souvenirs in Wood' by John S. Buist in **The Scots Magazine**, July 1971.
Tunbridge and Scottish Souvenir Woodware by Edward H. and Eva R. Pinto, London, 1970.
'Knick-Knacks in Clan-Tartans' by G. Bernard Hughes in **Country Life**, 20 August, 1964.

Viking Studios

Silver & Jewellery in Scotland

Ian Finlay

Viking Studios

3

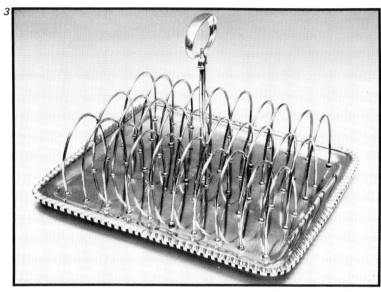

Museum Photo

Fig. 1 **Snuff-measure** by Ferguson and McBean, Inverness, 1880. Whalebone handle with silver tip containing Cairngorm stone. (Museum and Art Gallery, Dundee.)

Fig. 2 **Cake-basket** by William Scott, Dundee, 1776. Silver, saw-pierced. (Museum and Art Gallery, Dundee.)

Fig. 3 **Bannock-rack** by Patrick Robertson, Edinburgh, 1773. Silver. (The Royal Scottish Museum.)

Scottish silverware, although following southern fashions, still retained an elusive Scottish element which intrigues the collectors of today

Throughout the eighteenth century, and still more in the nineteenth, Scottish silver tended to follow southern manners. Even characteristic pieces such as the quaich and the thistle cup either compromised with southern shapes or disappeared entirely. Yet there is nearly always something subtly different about the northern work. The Romantic Revival of the nineteenth century, which Sir Walter Scott did so much to bring about, at times produced silver with an accent as bogus as that of neo-Scots-baronial architecture and these pieces, already acquiring respectability in the world of antiques, are quite easily recognised.

Edinburgh was always the main centre of silver-smithing, with Glasgow some way behind. It has to be remembered that Glasgow did not outstrip Edinburgh in size until after the Industrial Revolution established the heavy industries of the Clyde; even then, Edinburgh remained the capital city and seat of the kind of society which indulged in patronage of the arts; only towards the end of Victoria's reign did wealthy western magnates begin to encourage painting.

It is not surprising to find that, in Scotland, only Edinburgh had a system of hallmarking in any way comparable with London's. From 1681 tables of date-letters were introduced which were as reliable as those of London. From this date until 1759 the punch of the assay-master, the officer responsible for testing the purity of the metal, appears with the date-mark, the maker's mark and the town-mark, but from 1759 the assay-master's mark is replaced by the standard-mark, a thistle.

The Glasgow date-letter system does not begin until 1819. Prior to this, letters occur among the hallmarks which have been associated with certain years, but one has to rely on the maker's working dates. It is worth remembering that the Glasgow cycle, unusually, contains all twenty-six letters of the alphabet.

The other Scottish towns which made silver – and they are not a few – present an inexperienced collector with real problems; but, on the other hand, this field of provincial silver offers certain opportunities, and the lack of any proper hall-marking system makes it just possible now and then to discover prizes which others have not noticed. Often town and maker are the only marks. Date-letters are never present. In a great many cases, the piece will carry only the maker's punch. This is really a field for the specialist, but, as familiarity with the character of the marks grows, it will often be possible to recognise provenance at first glance. By no means all provincial pieces are of the recognised standard of purity, and perhaps inevitably this put an end to the prosperity of provincial workers. In 1836, an Act was passed requiring all Scots silver to be assayed in Edinburgh,

4

6

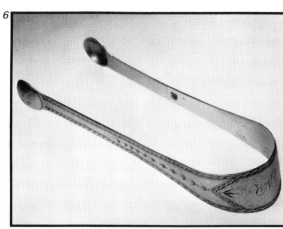

Author's Photo

5

Museum Photo

7

Fig. 4 **Quaich** *by Charles Blair, Edinburgh, 1736. Silver, diameter across lugs $11\frac{3}{10}$ ins. (Private Collection.)*

Fig. 5 **Teapot and stand** *by Coline Allan, Aberdeen, c.1750. Silver, height of teapot 6 ins., diameter of stand $6\frac{1}{8}$ ins. (Royal Scottish Museum.)*

Fig. 6 **Sugar-tongs** *by Benjamin Lumsden, c.1790. Silver, marked 'BL' on one leg, a rose on the other, and 'N' in script. (Museum and Art Gallery, Dundee.)*

Fig. 7 **Toddy-ladle**, *Canongate, Edinburgh, c.1800. Silver. (Museum and Art Gallery, Dundee.)*

in Glasgow or in London.

The most obviously Scottish vessel made in silver is the quaich. Originally, this was a wooden drinking-bowl, either hollowed out from the solid or built up with staves, and in time it acquired silver mounts; then it was copied wholly in silver. Early silver quaichs perpetuate the stave construction in lines traced on the surface. The low-slung lines of the true quaich disappear and a vessel which is merely a bowl, with twin opposed handles, takes its place. In the first half of the nineteenth century, there was something of a revival.

Late quaichs are usually miniatures, with a diameter of three inches or less, and there is often a reversion either to woods such as laburnum, yew or lignum vitae, or to horn, with only mounts of silver. No doubt they reflect the Romantic Revival. Embossed thistles and other evocative emblems of the kind appear on them, in marked contrast to the early quaichs which often carried engraved roses or tulips, symbolising hopes for William of Orange as a Protestant successor to Charles II or his brother, James II. Some of the early nineteenth-century pieces are not properly quaichs at all, but 'coggies' or 'luggies', humbler vessels in common use, with greater depth in relation to the diameter. Silver quaichs were made not only in Edinburgh and Glasgow, but also in smaller towns. Little ones, two or three inches in diameter, were made in Inverness, perhaps for the use of travellers, and were still

being made there early in the nineteenth century. These are now hard to find and are highly prized.

Though quaichs were used for strong liquor, tea- and coffee-drinking provided the silversmiths' craft with a much greater stimulus. Scottish silversmiths, and indeed goldsmiths, made teapots which were essays in pure, functional form. They have bullet-shaped bodies, though not quite spherical; tapering or curling spouts and bands of engraving around the lid. They rarely occur complete with sugar-basin, cream-boat, teapot-stand and, occasionally, a salver. Elegant domesticity was never better symbolised.

Contemporary with these teapots were some beautiful coffee-pots. They were either of tapering form, as in England, or oviform urns fitted with taps and curious snake handles, the urn supported on curved legs over a burner. Such urns are usually very plain, with decoration perhaps limited to a coat of arms.

With the second half of the eighteenth century came a rococo phase; outlines were contorted and surfaces covered with embossed scrolls. A little later, in the 'seventies, when the neo-classical New Town of Edinburgh was being planned and built, silverware was made to match and included such noble pieces as the great tea-urn by Patrick Robertson now in the Royal Scottish Museum (Fig. 13).

Teapots often had stands, to catch drips and to serve as insulators (Fig. 5). To find a teapot with its

Museum Photo

Fig. 8 *Highland plaid-brooches:*
Left: *1727, bearing initials I.R.
Silver, diameter $2\frac{7}{16}$ ins.
Right: 1787, bearing initials
J.McD. and C.McC. Silver,
diameter $2\frac{3}{4}$ ins.
(National Museum of Antiquities
of Scotland.)*

Fig. 9 *Sauce- or gravy-tureen
with lid (one of a pair) by Robert
Gray and Son, Glasgow, 1813–14.
Silver, height including lid
$5\frac{7}{10}$ ins. **Teapot** by William
Marshall, Edinburgh, 1865–66.
Silver, height $7\frac{4}{5}$ ins.
(National Museum of Antiquities
of Scotland.)*

Fig. 10 *Bowl by Robert Gray and
Son, Glasgow, 1832. Silver.
(Glasgow Museum and Art
Gallery.)*

9

Museum Photo

10

Rupert Roddam

original stand is not easy, but stands are to be picked up which can be matched with, and which much enhance, a pot. Stands were made throughout the eighteenth century, no matter how teapot styles might change. At that period tea-sets included some pretty sugar-bowls and, rarely, a spherical cream-jug with lid.

The elusive, truly Scottish element, which one can learn to recognise, appears in domestic silver in some salvers and small trays. As one might expect, the accent grows stronger as the source goes further north, and there is a type of Aberdeen salver at once recognisable by its deeply indented rim and the belt of close, intricate engraving fringing the inner edge of the rim. Candlesticks, too, tend to have a slight accent. As a rule, the Scottish candlestick is a little less elaborate than the English, although this applies less often to an Edinburgh piece. Comparative simplicity is even more true of humbler things such as hand-candlesticks. Mention must be made of that rare, though once common, article – the bannock-rack. This is just an outsize toast-rack, made for the thick oatmeal bannocks once served hot in Scottish houses, which are now, unhappily, nearly as rare as the old racks themselves (Fig. 3).

Two categories of Scottish silverware which can provide collectors with some rewarding finds for a relatively modest outlay are provincial pieces and flatware, which in this case means spoons. It is

11

12

Fig. 11 **Brooches:** Top, l. to r: Heart-shaped brooch, *Perthshire. Silver, length 1½ ins.* Double heart brooch, *inscribed 'K.M.' Silver, length 3 ins.* Heart-shaped brooch *inscribed 'D.C.' Silver, length 1 3/16 ins.* Bottom, l. to r: **Heart-shaped brooch,** *having in its centre the letter M and a fleur-de-lis, surmounted by a coronet. Silver, length 2⅝ ins.* Oval brooch with a smoked amethyst, *given by Queen Victoria to her lady-in-waiting, Flora Macdonald. Said to have belonged to Mary Queen of Scots. Length 2⅓ ins.* Annular brooch *of silver set with pebbles and topazes, a nineteenth-century version of the Hunterston brooch shape, length 2 7/10 ins. (National Museum of Antiquities of Scotland.)*

Fig. 12 *Sugar-castors by James Kerr. Silver.*
(Edinburgh Corporation Museum.)

Fig. 13 *Tea-urn by Patrick Robertson. Silver,*
height 19½ ins.
(The Royal Scottish Museum.)

13

Fig. 14 *Scottish Silver*
Hallmarks.
Top left: Sterling silver.
Top right: Edinburgh.
Bottom: Glasgow.

such as Aberdeen and Dundee, to tinker-made pieces with much artless charm; towns like Banff, Elgin, Inverness, Perth and Greenock were, perhaps surprisingly, capable of producing beautiful work. While the great landowners went to Edinburgh, Glasgow or London for their silver, the small laird and the minister would turn to the local silversmith, if he existed. Their needs, apart from tableware, were perhaps mainly for practical things such as mugs, bowls or a baby's feeding-cup. The men they patronised, however, could excel themselves when put to it, and some very attractive Communion cups in Scottish churches were made in smaller towns.

There is one branch of silverware which is properly a separate subject: brooches. There are many fakes about, and some of the later jewellery may be difficult to distinguish from the earlier, especially as they are not usually hallmarked.

There are two broad classes of brooch. The first is the plaid-brooch (Fig. 8). In the seventeenth and eighteenth centuries these appear to have been made in the Highlands by clan craftsmen of varying skill. They take the form of a flattened ring with long transverse pin to pierce the loop of cloth brought up through the ring; the upper surface is decorated with rather crudely engraved patterns, derived ultimately from traditional Celtic motifs as found on West Highland gravestones. Sometimes they are inlaid with niello, a black compound of silver, copper, lead and sulphur. Among the inlaid brooches are the so-called 'anchor' type.

From the late eighteenth century, the town silversmiths imitated the Highland brooches. In the nineteenth century, particularly in Victorian times, the plain silver brooches did not satisfy the current taste for elaboration, and silver was often replaced by gold, and niello by inlays of bloodstone and similar materials. Cairngorms were also introduced, sometimes at the end of the pin.

The other type of brooch, more commonly found and even more imitated today, is the heart-brooch (Fig. 11), also known as the 'Luckenbooth' brooches, in reference to the shops (locked booths) built against St. Giles' Kirk in the High Street, Edinburgh. Usually quite small, these brooches were formed either as a heart or as twin hearts interlocked, cut from sheet-silver, or cast and hand-finished, the heart frequently with a twist to its 'tail'. A few have the punch of the maker or of the town. Initials on the back indicate the donor and the recipient, and there is no doubt that such brooches were used as betrothal tokens. There is also a tradition that mothers pinned them to children's skirts as protection from the evil eye.

usually possible to pick up odd spoons, and sets of six of the later types are not uncommon. Most of the later spoons were made for practical use, not for show, and are uncompromisingly simple and functional; the metal may be rather thin, but they have the feel of the craftsman-made article, and spoons of the same set vary slightly in size and shape.

One of the reasons for collecting spoons is for the sake of their marks; one may combine the two categories of collecting mentioned above and aim to find as wide-ranging a series of provincial spoons as possible. Spoons with the town-marks of larger centres such as Aberdeen, Dundee or Perth are not rare, but more patience is needed in searching for the products of smaller towns such as Banff, Elgin, Montrose or, in the far north, Wick and Tain. Some of the northern towns seem to have been served by wandering silversmiths, whose initials appear with more town-marks than one. Some towns simplify matters for collectors by using the town name, or an abbreviation of it, for their punch.

As for provincial silver in general, this will range from sophisticated wares of many types from places

MUSEUMS AND COLLECTIONS
Scottish silver may be seen at the following:
Aberdeen: Art Gallery and Museum
Dundee: City Museum and Art Gallery
Edinburgh: Huntly House
 National Museum of Antiquities
  of Scotland
 The Royal Scottish Museum
Glasgow: Art Gallery and Museum

FURTHER READING
English and Scottish Silver Spoons by G. E. P. and
J. P. How, 3 vols., London, 1952–57.
A History of Scottish Gold and Silver Work by
Ian Finlay, London, 1948.
Scottish Crafts by Ian Finlay, London, 1948.

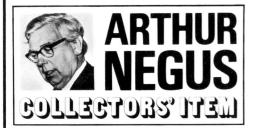

ARTHUR NEGUS
COLLECTORS' ITEM

SCOTTISH PEBBLE JEWELLERY

Although Scottish jewellery, developed from Celtic and Runic designs, has been in existence for many centuries, 'pebble jewellery' was peculiar to the romantic period of the Victorian era. Victorian society, greatly influenced by the writings of Sir Walter Scott, idealised the romantic Scotsman, but it was Queen Victoria who was mainly responsible for the popularity of this type of jewellery.

The 'pebbles' used were mainly of the agate family and were native to Scotland. The most usual were sard, cornelian, bloodstone, grey striped agate, moss agate, jasper, marble, Iona marble and even granite. They were set into their mounts in pitch or shellac with which their settings were filled. Shellac was not visible once the stones were set and also lightened the weight of an otherwise heavy looking jewel. In better pieces, the workmanship of the mount was fine and the stones well cut and fitted and subtly matched. Sometimes little or no metal was visible, the stones were cut to shape and fitted together like a mosaic and attached to a slate backing with shellac. The whole was then set in, or on, a simple mount of silver or gold.

The mounts for the pebbles were made mainly in silver, but gold was used for very fine pieces. The pebbles were either set on their own or combined with clear stones such as cairngorms, amethysts, smoky quartz, crystals, fresh-water pearls and to a lesser extent garnets, all of Scottish origin, the former four stones often being faceted. However, with the quantity of pebble jewellery produced at this time, it is believed that many of the stones were imported from Germany.

Brooches were the most prolific form of pebble jewellery made, and varied in shape from simple annular styles to strap and buckle brooches, shields, crests, clan symbols, the St. Andrew's cross, knots, miniature daggers, claymores and *skean dhus* (the latter three usually for use as kilt pins) — hearts, thistles, grouse claws and deer hoofs — natural claws and hoofs being sometimes mounted or copied in silver and gold and set with stones.

Bracelets, necklets, pendants, ear-rings, buttons, cuff-links, buckles and stock-pins were also made in fair quantity and more rarely hair ornaments, chatelaines and purses.

The fashion for pebble jewellery lasted until the end of the nineteenth century. Today the traditional designs continue to be made and also mass-produced imitations in metal and glass.

Collecting Hints

Not all Scottish jewellery bears identification marks but some pieces were hallmarked and some made between 1842 and 1883 bear the diamond shaped registration mark of the British Patent Office: this gave copyright protection for three years. After 1883 registered pieces bore numbers only, e.g. Rd. No. 12345.

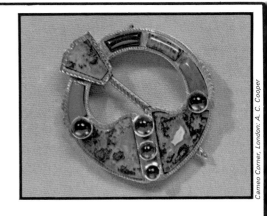

Current Prices

Silver-set pebble brooches of good quality from about £10 upwards.
Gold set brooches from about £40 upwards.
Silver set bracelets and necklaces from £20 and gold proportionately higher.
Pebble jewellery set with additional stones such as cairngorms, amethysts, etc., are usually more valuable; silver brooches can cost in the region of £40 upwards and gold, £80 upwards.

Above: **Brooch,** gold mounted, set with semi-precious stones, based on an ancient Celtic design. £62.50.

Below left: **Chatelaine.** Each of the silver chains is decorated with a faceted agate bead. £45.

Below right: **Sheathed dagger brooch and two bracelets:** £25 (middle), £30 (left), £20 (right).

Opposite: **Hair-comb and two daggers:** hair-comb £55, claw-handled dagger £15, carved-handled dagger £15.

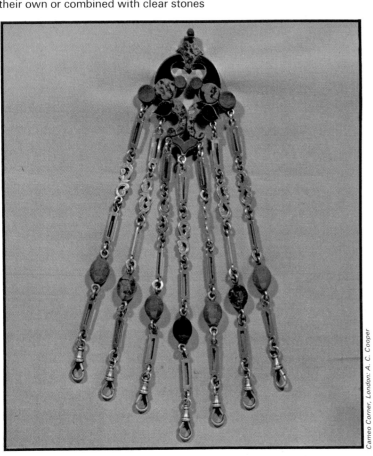

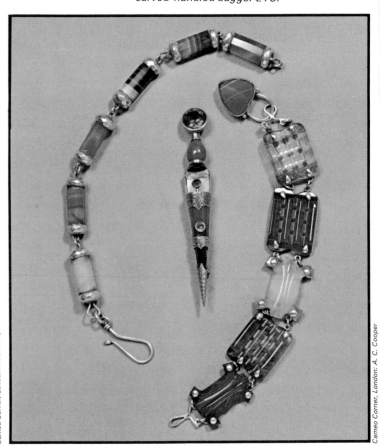

Fig. 1 Left: **Henry Dundas, first Viscount Melville** by Josiah Wedgwood (1730–95) after James Tassie. Right: **Henry Dundas, first Viscount Melville** by James Tassie (1735–99). Unless otherwise stated the objects illustrated are in the Scottish National Portrait Gallery, Edinburgh.

Fig. 2 Left: **James Tassie** by William Tassie (died 1806). Paste, $3\frac{1}{2}$ ins. x $2\frac{3}{4}$ ins. William Tassie was the nephew of James Tassie. Right: **Randolph Eric Raspe** by James Tassie. Paste, 3 ins. x $2\frac{1}{2}$ ins.

4

A. C. Cooper

Fig. 3 **Robert Harker** by James Tassie. Wax, 5 ins. x $3\frac{7}{10}$ ins. Tassie made a red wax modello such as this as the preliminary stage in the making of a portrait medallion. The final casting of the medallion was done either from a plaster mould of the modello or from a mould of a cast in relief of the modello.

Fig. 4 **Engraving of a gemstone,** an illustration by David Allan to R. E. Raspe's two-volume catalogue of Tassie's 'ancient and modern engraved gems', 1791. (Victoria and Albert Museum, London.)

CAMEOS, MEDALS & IMITATION GEMS

Robin Hutchison

Museum Photo

Fig. 5 **James Tassie** by David Allan (1744–96). Oil on canvas. Tassie was born in Glasgow and died in London. He attended the Foulis Academy in Glasgow, where he was a fellow student of Allan, the painter and engraver (see Figure 4). Tassie holds in his hand a miniature portrait head derived from an antique model. He learnt the skill of making casts from antique gems from Dr. Henry Quin, a Dublin medical man, and with him developed a white paste which imitated the appearance of marble.

James Tassie, excelling as a portrait medallist, was an expert imitator of antique and contemporary engraved gems and cameos

James Tassie was born in Pollockshaws, near Glasgow, in 1735; he died in London in 1799. None of the biographical material available to us gives much indication of the sort of man he was, except that he was hard working and business-like. It is what he produced that provides his monument. He modelled and cast in imitation of marble over five hundred medallion busts, and he reproduced over fifteen thousand antique and contemporary engraved gems, cameos and medallions, using a translucent form of the same paste, coloured to imitate the original gem.

James Tassie's father was a skinner, who apprenticed him to a stonemason. The young Tassie was not satisfied with such a limited career and attended the Academy in Glasgow, run by the Foulis brothers. There he studied modelling under an Italian named Torri.

In 1763, Tassie moved to Dublin with the intention of setting up as a sculptor and modeller. There he met Dr. Henry Quin, a distinguished medical man who, as a hobby, made casts from antique gems. Quin was impressed by Tassie's abilities and took him on as an assistant, and together Quin and Tassie developed a white opaque vitreous paste with a low melting-point suitable for producing miniature portrait heads in imitation

of marble. It was probably also in Dublin that Tassie developed and perfected the use of this same paste, both translucent and coloured, not only to take casts from antique and contemporary engraved gems but also to imitate the precious and semi-precious stones of the originals. He became so expert in this that he was able to reproduce the various layers of a cameo or the variegated colour of a semi-precious stone.

In 1766, encouraged by Dr. Quin, Tassie moved to London, where he set up as a sculptor of small-scale portraits in relief and as a supplier of imitation gems which were used by jewellers for rings and other trinkets. His reputation grew and, from 1769 to 1791, he regularly exhibited at the Royal Academy. Meanwhile, he was building up a remarkable cabinet of reproduction gems which still survives in the collection of the Scottish National Portrait Gallery.

James Tassie first produced a catalogue of his reproductions in 1775 containing just over three thousand items; by 1791, his cabinet contained over five times that number. It was in this year that Rudolph Eric Raspe, the German antiquary, perhaps best known as the creator of Baron Munchausen, compiled a monumental catalogue of Tassie's cabinet. This two-volume work, illustrated with engravings by David Allan, (Fig. 4), is by far the most valuable source of information about Tassie's reproductions and is the main source of information about the man himself and his methods.

From Raspe's catalogue, it can be seen that he had access to many of the most important collections of engraved gems and, in about 1783, had received an order for a set of ten thousand gems

Fig. 6 *David Hume* by James
Tassie.

Fig. 7 *Mrs. Alexander Wilson*
by James Tassie.

Fig. 8 *Sir Henry Raeburn*,
modelled by Raeburn, cast by
Tassie.

6

7

Museum Photo

8

Museum Photo

Fig. 9 Top: (right) *Earl Howe*,
a mould in paste by James Tassie
from a metal medallion: (left) *a*
modern cast in resin from the
mould.
Centre: (left) *Lt. General*
Monkton by James Tassie: (right)
the same head cast in paste in
imitation of a gemstone designed
to be seen from the reverse.
Bottom: (left) *First Earl*
Spencer by James Tassie: (right)
the same head cast in paste in
imitation of a gemstone designed
to be seen from the reverse.

Fig. 10 Top: (left) *Thetis*, cast
from an antique cameo: (right)
the same gem cast as an intaglio.
Centre: (left) *Greek gem*, a cast
in sulphur wax: (right) *Leda and*
the Swan, *cast in intaglio and*
designed to be seen from the
reverse. Bottom: (left) *Paste*
gem, *probably by William*
Tassie, based on a design by
Henry Fuseli (1741–1825):
(right) *Osiris*, *a reproduction of*
an Egyptian seal.

Fig. 11 *Robert Adam* by
James Tassie.

Fig. 12 *Robert Adam*, a modern
replica in resin.

from Catherine the Great of Russia. Tassie not only
produced his reproductions in coloured paste, but
also made up sets cast in red sulphur wax. Small
sets of gems and wax casts can still be found, but
other craftsmen were producing the same sort of
thing and the identification of Tassie's work in this
medium is difficult.

The mass of reproductions by Tassie tend to
overshadow his production of original portraits,
which are his most important works. Although
most of the heads were produced in numbers
varying according to the demand, they are originals
and some must rank with the best portrait sculpture
produced in the second half of the eighteenth
century in Britain.

Tassie's method of producing his portraits was
very simple; he made no preliminary drawing
but worked direct from his sitter, making his
modello in red wax (Fig. 3). It is not certain how he
proceeded after he had completed the wax: one
authority states that he made a mould in plaster
from the *modello*, that from this he produced a
plaster cast in relief and from this, in turn, he made
a mould in paste from which the final head was cast.
However, although a few original waxes have
survived, no paste moulds of his large portrait
heads are known. J. M. Gray, who wrote an account
of James Tassie in 1894 and compiled a catalogue of
his portraits, suggests that Tassie somewhere cast
the paste head direct from the first plaster mould.

At first, Tassie's cast portraits were mounted on
an oval of slightly frosted glass backed by a piece
of blue paper to provide a coloured background.
Later, he cast the figure and background in one
piece to give the effect of a marble plaque in
miniature. Initially, he apparently experienced
some difficulty in doing this. The Scottish National
Portrait Gallery possesses a portrait of Sir John
Dolben of Finedon which is labelled on the back in
an eighteenth-century hand: 'This was the very
first attempt of making large Paste impressions
but cracked by not being long enough annealed'.

The majority of Tassie's portraits consist of a
figure in low relief and in profile, cut off just below
the shoulder; the figure approximately one and a
half inches high, mounted on an oval four by three
and a half inches. This format varies occasionally,
some are heads alone and there are a very few where

the sitter is shown three-quarter face. Occasionally,
the backgrounds are round. Many of the portraits
are signed on the truncation of the shoulder with
an inscribed 'Tassie F', or a plain 'T'. In some
portraits the name of the sitter and the date are
included. The finished medallion is generally in a
turned boxwood frame designed to hang on the wall.

For a period, James Tassie supplied Wedgwood
with moulds from his own medallions, which were
produced by Wedgwood in his own paste. The
Scottish National Portrait Gallery possesses identical
medallions of the first Viscount Melville by both
Tassie and Wedgwood (Fig. 1). One of the most
interesting medallions cast by Tassie is that of the
young Henry Raeburn (Fig. 8). By tradition, this
was modelled by the painter and cast by Tassie.
Because no other piece of modelling by Raeburn is
known, some doubt has been thrown on this tradition, but examination of the medallion shows a very
different technique of modelling from all other
examples of Tassie's work.

After James Tassie died, his nephew William
Tassie, who had worked with him, carried on the
business, both as a portraitist and in the reproduction of antique gems (Fig. 2). His reproductions are
indistinguishable from those of his uncle, but his
portraits lack the precision of the older man's work.

Portrait medallions in paste by both Tassies still
occasionally appear in salerooms, but there also
exist many plaster casts, often of quite late date. The
Scottish National Portrait Gallery and one or two
other institutions produce very convincing replicas,
made in modern resins which are available to the
public (Fig. 12). Tassie's original paste is very hard
and cold to the touch, while the replicas in plaster
on resin are much softer.

MUSEUMS AND COLLECTIONS
The principal collection of portrait medallions
and reproduction gems is in the Scottish National
Portrait Gallery, Edinburgh.

FURTHER READING
James and William Tassie, pamphlet for the
National Galleries of Scotland, 1960.
James and William Tassie, by John M. Gray,
Edinburgh, 1894.

10

12

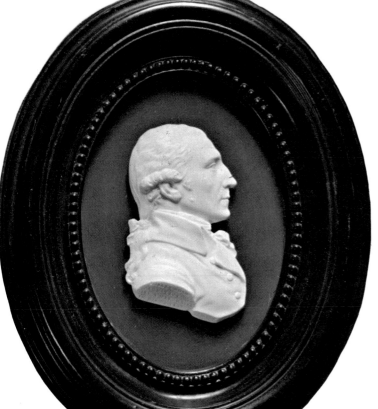

CLUTHA GLASS

K. Hoddle

K. Hoddle

Figs. 1 and 2 **Vases**, *Clutha glass made by James Couper & Sons, Glasgow, c.1885–1905. Clutha was bubbled and streaked; it was different to Thomas Webb's Old Roman, which, in 1888, Couper's were complaining was a deliberate imitation of Clutha. Height 6½ ins. and 12¼ ins. (Private Collection.)*

Fig. 3 **Four-handled bottle**, *designed by Christopher Dresser (1834–1904) with Couper's mark on the base consisting of a flower and the words 'Clutha designed by CD'. 'Clutha' is an old Scottish word meaning cloudy. Height 5 ins., diameter 5 ins. (Victoria and Albert Museum, London.)*

A. C. Cooper

The latter part of the nineteenth century saw a completely original development in the glass industry from the *avant-garde* firm of James Couper & Sons in Glasgow. Working in a modern style, they evolved a new material incorporating a streaky and bubbly effect to which they gave the name of 'Clutha glass', Clutha meaning cloudy. The primitive shapes are based on antique models and many can be credited to the famous designers, Christopher Dresser and George Walton

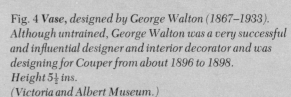

Fig. 4 **Vase**, designed by George Walton (1867–1933). Although untrained, George Walton was a very successful and influential designer and interior decorator and was designing for Couper from about 1896 to 1898. Height 5½ ins. (Victoria and Albert Museum.)

Fig. 5 **Vase**, designed by Christopher Dresser with Couper's mark on the base. Christopher Dresser was perhaps the greatest of the commercial designers of this period and Clutha shows him at his best and most inventive. The material was ideal for the exploitation of his considerable botanical knowledge. Height 5½ ins. (Victoria and Albert Museum.)

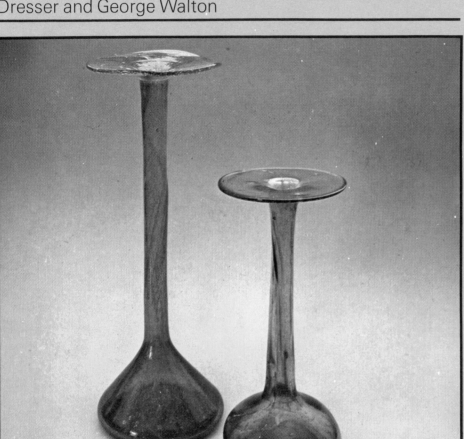

9

10

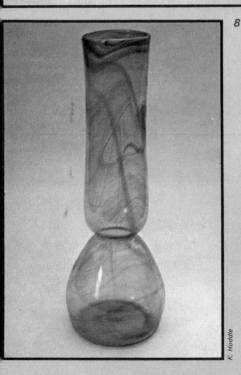

8

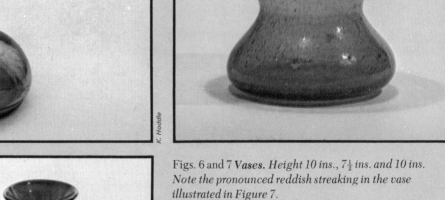

Figs. 6 and 7 **Vases**. Height 10 ins., 7½ ins. and 10 ins. Note the pronounced reddish streaking in the vase illustrated in Figure 7. (Private Collection.)

Fig. 8 **Vase**, of a very unusual type of black Clutha glass. Height 7¼ ins. (Private Collection.)

Fig. 9 **Two vases**, the one on the left with patches of aventurine (copper crystals) in the metal. This is a characteristic of Clutha in the 1890s. Height 3½ ins. and 2¾ ins. (Private Collection.)

Fig. 10 **Vase**, designed by Christopher Dresser, with Couper's mark on the base. All pieces designed for Coupers by Christopher Dresser bear their mark. Height 3 ins. (Victoria and Albert Museum.)

Paisley Shawls

Rupert Roddam

Rupert Roddam

James Hunter

Patronised by Queen Victoria, many of the Paisley weavers worked in their own homes making fascinating patterns which were derived from Kashmiri shawls

Fig. 1 **Shawl** *with 'pine' motif and white centre, perhaps Paisley, 1825–30. Wool and silk, 62 ins. x 65 ins. Shawls made at Paisley usually had a silk warp and a wool weft carrying the pattern. (Museum and Art Galleries, Paisley, Renfrewshire.)*

Fig. 2 **Shawl** *woven on a Jacquard loom, Paisley, c.1850. Wool, 71 ins. x 71 ins. The Jacquard machine loom was developed in France at the start of the nineteenth century. (Museum and Art Galleries, Paisley.)*

Fig. 3 **Shawl** *with overall pattern, perhaps Edinburgh, c.1815. Wool and silk, 31 ins. x 105 ins. (Museum and Art Galleries, Paisley.)*

Fig. 4 **Shawl** *with 'spade' motif, c.1815. Silk background, pattern in wool, 58 ins. x 55 ins. (Museum and Art Galleries, Paisley.)*

For a century, from about 1770 to 1870, Western European female fashion was heavily influenced by the garment that has become known as the Paisley shawl. The term is loose, and it covers not only a wide range of sizes and shapes of shawls worn in various styles, but also shawls made in many places other than Paisley, Renfrewshire.

All these various shawls had, however, a common ancestry in Kashmir. The flourishing, luxury weaving industry of that area produced high quality shawls, originally for local male attire, but from the 1770s they were exported for European female use. The fine yarn used was spun from the fleece of the Kashmir goat, dyed to give a great range of colours, dazzling and subtle. The complex patterns were created by weaving in tapestry technique, so that, instead of throwing shuttles to and fro to produce a weft of horizontal threads, bobbins were intertwined with the warp by hand. The results were spectacular, but the process was painfully slow and expensive.

As Indian shawls grew in popularity, various weaving centres in Europe experimented with imitations – Edinburgh in 1777, soon followed by several small Scottish towns, Norwich and Lyon. Paisley joined in about 1800, and within twenty years had such a commanding lead in bulk production that its name became identified with the product and most of its competitors were eventually forced out of business. Likewise, the pattern most closely associated with the Paisley shawl, the Kashmiri 'pine' motif (Figs. 1 and 3), became the Paisley pattern.

European imitators of Kashmiri shawls had two main problems: producing a yarn as fine and soft as the original, which was strong enough to weave on a European loom, and equalling the intricacy of

Kashmiri design, using mechanical control instead of manual skill. Large quantities of Kashmir fleece were in fact imported and spun, chiefly in France, but various substitutes were developed which proved acceptable. Shawls made in Paisley usually had a warp of silk and a weft (carrying the pattern) of fine wool. Similar arrangements were used elsewhere, and these substitute fabrics were generally described as 'cashmere'.

The extent of pattern was usually fairly limited in the early shawls. Often the whole centre was left plain, red and white designs being a common choice. Long narrow shawls were popular, and these usually had a narrow patterned border with larger areas of pattern at either end. The patterned parts were usually woven separately, and sewn on to the plain centre. The 'pine' was the popular choice of motif for the ends, and a floral sprig for the border. More sophisticated (and expensive) versions of this style used the centre as a background for further patterns (Fig. 3).

A simplified form of this was the popular 'spade' shawl (Fig. 4), where a very simple motif was repeated all over the centre. Similar designs were employed for scarves and square shoulder-shawls.

By 1820, the original Kashmiri patterns were undergoing drastic modifications at the hands of French designers. The geometric precision of the detail gave way to more continuous, flowing lines.

The Jacquard loom, which had been spreading and developing in France since 1800, assisted this change in design, since the accuracy of its punchcard control mechanism allowed the production of much more ambitious and extensive patterns. Eventually it was possible to cover the whole surface of the shawl with an overall 'harness' design of great complexity.

Paisley was rather slow to adopt this machine, which did not make its appearance until the late 1830s. The old manually controlled draw-loom which continued in use almost until mid-century, despite numerous locally developed refinements, did impose limitations on both designer and weaver. The evidence indeed suggests that until the 1830s the quality of shawls produced in Paisley was not comparable with those of Edinburgh or

3

Rupert Roddam

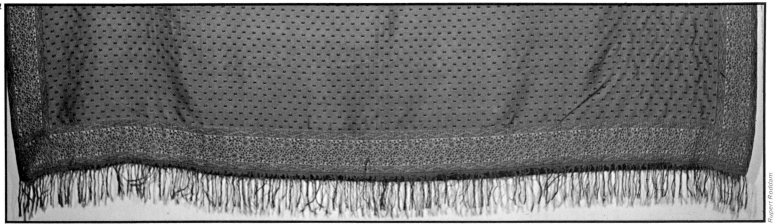

4

Rupert Roddam

5

Rupert Roddam

6

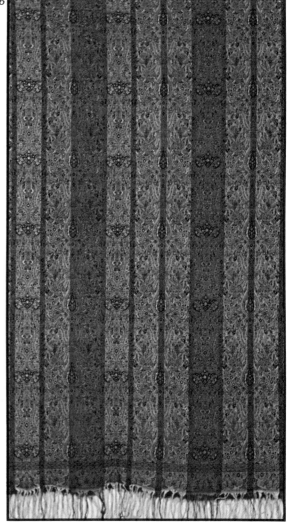

Rupert Roddam

Fig. 5 **Shawl**, *Jacquard-woven with overall 'harness' pattern, Paisley, 1861. Wool and silk, 61 ins. x 142 ins.*
The Jacquard loom permitted the weaving of more ambitious and extensive designs. Paisley did not adopt it until the late 1830s and was consequently slower than Edinburgh and Norwich to produce really fine shawls. Large plaids of this type survive in quite large numbers; they represent the highest artistic and technical achievement of the industry. (Museum and Art Galleries, Paisley.)

Fig. 6 **Shawl** *with 'zebra' pattern, Paisley, 1850–65. Silk, 67 ins. x 134 ins.*
A model for this design is to be found in Turkish fabrics, but it also derives in part from Kashmiri patterns, the source of the true Paisley pattern. In Kashmir these patterned shawls were worn by men, but from the 1770s they were exported to Europe as female attire. The first European imitations were made in Edinburgh in 1777. (Museum and Art Galleries, Paisley.)

Norwich, and really fine early shawls (Fig. 3) are not likely to have been made in Paisley. Due to copying of patterns and migration of weavers, however, it is very difficult to identify the source of most shawls with any certainty; the quality of design and craftsmanship in Paisley steadily increased.

In the 1830s most local firms employed their own designers, many turning out work of a high standard, although the excellent French designs continued to be bought in large quantities. The introduction of the Jacquard loom allowed the weaving of all-over 'harness' shawls; large plaids of this type are typical of the later period of production, and they survive in considerable numbers. The best of these (Fig. 5) represent the peak of the artistic and technical achievement of the industry.

During the seventy years of manufacture in Paisley many types of shawl were produced in addition to the mainstream of development. Turkish fabrics were the model for the striped 'zebra' shawls (Fig. 6) but since these also made use of the familiar Indian patterns, they can be regarded as a variety of Paisley shawl. Similarly, Chinese influence is quite marked on many Paisley shawls. Among a number of minor woven types, mention should be made of the reversible shawl, which was patterned on both front and back.

The development of such variations in production was organised by local manufacturers, who, in fact, did not undertake the bulk of the weaving directly. Most manufacturers had a small factory with a dozen or so looms, but contracted out most

of their work to independent weavers working on their own machines in their own homes. A highly skilled, educated and articulate section of the community, they represented one of the last major stands of individual craftsmanship against the onset of factory production.

But the commercial expertise of the manufacturers and the technical skill of the weavers were equally at the mercy of fluctuations in trade and in fashion. One of the most severe depressions, from 1842 to 1844, was overcome by a highly organised campaign in Court circles, as a result of which Queen Victoria and many of the nobility purchased large numbers of shawls from Paisley, helping to stimulate a revival, and from about 1848 to 1865 the industry was at its peak. An irrevocable change in fashion struck in 1870, the bustle skirt making the shawl obsolete, and within a few years the industry was extinct.

MUSEUMS AND COLLECTIONS
Paisley Shawls may be seen at the following:
London: Victoria and Albert Museum
Norwich: Castle Museum
Paisley: Museum and Art Galleries

FURTHER READING
Paisley Shawls by C. H. Rock, Paisley, 1966.
Centuries of Scottish Shawl-making by Muir and Patterson, Edinburgh, 1962.
Shawls by John Irwin, London, 1955.
The Paisley Shawl by Matthew Blair, Paisley, 1904.

Scottish Pistols

John Wallace

Fig. 1 **Lemon-butt snaphaunce pistol,** *lock-plate stamped with the maker's initials 'IL', the fence dated 1634. Iron stock, brass lock-plate, length $16\frac{3}{4}$ ins. Because the pistol is fitted with a left-hand lock, it must originally have been one of a pair. (Art Gallery and Museum, Glasgow.)*

The art of pistol-making flourished in Scotland for some two hundred years, providing some of the most graceful firearms ever made

'This art [pistol-making] was introduced to Doune about the year 1646, by Thomas Caddell . . . He taught the trade to his children, and several apprentices, of whom was one John Campbell, whose son and grandson carried on the business with great repute, the trade is now carried on by John Murdoch . . . There is now very little demand for Scottish pistols, owing to the price of the pistols made in England; but the chief cause of the decline is the disuse of the dirk and pistol as part of the Caledonian Dress; and when Mr. Murdoch gives over business, the trade, in all probability will become extinct.'

In these words from the entry for Doune in the *Statistical Account of Scotland*, 1798, set down no doubt by the local Minister of the Church, are enshrined the deathbed scene and the obituary of an industry which had flourished in Scotland for some two hundred years.

The exact date when pistols were first made in Scotland is still unknown. Certainly the country's gunmaking industry was flourishing at the end of the sixteenth century, when Dundee was an important centre of the trade. In 1587 no less than eight of a total Hammermen Craft membership of

thirty-five were gunmakers, the Deacon himself being one. There were also others; a considerable number of the small towns on the North East coast and in the Lowlands that border the eastern flank of the Highland massif had gunmakers among their Hammermen members.

Since the publication in 1923 of a treatise on Scottish firearms by the late Charles Whitelaw, it has been customary to group or classify Scottish pistols by their most dominant characteristics – the shape of their stocks and the butt-profile in particular. Whitelaw established the following five groups: fishtail; lemon-butt; heart-butt; scroll-butt; lobe-butt. Although one cannot say for certain that any one group evolved directly from another, it might be suggested that the scroll-butt was a related manifestation of the fishtail, and the heart-butt of the lemon-butt.

Whitelaw suggested that the dominant characteristics of the Scottish pistol, the fishtail and lemon-butt, evolved from imported Dutch pieces. Subsequent research, however, has made a strong case for singling out contemporary English pistols as the major influence in points of shape and style, though it is possible that both English and Scottish models derived separately from a Continental prototype. Certainly the English and Scottish pistols of the late sixteenth and early seventeenth centuries display similarities, such as a belt-hook, no guard to the trigger and the frequent use of brass for barrels and lock-plates. In Scotland, however, there was an early predilection for all-metal stocks, at first mainly in brass, then in steel. A relatively large number of these weapons has survived, both

2

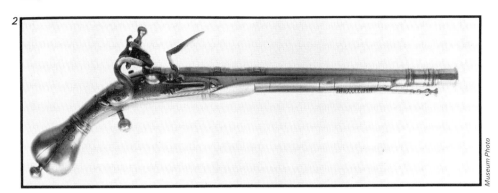

Museum Photo

3

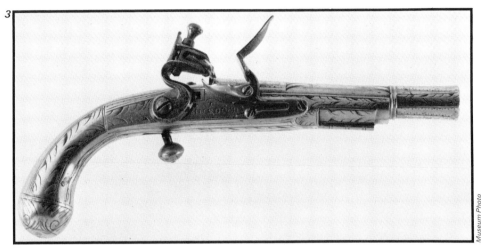

Museum Photo

4

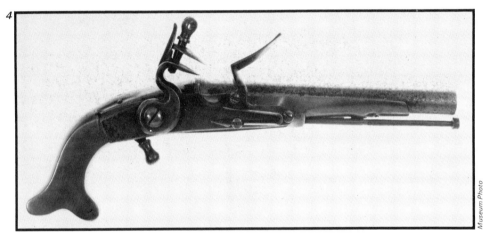

Museum Photo

5

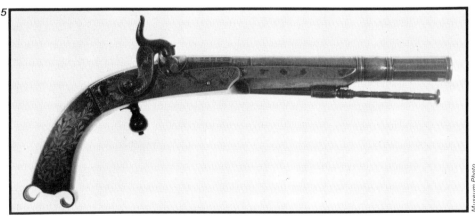

Museum Photo

in fishtail and in lemon-butt styles. One explanation for this preference is that Scottish pistol-makers were members of the Hammermen Craft, and thus found no problem in working with the basic materials of their trade.

Many of these pistols bear dates on the fence of their snaphaunce locks and across the breech of the barrel. Surviving examples of the fishtail type bear dates ranging from 1598 to about 1625; the lemon-butt type appears to have been made until

about 1650. These early pistols generally carry the makers' initials, some of which have been identified; a high proportion are Dundee Hammermen. The fishtail and the lemon-butt styles appear to have been discontinued at a time when the fortunes of Dundee were at their lowest ebb following the sack of the city by Monk's army in 1651.

Invariably the pistols were made in pairs, with right-hand locks and left-hand locks, a peculiarly Scottish practice that was applied to pistols throughout the seventeenth century but ceased shortly after 1700. Some of the surviving all-brass lemon-butt pistols are remarkable for their extreme length. An English private collection includes one such pair, dated 1614 and made by James Low of Dundee, the pistols being nearly two feet in length. In addition, the pommels unscrew and extend a further four and a quarter inches. Like all Scottish pistols of this period they are extensively decorated with strap-work and scrolls.

Butts shaped like the accepted stylisation of the human heart were a feature of a class of pistol that emerged in the third quarter of the seventeenth century (Fig. 2). They were made exclusively in towns along the east coast of Scotland, from Inverness in the north to Edinburgh in the south, and mainly of steel, though some with brass barrels (and, more rarely, with brass stocks to match) do survive. Decoration was usually simple, consisting of panels and bands of engraved silver let into the barrel and sometimes into the stock. The workmanship and ornamentation are rarely of the best, but they have a certain strength of character.

Heart-butt pistols vary considerably in size. Their barrels can be anything from twenty inches long, down to little more than six inches. The short-barrelled, stubby form of heart-butt pistol survives in some numbers. Most of them are signed IA MK, the initials of James MacKenzie, pistol-maker in Brechin, working in the 1730s.

The scroll-butt pistol, another type peculiar to Scotland, seems to have emerged shortly before the heart-butt, but it remained in production in one form or another for a good century longer.

The scroll-butts of the late seventeenth century are rough and ready in their workmanship compared to, say, the contemporary products of Doune. H.M. Tower of London Armouries have two scroll-butts of early form, where the scrolls are constructed merely of a narrow strip of iron attached to the end of the butt and rolled up at each end. From between the scrolls protrudes the head of a detachable pricker used in cleaning the touch-hole. The butts have slab sides, and there is very little curvature to the stocks as a whole. There is a similar pistol (the left-hand survivor of a pair) in the Kungl. Livrustkammar, Stockholm. It is dated 1670, and bears the initials A.W. These could be of Alexander Wilson of the Canongate, Edinburgh, who was admitted Freeman of the Incorporation of Hammermen in 1643, his Assay or test piece being an 'irne pistolet'.

By the end of the century, when makers such as Daniel Stewart, John Stuart and Thomas Caddell were signing their pieces in full, the scroll-butt was becoming less angular and more elegant, with engraving and silver inlay on the barrel and stock. During the ensuing twenty years or so, the scroll-butt developed the characteristic curve of line and profile that was to achieve its greatest refinement in the 1730s and '40s (Fig. 9). However, in terms

Fig. 2 **Heart-butt flint-lock,** lock-plate inscribed 'And. Strachan/Edzel', c.1700. Steel with silver-inlaid barrel and engraved stock, length 17½ ins. *(Art Gallery and Museum, Glasgow.)*

Fig. 3 **Flint-lock pistol,** lock-plate inscribed 'T. Murdoch', c.1780. Brass, length 9½ ins. This is an example of the lobe-butt, Whitelaw's fifth group. Murdoch left Doune for Leith in 1774. He appears to have specialised in making pistols of this kind. *(Art Gallery and Museum, Glasgow.)*

Fig. 4 **Flint-lock pistol,** c.1785. Bronze stock, length 11½ ins. This is one of the so-called 'Scottish' pistols made in England for issue to the Highland regiments. *(Art Gallery and Museum, Glasgow.)*

Fig. 5 **Percussion pistol,** mid-nineteenth century. Steel, engraved and with silver inlays, length 11¾ ins. This pistol would be one of a pair to be worn as an ornamental part of Highland Dress. *(Art Gallery and Museum, Glasgow.)*

Fig. 6 **Kenneth Sutherland, Lord Duffus,** by Richard Waitt, c.1700. Oil on canvas. The position of the pistol is slightly unusual. More often it is worn on the left side, either on the waistbelt, or slung from a separate shoulder belt. *(Scottish National Portrait Gallery, Edinburgh.)*

Fig. 7 **Fishtail pistol with snaphaunce lock,** one of a pair, the lock-plate with maker's initials 'IL' (see also Figure 1), the fence dated 1624, the barrel dated 1626. Brass, length 17½ ins. *(Art Gallery and Museum, Glasgow.)*

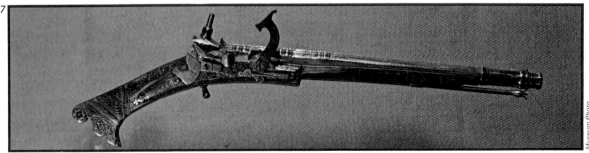

8

Museum Photo

Fig. 8 *The Highland Chieftain* by *Michael Wright,* c.*1660.*
(*Scottish National Portrait Gallery.*)

Fig. 9 *Scroll-butt flint-lock pistols, Doune,* c.*1730–40.*
Steel, length 14¾ *ins. and* 14¼ *ins.*
These are examples of Highland steel pistols at their very best.
(*Art Gallery and Museum, Glasgow.*)

of technical finish and impressive overall decorative treatment where 'lines appear to have been drawn with a pen dipped in silver', as one writer has put it, Doune pistols of the immediate post-1745 Rising period must be awarded the palm.

The same period saw the emergence of a considerable new industry directed at the military market, since it was agreed that privates in Highland regiments should be furnished apiece with a single metal pistol. Hence the existence in some quantity of plain but serviceable scroll-butt pistols, stamped or engraved with initials and numerals, identifying the regiments and battalions of their owners. The majority of these weapons were made not in Doune or even Scotland, but in English industrial centres. Isaac Bissell, whose name appears frequently on the lock-plates of such pistols, was only one of several English manufacturers who managed to get orders direct from battalion commanders for their 'Scottish' pistols.

By now one can see the writing on the wall for the Doune industry. The lack of Highland clients for their superb products (The Proscription Act of 1746, forbidding the wearing of Highland dress and arms, was not repealed until 1782) and the swamping of the military market by cheap English imitations forced the Doune makers to close down, or to move elsewhere.

Flint-lock steel pistols continued to be made for dress purposes in all the large towns until well into the nineteenth century. Nevertheless, with the old school of pistol-makers losing heart as well as custom, it was inevitable that the standards within the industry would deteriorate. Except when special orders demanded a high degree of craftsmanship, Scottish pistols in general became increasingly clumsy in appearance and coarse in finish, with stocks of malleable cast iron or low-grade silver instead of steel.

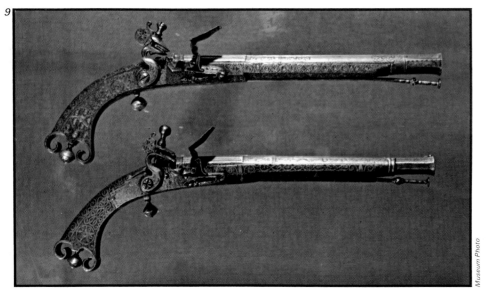

9

Museum Photo

MUSEUMS AND COLLECTIONS

Scottish pistols may be seen at the following:

Edinburgh:	National Museum of Antiquities of Scotland
	The Royal Scottish Museum
Glasgow:	Art Gallery and Museum
London:	H.M. Tower of London Armouries
	Victoria and Albert Museum

FURTHER READING

'Scottish Pistols' by Geoffrey Boothroyd, **Journal of the Arms and Armour Society,** Volume VI No. 5, London, 1969.
Pistols of the World by C. Blair, London, 1968.
'Scottish Firearms' in **Encyclopedia of Firearms** edit. by H. J. Peterson, London, 1964.
European Hand Firearms of the 16th, 17th & 18th centuries by Herbert Jackson, with a treatise on Scottish Hand Firearms by Charles E. Whitelaw, London, 1963.

The Glasgow Style

Roger Billcliffe

Keith Gibson

Fig. 1 **High-back chair**, one of a pair designed by Charles Rennie Mackintosh (1868–1928), 1899–1900. Oak. Made by Mackintosh for his own dining-room, these tall chairs have the stylised shape of a swooping bird pierced in the oval back-rail, a motif often used by The Four. (University of Glasgow, Mackintosh Collection.)

'The Four', consisting of C. R. Mackintosh, H. MacNair and the Macdonald sisters, created in the years around 1900 a thoroughly Scottish Art Nouveau style which was to influence the world

Glasgow was already famous in artistic circles throughout Britain and Europe in the 1890s, but that fame rested upon the work of a group of artists who came to be known as 'the Glasgow Boys' or 'the Glasgow School'. The Glasgow Style was a movement entirely different from the Glasgow School, but it too was to be noticed far beyond the confines of Glasgow. In fact, its reputation abroad was higher than it was in Britain and the four main protagonists of the style were welcomed and acclaimed in Paris, Vienna, Berlin, Turin, Rome, Munich and even Moscow; at home they were rejected in London in 1896, and Glasgow turned its back on them after 1914.

The most important of these young artists – 'The Four', as they were known to their friends at the Glasgow School of Art – was Charles Rennie Mackintosh (1868–1928). Mackintosh was trained as an architect and his decorative work is usually ancillary to an architectural commission. His close friend, Herbert MacNair (1868–1955), was also trained as an architect, but he never practised as such and always called himself a designer. The other two members of The Four were Margaret (1865–1933) and Frances (1874–1921) Macdonald (who were later to marry Mackintosh and MacNair respectively); they were students at the Glasgow School of Art, where they studied embroidery, metalwork, jewellery and the other applied arts. It was at the Glasgow School of Art that the architects met the two girls, probably in 1893. They were introduced by the Director of the School,

Francis H. Newbery, who had noticed a similarity in their works.

The early works which survive are nearly all water-colour drawings. These drawings are all similar and one overriding influence is apparent, that of the Dutch artist Toorop, whose painting *The Three Brides* had been reproduced in *Studio* in 1893. The girls, in particular, were intoxicated by his imagery, and the swirling draperies, elongated figures, the spiritual and the malevolent, were all adopted by them. Their imagery was often taken from Celtic myth, as was much of their decorative detail, and eventually their style was to be known as the 'Spook School' Mackintosh also produced water-colours, but he rarely produced the full-blooded symbolism of MacNair and the Macdonalds.

Their work at this stage was on the boundaries of Art Nouveau, the decorative style which spread from Paris to every country in Europe, each one adapting the style and producing its own variation. Art Nouveau is much more an architectural and design movement than a painting style, and it is in their designs for furniture and other objects that The Four come closer to their European contemporaries. Mackintosh and MacNair were producing furniture designs from the early 1890s, but their work owed much to the English Arts and Crafts Movement. The Macdonald sisters did not design furniture, but confined themselves to beaten metalwork, leaded glass, embroideries, jewellery and painted gesso panels. Much of the furniture designed by the men incorporated decoration made by the girls, usually in the form of repoussé metal panels or embroidered covers and curtains.

By 1896 Mackintosh's furniture had moved sufficiently far away from Arts and Crafts for him to be decried by the members of that movement at their London exhibition. MacNair and the Macdonalds suffered the same fate too, and none of the group exhibited similar work in London again. The editor of the magazine *Studio*, Gleeson White,

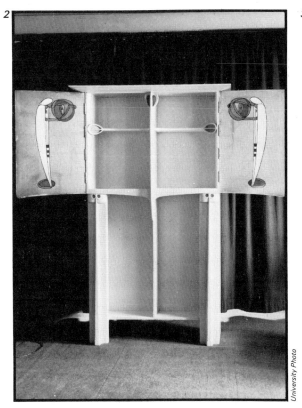

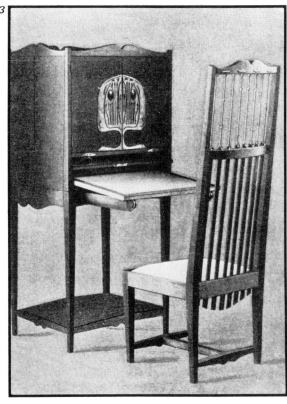

University Photo

Fig. 2 **Cabinet**, *one of a pair designed by Charles Rennie Mackintosh, 1902. Wood painted white, with metal handles, the inside door panels painted silver and inlaid with opaque coloured glass, small panels of opaque coloured glass inside cupboard. The most delicate and feminine of Mackintosh's cabinets, this was commissioned by Francis Newbery's mother-in-law. The Mackintoshes, however, seem to have kept the pair for themselves. (University of Glasgow, Mackintosh Collection.)*

Fig. 3 **Writing-cabinet and chair**, *designed by Herbert MacNair (1868–1955), 1901–2. Oak, beaten metal and glass. Although more awkward and ornate than Mackintosh's work, MacNair's furniture never broke away from the Glasgow Style. This set was made for the Turin Exhibition of 1902. The bead and string back on the chair is highly inventive, and the metalwork panel on the cabinet is typical of the work of Margaret and Frances Macdonald. (Private Collection.)*

disagreed with the treatment The Four had received, and he visited Glasgow to see more of their work. In 1897 he included two articles in *Studio* which showed their work in depth, and also that of some of their friends in Glasgow including E. A. Taylor and Talwin Morris. The following year, articles on The Four appeared in several Continental magazines devoted to the decorative arts, notably *Deutsche Kunst und Dekoration* and *Dekorative Kunst*. The Four were now known throughout Europe and were invited to show in several major exhibitions of decorative work; in London they were ignored, and Glasgow, too, with the exception of three or four committed patrons, found them too unconventional for its taste.

It has already been stated that Mackintosh's decorative work was usually ancillary to his architecture. This does not mean that he produced only a small amount; in fact the reverse, for Mackintosh believed in designing the furniture, lampshades, carpets, curtains and all the other items connected with his buildings; for his restaurants he even designed the cutlery, for his houses the gardens, for the Glasgow School of Art a variation of the Glasgow coat of arms. He wanted to create a total environment and was fortunate enough to have clients who allowed him to do it (Fig. 4). For fifteen years his output was prodigious – not a great number of commissions, but each one was treated in the same manner, each one was worked out to the last detail.

Mackintosh's architecture and furniture is often called Art Nouveau, but this is misleading. His architecture in particular, although often drawing its inspiration from the Scottish Middle Ages, is forward-looking. His buildings are functional, and from the outside rather plain. They were designed from the inside out, and decoration is applied to the form of the building rather than the form being hidden by the decoration. The same applies to his furniture; Glasgow Style decoration often appears on it, but usually it is the work of Margaret Macdonald. Unlike the French and Belgian Art Nou-

veau designers, his work is restrained and light, slender and willowy. Mackintosh said that he wanted to be thought of as a purifier of form.

His early furniture designs, like MacNair's, tended to be similar to those produced by the Arts and Crafts Movement. Later works are much more individual and have less of an obvious debt to the past or his contemporaries. The most famous pieces are the tall-backed chairs, which are always accused of being uncomfortable and incongruous. All the high-back chairs were designed as part of an overall scheme, usually for one of Miss Cranston's Tea Rooms. To see a room full of chairs like these explains their height. They surge upwards like a forest of young trees, gently curved and gracefully proportioned. Nor are they uncomfortable if one considers them in the light of their purpose – they are certainly not easy chairs, but they would not tire their occupants for the length of time that Edwardian ladies spent in tea-rooms.

In Mackintosh's own dining-room, he had two high-backed chairs with an oval back-rail, but these are of plain oak (Fig. 1). The back-rail is pierced by the shape of a stylised swooping bird, a motif which The Four often used. Other oak chairs were made for the Ingram Street Tea Rooms, Glasgow; in one of the rooms he used two chairs of basically the same design, one of which had a low back and the other a high back. He later painted white one of the high-back chairs and kept it for himself. The white chairs are generally far more graceful and delicate than the oak ones. Usually they were made for domestic use, or for display in exhibitions. Possibly his most beautiful chair was designed for the Wärndorfer music-room in Vienna (Fig. 6); unfortunately all the furniture in this room has been disbanded, but Mackintosh again kept one example for himself.

Other items of furniture tend to have more decoration, although it always complements the form rather than overwhelms it. The construction of Mackintosh's furniture is always simple and direct; he did not often work with cabinet-makers and

Fig. 4 **Project design** *for the dining-room of the House of an Art Lover by Charles Rennie Mackintosh, 1901–2. Colour lithograph. Mackintosh was lucky throughout his career in that he had clients who allowed him to create total environments for them. In this project he has provided for every detail of the decoration as well as the furniture. (University of Glasgow, Mackintosh Collection.)*

Fig. 5 **Door-handles** *for Dunglass Castle, designed by Talwin Morris, 1898-99. Brass. A minor designer working in the Glasgow Style, Talwin Morris had relatively limited talents and often produced altered versions of traditional designs. (University of Glasgow, Mackintosh Collection.)*

Fig. 6 **Chair**, *designed by Charles Rennie Mackintosh, 1901–2. Oak painted white with stencilled canvas back. Possibly Mackintosh's most beautiful chair, this was designed for the Wärndorfer music-room in Vienna. The actual pieces from this room have unfortunately disappeared, but Mackintosh kept this one example for himself. (University of Glasgow, Mackintosh Collection.)*

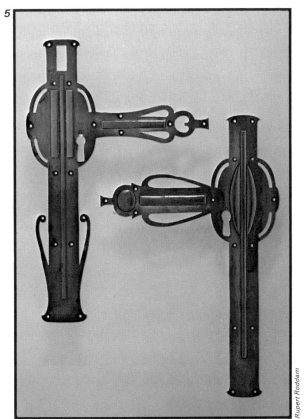

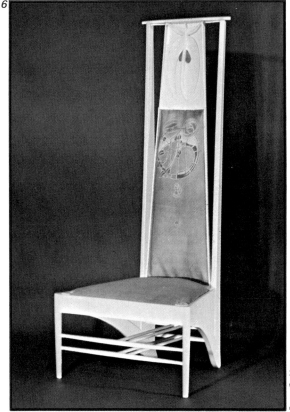

Fig. 7 **Decorative panel** *by Margaret Macdonald (1865–1933), 1898–99. Beaten metal. Panels of this sort were a frequent feature of Glasgow Style design. Made of various metals, they were incorporated into all kinds of furniture. (University of Glasgow, Mackintosh Collection.)*

Fig. 8 **Lampshade**, *designed by Charles Rennie Mackintosh, c.1900. Plated brass and coloured glass. Artificial lighting was an integral part of Mackintosh's overall plans. This cleverly conceived example was made for his own house in Mains Street. (University of Glasgow, Mackintosh Collection.)*

Fig. 9 *Fish-knife and fork,*
designed by C. R. Mackintosh,
c.1903. Silver-plated nickel.
The simplicity of design and the
linear shapes of Glasgow Style
objects suggest the Art Deco of
the Twenties.
(University of Glasgow,
Mackintosh Collection.)

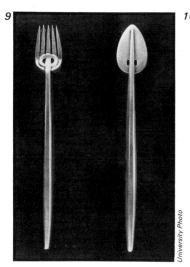

Fig. 10 **Willow Tea Rooms,**
Glasgow, furniture and
decoration designed by
The Four, 1903–4.

rarely produced fully worked-out drawings for an object. Fairly detailed drawings do exist for some pieces, but Mackintosh usually stood by his joiner as the piece was made, directing him away from the drawing as he worked, so that in some cases no two chairs of the same pattern are identical in dimensions.

Possibly because of their unusual method of construction, the chairs have proved fragile, although certain types are very solidly made. His tables and cabinets, however, are finer pieces of craftsmanship.

The most delicate and feminine of his cabinets (Fig. 2) is again painted white, and was made in 1902. It is one of a pair which were commissioned by Francis Newbery's mother-in-law, but which the Mackintoshes seem to have kept for themselves. The decoration on the outside is elegant and discreet, with pieces of coloured glass let into the legs and brass handles on the doors. The interior, however, is very different, for the back of each door is painted silver and has a design of inlaid coloured glass showing a stylised figure holding a rose ball, a favourite motif of the Glasgow Style.

Mackintosh also took great pains to ensure that the artificial lighting of his interiors formed a coherent part of his design. His lampshades were simple. That illustrated in Figure 8 is from his own house in Glasgow, and shows his skilful use of leaded glass. Other light-fittings for the Glasgow School of Art and Hill House, Helensburgh, are much larger, but they are equally effective in their setting.

MacNair's furniture often has a more decorated surface but it is rarely as graceful as Mackintosh's. The writing-table and chair illustrated in Figure 3 were made for the Turin Exhibition of 1902, and they show that he had not broken away from the Glasgow Style. The pierced metalwork panel on the writing-table is particularly typical of the work of Margaret and Frances Macdonald. The chair, however, has the novelty of a bead and string back in the upper half. MacNair produced many designs for jewellery and silverware, and he also used much leaded glass in his furniture. Like Talwin Morris (Fig. 5), his talents were more limited and he often took traditional designs and altered them in some fashion.

Much of the decorative work of the Macdonald sisters was linked to pieces designed by their husbands. They also produced works in beaten metal such as sconces, candlesticks, panels (Fig. 7) and pieces of leaded glass. Margaret also produced a number of gesso panels, two of which were incorporated in the Room de Luxe at the Ingram Street Tea Rooms, Glasgow. The phase of the Glasgow Style called the 'Spook School' is evident in much of their decorative work until about 1904, when they began to develop away from it. Neither of them designed furniture, and until about 1899 their work was limited to watercolours and objects such as candlesticks, mirrors, jewellery, firescreens, even metalwork book-covers. As they became more involved with the two architects, they began to produce articles which complemented their designs. Margaret, in particular, worked very closely with Mackintosh on most of his commissions. She designed and made the embroidered curtains for Hill House and made leaded glass panels which Mackintosh appears to have incorporated in light-fittings. They both designed menu-cards for Miss Cranston's Cafés at the 1901 and 1911 Glasgow International Exhibitions.

After the Mackintoshes left Glasgow, Margaret produced many fabric designs, some of which were bought by important manufacturers such as Foxton's. These later designs are much more formal than her Art Nouveau work produced in Glasgow, and their linear shapes suggest the major decorative style of the Twenties, Art Deco.

The Glasgow Style of Mackintosh and MacNair is quite different from that of the Macdonald sisters, especially in the three-dimensional designs which they produced. The two styles have sufficient in common, however, for them to complement each other in their decorative schemes. Mackintosh must be considered separately from the group for his status as an architect forces one to apply different criteria to his work. Every line and curve has a purpose in his design and everything is part of a far larger scheme. His work is simple, pure in form, and always on the right scale, while MacNair often gives in to impetuosity which dilutes his designs.

The Four were a phenomenon; at any other time their genius would have been crushed by the Establishment, but they were part of a movement which spread all over Europe. Their style was not European, however, and their work could never be mistaken for that of other Art Nouveau designers. Its roots were Scottish, its concept and handling were Scottish, but Scotland turned away from it while the whole of Europe hailed it for its genius. 🏶

MUSEUMS AND COLLECTIONS
The work of the Glasgow Style designers may be seen at the following:
GREAT BRITAIN
Glasgow: Glasgow Art Gallery and Museum
                Glasgow School of Art
                University Art Collections
London: Victoria and Albert Museum
Edinburgh: National Museum of Antiquities of
                Scotland

FURTHER READING
Charles Rennie Mackintosh by Robert MacLeod, London, 1968.
Charles Rennie Mackintosh, an Edinburgh Festival Exhibition catalogue by Andrew McLaren Young, Edinburgh, 1968.
Charles Rennie Mackintosh and the Modern Movement by Thomas Howarth, Glasgow, 1952.
Charles R. Mackintosh by Nikolaus Pevsner, Milan, 1950.

Wooden Ladles

Although literary references occur earlier to spoons than to ladles, this proves neither that spoons were born before ladles, nor that ladles were an offshoot from the spoon family. They may always have been separate, because ladling out and spooning up are different functions. Fifteenth-century references occur to the ladling of gun-powder, molten metals and molten glass, but wooden culinary and serving ladles for soups, stews, porridge, etc. must have been in common use before then.

For serving spiced alcoholic drinks from lignum vitae wassail bowls and other seventeenth-century community vessels, the dipping of lignum vitae, horn, or silver dipper cups seems to have been usual. Our ancestors' habits were not hygienic: they dipped and refilled their cups probably many times from the community bowl.

Punch and toddy ladles date mainly from the 1760s, when hot spiced rum drinks came into fashion; hard-wood ladles were used more than silver. **Typical English eighteenth-century specimens, made in one piece, are shown in the illustration (8 and 9).** Note the lug or hook on the back of the handle, to prevent the ladle slipping into the bowl; this was quite a common feature of eighteenth-century ladles, but was hailed as a new improvement on twentieth-century jam spoons.

The pearwood ladle (7) is a muffin ladle, holding the correct amount of batter for one muffin. **The kitchen ladle (10) doubtless served many purposes.** Ladles of this type were frequently provided with hook-ended handles, to prevent them slipping into the bowl or pot. **The ladle with a 6½-inch diameter bowl (11)**—a lovely one-piece object of honey-coloured maple—has been cleverly cut so that the bowl comes out of a handsomely marked burr, while the handle is straight-grained. **The carved ladle (1) is Scandinavian;** also cut from a burr, it shows an ingenious use of the twisted grain to form a thin but quite strong side lip, a very rare feature in wood. Next **(2) is a Scottish eighteenth-century punch ladle,** which differs from the English by being made in two parts: the handle, twist-turned to give a grip, is threaded into the side of the bowl. Many silver and Sheffield-plated ladles of the 1780s follow basically the same practice, with twisted whalebone handles fitted into silver or plate sockets. **The two ladles with open-twist handles (3 and 4) date from the early 1800s,** when oval bowls, with their length at right angles to the handles, were fashionable. The carved double-twist example **(3),** may be English; the triple-twist **(4),** decorated with a pen-and-ink picture, is Scottish; next to this is **a neat, one-piece, English eighteenth-century punch ladle (5),** with a feature rarely found in wooden ladles, a double connection to the bowl.

The hook-handled ladle (6), its handle carved with the traditional heart and roundels denoting a love token, was also meant to be used, and shows signs of wear. Its hook, its graceful side curvature and the twist on its stem, which make it easy to flick over when serving, are dictated by the tortuous contours of a piece of yew-wood.

EDWARD PINTO

Highland Lore

The romantic attitude to Scotland in the nineteenth century, fostered by the novels of Sir Walter Scott and Robert Louis Stevenson, helped to disguise the changes and hardships which engulfed the Highlands after the '45 rising. These changes led to the dispersal of clan relics and the arrival of Scotsmen in distant parts of the world, carrying with them traditions and mementos of their ancient culture. Alexander Gordon describes the development of aspects of Scottish dress and manners from the time of the 'clearances' to the era of coach tours.

During the bleak period of English military domination in the Highlands of Scotland after the uprising of 1745, an insidious companion to the army of George II was the Englishman's idea of property. Imposed on the social structure of the clan system, with its customary law, was the concept that property—whether land or movable—should belong to an individual, unencumbered by the interest of any other person. Admittedly this doctrine took many years to take root, but gradually the old interests of clansmen and the responsibilities of their chief declined.

Sales of Clan Relics

Some chieftains were sufficiently old-fashioned and near to their people not to evict during the time of the 'clearances' of the end of the eighteenth century. However, despite the wisdom of men like Old Cluny, Chief of the Clan Chattan, who died as late as 1885, this property idea had taken hold. On the death of one of Cluny's sons, some of the most precious clan relics, including the green banner and the Black Chanter (*Pheadan Dhu*), two mascots of many a battlefield and regarded by the clansmen as the property of the Clan, were sold to the highest bidder. These relics have fortunately been bought back by the Clan, and placed in their museum.

Dispersal of the Clansmen

The same unhappy fate seems to have overtaken many of the Highland clans. A great many Scots went overseas in the years following the '45 uprising and took service in the armies of Prussia, Sweden or Russia if they were of the Protestant faith, and France or Austria if Catholic. Famous commanders, such as Andrew Keith, Frederick the Great's able general, attracted large numbers of Scots into the service. They brought their weapons and other family relics with them, and in many cases they left them behind, to be seen today in Continental museums.

Taking into account sales, emigrations and theft, it is certain that relics of the old culture of the Gael are to be found throughout the world.

The Music of the Scots

The Scots who left for foreign parts also took with them, and made popular in their countries of adoption, the music of their motherland. Today the light music—ballads, marches, strathspeys and reels—is very popular throughout the English-speaking world. It is notable that the sound of the bagpipes, even in a London street, will bring people at a quickened pace towards the source. Wits would explain that they were taking avoiding action but were confused by the echo.

The Bagpipe

The classical music of the bagpipe, with a history going back to the shepherds of Ur, is known as the *Piobaireachd*. It is impossible to ignore this, their greatest artistic achievement, when discussing the old life of the Highlanders. Because of the unusual scale of the pipe chanter and the irregularities in tempo, for

Gentleman in the dress of the Hebrides c. 1745.

which no satisfactory notation in written music exists, the *Piobaireachd* presents a puzzle to western European ears indoctrinated with tonic solfa and common time.

The Tartan

John Major, a sixteenth-century historian, describes the Highlanders as 'rushing into battle in a garment of linen with pleats sewn in and daubed with pitch and with a deerskin covering'. These materials were replaced when wool became more readily available. The threads were dyed in locally obtained lichen dyes and woven in intricate patterns. It has been suggested that it was in the wars of Montrose and the Viscount Dundee in the seventeenth century that it became convenient for the various clans, or companies, from a particular locality to be identified by the pattern, or tartan, of their clothes. The emergence of these distinctions, and the pride with which a tartan was worn, led to the rigid classifications of later times.

The Kilt and Plaid

At that time the breacan *felie* (belted plaid) was worn. This was a long piece of tartan cloth, carefully pleated and secured by a belt so that the lower part formed the kilt and the other half, worn over the shoulder, formed the plaid. This garment was certainly cumbrous, but it appears that no substantial change was made in style until after the uprising of 1715, when, according to the contemporary account of Evan Baillies of Abriachan, the change came about by the inspiration of Thomas Rawlinson, an English Quaker who managed the iron-smelting works at Invergarry in Inverness-shire: He was a man of genius and quick parts, and thought it no great stretch of invention to abridge the dress, and make it handy and convenient for his workmen; and accordingly directed the using of the lower part plaited of what is called the felie or kilt (as described above), and the upper part was set aside; and this piece of dress so modelled as a diminution of the former, was in the Gaelic termed "felie beg" ("beg" in their tongue signifies "little"), and by our Scots termed "little kilt"; and it was found so handy and convenient, that in the shortest space the use of it became frequent in all the Highland countries, and in many of our northern low countries also'.

This new style can be seen from the accompanying photograph taken before World War I of that great Piper, Malcolm Macpherson, piper to the Chief of Clan Chattan: the plaid is worn separately, as it is today.

ALEXANDER GORDON

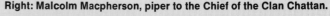

An autumn morning in the Highlands.

Right: Malcolm Macpherson, piper to the Chief of the Clan Chattan.

Mansell Collection

Oban Times

A Museum of Childhood

Toy collecting has grown into a popular hobby over the past few years. Nowadays such things as automatons and early model railway engines often command high prices in salerooms and even the once humble lead soldier has become a much-sought-after prize for many people.

Toy collecting is a fascinating subject; and anyone who is at all interested in it would find a visit to Edinburgh's Museum of Childhood equally fascinating. For this four-storied building in the city's famous Royal Mile has a wealth of exhibits on display that can be practically guaranteed to please the enthusiast.

The scope of the Museum is enormous. Puppets, puzzles, games, cigarette cards, magic lanterns, mechanical savings-banks, musical instruments, clockwork cars, model aeroplanes, miniature tea sets...these are only a few examples of the kind of articles that pack the showcases on each floor. There is something for everyone here, in a very extensive collection that ranges from rocking horses to penny-in-the-slot machines and nursery medicines.

A professional marionette theatre with seventeen figures occupies almost the whole of one wall on the second floor. Taking up about the same amount of space on the third floor is **'Stanbrid Eorls', an English dolls' house** which has electric light, an internal water supply and over two thousand pieces of furniture and furnishings for its twenty rooms. Realism has been carried so far with this dolls' house that it has even had a fire and a burst water-pipe.

A very fine collection of **model soldiers** remains on permanent

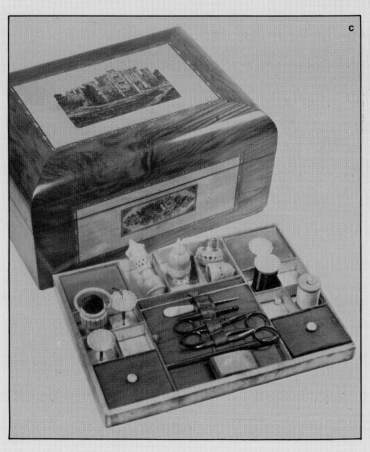

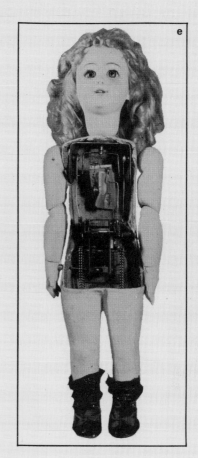

parade, including numerous mint sets which are still secured inside their original containers. Naturally Britain's is well represented, from early sets onwards, and the Museum displays prominently one of the last boxes of metal soldiers that this famous firm produced in 1966.

The library shelves around the top floor are filled with one of the finest representative collections of **children's books** in the world. Their attractive covers bear famous names such as Lt.-Col. Brereton, Percy F. Westerman and Captain Marryat, as well as names of authors who are unknown today except to students and researchers.

In this room, too, are displayed the popular boys' and girls' papers of the past; *Hotspur, Beano, Dandy, Magnet* and *Gem,* for instance, which used to delight children many years ago.

No history of childhood would be possible without **dolls,** and these are well represented. Starting with *Nefrett*—a very rare 2000 B.C. Egyptian grave doll—the Museum presents a very representative selection of examples, ending with one of the ultra-sophisticated American dressing dolls, a range that should satisfy even the most ardent enthusiast.

The Museum of Childhood is open from 10 a.m. to 5 p.m., Mondays to Saturdays. GEORGE CAMERON

Fig. a. American cast-iron locomotive, circa 1885.
Fig. b. Mechanical toy bank, English cast-iron, 1900.
Fig. c. Tunbridgeware inlaid workbox, circa 1890.
Fig. d. Butcher's shop, English, circa 1840. These were usually made in Germany or France.
Fig. e. Walking and talking doll, German, 1895.

The Folk Art Of Greece

Sleeve embroidery, c. 1880.

Greek folk handicraft has, until quite recently, received scant attention even in its native land. This art is surprisingly sophisticated in view of the fact that from the fall of the Byzantine Empire onwards it was denied the patronage and encouragement of a ruling secular elite. Thus there was little chance for a strong, distinctive and eponymous national school of art to develop. European influences were prevented from filtering through by the insulating effect of the dominant Ottoman power and culture.

Folk Art vs. Western Traditions

Creativity was channelled into folk art; utilising its own legacy, modified by the Islamic traditions of the Turks, it was kept alive by the Orthodox Church. In this way the Church became the guardian of the ethnic consciousness of the Greeks as well as of their religious faith. This national art survived four centuries of Turkish domination only to be neglected after 1821 in favour of Western traditions that seemed to the new, largely foreign educated national elite, to embody all that was modern, progressive and civilised.

It is only recently that scholarly and collecting interest has focused on the modern Greek tradition. The fact that there is only one museum, the Benaki in Athens, which specialises in this subject, is an indication of the general indifference.

The Role of the Orthodox Church

The importance of the Church in the development of Greek folk art can hardly be overstated. Many folk products such as chalices, crosses and gospel covers came into existence in response to a continuous demand from the Church. The long unbroken relationship between Church and craftsmen accounts in large measure for the transmission of the Byzantine tradition to modern Greece. The distinctive style of Byzantine iconography, for example, depicting spiritual yearning by a kind of physical immobility, is widespread in representations of the human form in embroideries and metal surfaces in the eighteenth and nineteenth centuries.

The Church did more than pass on traditions of the past; its requirement of ceremonial objects for which dignity, richness and pomp were essential. helped to foster a tradition of combining functionalism with ornament. Because their use is ceremonial, objects came to be decorated in this way; yet decoration never became an end in itself but was informed and inspired by the symbolic meaning of the object's function. Thus the interaction between form and content produces a harmonious organic whole. Silver gospel covers decorated with representations of the miracles, and priests' sleeves adorned with ornate crosses, are perhaps the most obvious examples.

Robert Kirk

Below: Embroidered waistcoat c. 1780.

Top, left: Silver snuff-box, c. 1820. Above: Bottom of same box, decorated in Turkish style. Bottom, right: Top of box, handsomely embossed.

Some of the decorative patterns are geometric in form but others depict peacocks and double-headed eagles which can be traced directly to Byzantium; some others are in the form of rising spiral plants, a design going back to the Hellenistic period. The strong preferences for densely worked patterns and curves are the main influences of Ottoman art.

The Influence of the Merchants

The craftsmen whose style may be regarded as having been fashioned by the influence of the Church came also to supply the merchants whose number and wealth were increasing in the eighteenth and nineteenth centuries. Decoration was still used to add ornament and dignity to objects of everyday use and this trend reached exaggerated heights in dress. Silver buckles, gold embroidery on belts and coats, loose, noisy, silver bracelets and necklaces of thin chain-work with pendant coins were some of the signs of rising prosperity. The colours used were generally muted, pastel shades unlike the vivid tints used in the otherwise similar dress of neighbouring Balkan countries.

Folk Art and the Soldier

The arms and dress of irregular soldiers gave further opportunity to the craftsmen. Their *pallaskes* (powder horns) were especially attractive; they take the form of triangular metal boxes with the two sides curving towards a wide angle, the whole crowded with elaborate geometric patterns in high relief. Some of these fine examples can be seen in the house of Ali Pasha of Yannina on the island in the Homonymous lake. Ali Pasha gave strong support to local craftsmen and silversmiths in the early nineteenth century when his court was second in splendour, as it was in intrigue, only to the Sultan's own.

Greek folk art is as yet relatively unexplored. Its investigation is proving a demanding task because of inadequate documentation. There are no reliable records and few if any devices such as silver hallmarks or other symbols. Interest in it is rising fast, particularly among modern Greek art historians. If the attraction of a virgin field and the opportunities it affords for one's pioneering instincts are diminishing, it is at least becoming easier to derive informed aesthetic satisfaction from this graceful art.   THEODORE ECONOMOU

Below: Embroidered armlet, late eighteenth century. Right: Head ornament, in traditional style.

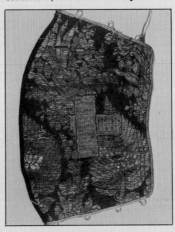

STRING BOXES

Balls of string were an invention of the early years of the nineteenth century. It was then, towards the beginning of the industrial revolution, that string-balling machines came into use. As a result, string boxes were soon devised for storing and using the new product.

Until the end of the eighteenth century it appears that string, like cotton, silk, and wool, was sold in skeins or hanks. **Balled string brought with it a demand for containers.** In the shops and warehouses they were large and generally plain. Usually made of cast iron, they took the form of perforated spheres or cages and they are of little interest to collectors. In the home they were far more attractive. String boxes had great novelty value and provided good scope for the imagination of woodworkers. In particular the wood turners benefited from the new demand. The illustrations on this page are examples of their work.

As a result a great variety of string boxes came on to the nineteenth-century market. There was a wooden doll which stored the string in the crinoline, a Dickensian fat boy, and a painted cottage with the string emerging through a chimney on the 'thatched' roof; a rosy-cheeked apple and a boxwood egg fixed in a lignum vitae egg cup. The Scots made tartan and transfer-decorated boxes.

Two patterns were particularly popular throughout the century: a miniature barrel with the string emerging through the tap, which was equipped with a steel cutter; and a sphere mounted on three ball feet. Both patterns were made in lignum vitae and boxwood and the barrels were placed both horizontally and vertically, on circular stands. String barrels made after about 1860 were often decorated with celluloid strips or ornamental brasswork.

Some barrels have spools fitted with projecting winders and they probably predate balling machines. No doubt they were designed to wind off string from skeins or hanks.

Many string boxes were given an ornamental turnery finish. Ornamental turning, an extra operation by which a surface pattern is added, was given a great fillip as a hobby for gifted amateurs in 1856 when Charles Holtzapffel published his *Turning and Mechanical Manipulation,* Volume 5.

String boxes are still available at reasonable prices, ranging between £2 and £18.

EDWARD PINTO

Centre top: An illustration from Turning and Mechanical Manipulation, an 1856 manual for amateur wood turners. Below: 1, 5, 6 and 10 are good examples of ornamental turnery. 2 is a more common box. It has a cutter on the knob and a hole in the base so it can be screwed down. 2 and 3 are made of lignum vitae; 4, 7 and 9 of masur birch. 8 is a 'weight' in satinwood with a brass mount and ring. 12 was a very popular pattern. It is made of boxwood, as are 11 and 13. 13 is an 1887 jubilee crown.

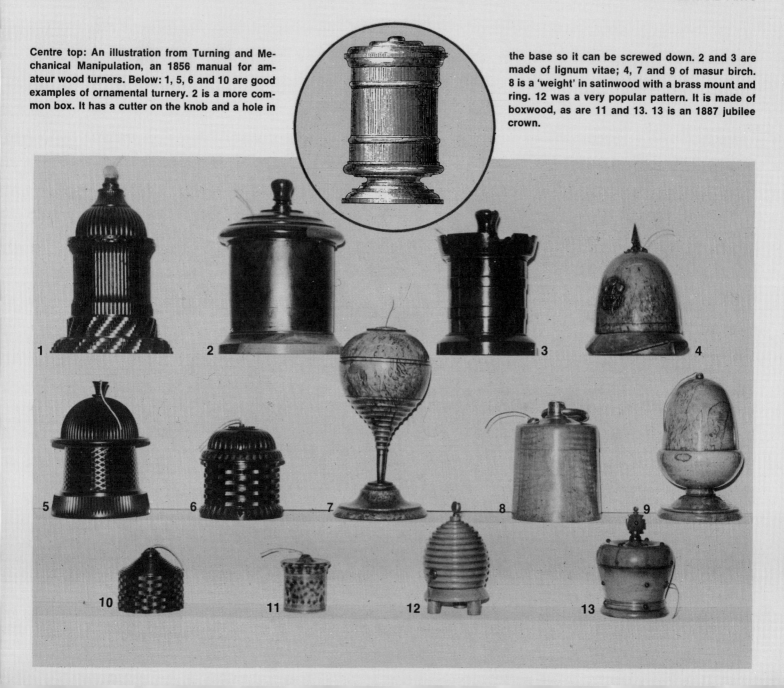

Market Trends

18TH AND 19TH CENTURY RUSSIAN ANTIQUES

Kovsh by A. Andreev sold by Christie's in Geneva in 1971.

Russian works of art have appreciated considerably in value in the last decade. Each change in European taste in the last two centuries was reflected and interpreted in Russian styles and techniques. The best-known Russian designer of European influence is Carl Fabergé. The trinkets and ornaments made for the Court of Tsar Nicholas II still have an enormous appeal today.

Perhaps the most interesting collection of Russian art to appear in the saleroom in recent years was that of the late Ambassador and Madame Jean Herbette sold by Christie's in Geneva in May 1971. Ambassador in Leningrad in 1924, Monsieur Herbette had an extraordinary opportunity to buy works of art. The *kovsh* (drinking-vessel) by Andrew Andreev, Moscow 1776, made about £1,000 while a parcel-gilt oval sugar-box and cover made £558. In 1957 a late seventeenth-century *kovsh* realised £220, while a set of four vase-shaped wine coolers by Frederick Joseph Kolb, St. Petersburg, 1820, offered at Christie's in 1967 made £1,700.

Malachite—that characteristically Russian stone—was an important element in some of the finest pieces of Russian decorative art. In 1962 a pair of large vases mounted in ormolu fetched £3,800 at Sotheby's. They would certainly be worth considerably more today especially as they were gifts from the Tsar and the only similar pairs are at Windsor Castle and in the Vatican. A large urn from the Herbette collection, also a gift from the Tsar, made about £6,000. In July 1970 a superbly extravagant malachite table supported on ormolu winged dragons was sold for £1,785.

Very few pieces of Russian furniture have reached the London market. In October 1968, £577.50 was paid for a set of four maplewood chairs with backs carved in stylised palmettes reminiscent of the Empire style. A maplewood secretaire of the time of Tsar Alexander I made only £399.

Russian porcelain is equally rare. In 1967, Christie's sold a magnificent banqueting service for the outstanding price of £65,750 although the *cachepots* from St. Petersburg which sold for £315 in the same year are a more accurate reflection of the market. Once again the Herbette sale mirrored the rise in prices when Lot 377, a single porcelain vase painted with flowers on a gilt ground, sold for £550.

ANTHONY DERHAM

Urn from the Herbette Collection.

SCOTTISH ANTIQUES

With the enormous interest in eighteenth- and early nineteenth-century silver which has been a major characteristic of London salerooms in the past decade, there has been a marked tendency to concentrate on the work of a particular silversmith or the output of a particular region. Following this pattern, Scottish silver as a whole has only recently come into focus.

Although the work of Perth smiths, such as Robert Keay and John Pringle, has always been highly regarded, lesser-known craftsmen working in Edinburgh and other Scottish towns have received scant attention outside their native heath.

Sotheby's sale at Gleneagles in August 1971 confirmed this trend when high prices were paid for Scottish silver of varying quality and type. Six tablespoons and seven dessert spoons by Robert Keay, dated 1799, fetched £70 in a lot with nine tablespoons by an earlier Perth craftsman named Alexander Gairdner. Twelve fiddle-pattern teaspoons made in Perth by John Pringle in 1830 sold for £48.

Silver from Edinburgh also made good prices, although it was not so much sought after as the work of the Perth craftsmen. Five tablespoons and twelve dessert spoons made between 1818 and 1828 by the firm of James and William Marshall were sold for

Right: Tassie glass paste medallion sold at Sotheby's for £110 in 1971. Left: Tassie portrait plaque of Lord Daer sold at Sotheby's for £135 in 1971.

£24, and six tablespoons marked Ker and Demster 1766 were sold for £52. Other larger objects attracted keener bidding and higher prices. A pair of rare George III Scottish lemon-squeezers made in Edinburgh in 1816 was sold for £280 and a pair of two-handled cups dated 1801 from the same city fetched £180. Most of the Scottish silver which comes on the market is nineteenth-century in origin. Queen Victoria's liking for Scotland, and the romantic interest in Scottish history generated by the novels of Scott and Stevenson, led to the widespread reproduction of seventeenth- and eighteenth-century designs.

Firearms

Scottish pistols always arouse considerable interest when they come up for sale. In July 1971 an extremely fine all-steel flint-lock belt-pistol made *c.* 1705, with heart-shaped butt decorated with silver, was sold for £540. This pistol is typical of those made on the east coast of Scotland, a type which can always be reckoned to make a high price at auction.

Glass Paste Medallions

There is also a revival of interest in glass paste medallions at the present time, and the work of James Tassie fetches high prices in the salerooms. In August 1971 a portrait plaque of Lord Daer signed 'Tassie f.' sold for £136 at Sotheby's, and a superb portrait of the horologist John Harrison was bought by the National Maritime Museum for £240.

DAMASCUS HOBNAIL

THE DECORATIVE ARTS IN SPAIN

Etching from a set of Los Caprichos (first edition 1799). Sold at Sotheby's for £6,000 in 1971.

Spanish art was not, with a few exceptions, particularly dependent on the art of other countries and seldom appears in salerooms.

Goya Etchings and Lithographs

An exception is provided by the work of Goya. During the last season of sales, sets of his etchings appeared regularly. Their social and satirical comment, combined with their subtlety of technique, has resulted in their continued popularity.

A first collected edition of *Los Caprichos* in book form can be expected to fetch between £6,000 and £10,000; in 1971, one such series reached £6,800.

Another famous set by Goya is *Los Disastres de la Guerra;* recently a first edition of eighty plates brought £2,800.

The price of engravings, prints and etchings is defined by the following factors: quality; whether they are an early edition or impression; what condition they are in; whether affected by damp or have cut-down borders.

The lithographs of Goya appear on the market occasionally and they make high prices; for instance, from the very rare *Tauromaquia,* a series on the art of bullfighting, (Gaulon edition), *Bravo Toro* and *Diversión de España* fetched £7,000 each recently and *Bullfight in Divided Ring* made £8,000.

Firearms

Because of their rarity, fine Spanish guns and pistols are much sought after by collectors. If, for example, a Spanish wheel-lock of the seventeenth century ever appeared on the market and could be identified as such, it would probably bring a very high price—£5,000 or more. More standard items, however, appear quite regularly in the salerooms, more so in England than abroad.

A pair of eighteenth-century brass- or steel-mounted miquelet-lock pistols can be bought for between £350 and £400; a pair of the former fetched £370 this season and may be considered a good buy. Similarly a fine Ripoll-lock blunderbuss pistol (Fig. 10 on page 2150 of Peter Hawkins article) fetched £820 in 1969 and was not overpriced. Firearms from the gunmaking centres such as Madrid, Ripoll or Barcelona are naturally the more expensive ones. Probably the finest pair of Ripoll pistols to come on the market in recent years was a seventeenth-century silver-mounted miquelet-lock pair of belt pistols sold for £2,730. Another reason for their high price was their silver mounts.

Porcelain

Buen Retiro porcelain rarely comes up for sale; the bulk of it is in museum collections, mainly in Spain. In 1961 a figure of a lady holding a fan brought £560. If that item were to appear in the catalogues again, it could go for four or five times that figure.

Prices can be measured against those of Capodimonte which is seen more regularly at porcelain sales. In this type of porcelain the paste was finer and the modelling almost sculptural, a quality never really achieved at Buen Retiro. A very exceptional documented Capodimonte figure of the *Mater Dolorosa* in white porcelain, signed by Gricci, brought £11,000 last season.

Armorial Dishes

Rare, too, are the fine Hispano-Moresque armorial dishes which are eagerly sought after by collectors. The famous Crèvecoeur dish made £1,800 in 1961 and could be expected to fetch perhaps four times as much if sold today. However, for those who do not wish to spend so much, eighteenth-century Spanish maiolica is not expensive. A good pair of Alcora *albarelli* (drug-jars) fetches between £100 and £150, while a Manises jar recently made £80.

KEITH POWNETT

ANTIQUES FROM TURKEY

In our own time the Ottoman Empire has finally, after a long illness, died. Its name is connected with decadence, its splendours are forgotten. But relics of its golden age still exist and are highly valued.

There was virtually no trade between Turkey and the West during the sixteenth and seventeenth centuries; the trickle that did begin was introduced to Europe through Venice. **Our knowledge about the applied art of Turkey has been acquired since the nineteenth century.** Initially, when this interest was aroused, these arts were not distinguished from those of Persia. Even today our state of ignorance remains considerable although recent events, including sales of the Chester Beatty collection at Sotheby's and the exhibition of Islamic pottery at the Victoria and Albert Museum in 1969, have stimulated more interest in this neglected field. An example of the uncertainty which still afflicts this market is illustrated by the sale in December 1970 of carpets from the Kevorkian Foundation: one lot catalogued as sixteenth-century and from Cairo was considered by several outside experts to be of later manufacture and produced in Turkey.

Pottery

Among the subjects covered in Volume 18 of *Discovering Antiques* only pottery is seen with some regularity on the market; Ottoman rugs and book bindings of the type described scarcely appear. Isnik pottery which ten years ago aroused little attention is now gaining in popularity and when pieces are auctioned—a rare occasion—competition is strong. The nine-inch-high jug illustrated here which, like the other pieces, dates from the sixteenth century made the high price of £651, although its condition was imperfect. It was less common than the dishes. The design of the dish on the right, painted in blue, green and red, is a style we associate perhaps most easily with the name Isnik; the dish on the left, however, is a considerable rarity with its architectural design and tall trees. It was justified in selling for £546.

The bright colours, elegance and very limited quantity of Turkish pottery available in the West will ensure that prices are maintained.

TOM MILNES-GASKELL

These four pieces of Isnik pottery were sold in March 1970. The dishes fetched (from left to right) £273, £420, and £546 and the jug £651.